The Ascendant, Volume 2
Copyright © 2018 The Association for Young Astrologers. All rights reserved.

THE ASCENDANT is the official journal of the Association for Young Astrologers. Submission guidelines may be found on our website: www.youngastrologers.org

Editor-in-Chief: Jennifer Zahrt, PhD
Deputy Editor: Danny Larkin
Deputy Editor: Nicholas Civitello
Charts Editor: Wade Caves

Layout and Design: Revelore Press
Cover Image: "Creation Palace" © 2016 Mariana Palova

First printed in 2018 through Revelore Press.

ISBN: 978-1-947544-11-6

The ASSOCIATION FOR YOUNG ASTROLOGERS is a registered 501(c)(3) non-profit organization dedicated to providing educational and networking opportunities for those interested in astrology, with a focus on young people, those new to the field, and aspiring professionals. Our mission is to ensure the continuity of the astrological tradition across generations. To this end we support aspiring astrologers and offer a social networking community where they can learn, be inspired and connect with both peers and mentors. We also publish a yearly journal, offer members access to free educational resources, scholarships to astrology conferences, and more!
Learn more at www.youngastrologers.org

Table of Contents

Letter from the Editors ~ 4
*Jennifer Zahrt, Danny Larkin,
& Nicholas Civitello*

Op-Ed: A Reflection on Disability in Astrology ~ 5
Michael MacLafferty

Wonder Woman Returns ~ 9
Wonder Bright

Art: Pilgrims in the Sky: Envisioning the Paths of the Wandering Stars ~ 20
Grant Hanna

Seven Reflections of Light: Considerations Upon the Seven Hermetic Lots ~ 25
Lars Panaro

Afflicted Syzygy and Daimon as Indicators of Violent Death According to Vettius Valens ~ 35
Tania Daniels

Medieval Timelords in Modern Life: The Firdaria Through the Life And Career of Madonna ~ 43
Cassandra Tyndall

Feature:
Cosmos and Chaos: Perpetual Tides of the Venus-Mars Epoch, Part II ~ 48
Gary P. Caton

A Critical Review of the Babylonian Berossus' Contribution to the History of Astrology ~ 60
Estabon S.R. Duarte

Hindutva and Indian Astrology's Modernization ~ 64
Freedom Cole

Feature:
Pluto's *Weird* History: Dumb luck? Dumb note? *Dumbell?* ~ 70
Kenneth D. Miller

An Astrological View of the Nuclear Age in Light of TNO Borasisi ~ 82
David Leskowitz

Telling the Story of Our Future: What Will Astrology Be Like in 2025? ~ 90
Kent Bye

From the Archives: Celestial Interpretation ~ 96
*Count Hermann Keyserling,
translated by Jennifer Zahrt*

☿

Letter from the Editors

Dear reader,

WELCOME TO THE SECOND VOLUME of *The Ascendant*, the literary outlet for the Association for Young Astrologers. Upholding our mission of intergenerational continuity and helping emerging astrologers enter and excel in the field, we present an ad-free blend of technical, theoretical, and historical articles with astral-inspired images by authors and artists of all ages.

Our timing for this volume, and perhaps the journal as a whole, carries a significant astrological signature. As we set about creating a new Ascendant in time for the 2018 United Astrology Conference; in Chicago, Mars conjoined Saturn in Capricorn in the ambient, which echoed the Mars/Saturn conjunction in Scorpio in 2014 that occurred when we worked on the first issue. The process has been quite intense.

As of this volume, we welcome Wade Caves, as charts editor, and Danny Larkin, the current AYA president, to our editorial board. We would also like to acknowledge the pivotal labors of our outgoing president, Alia Wesalia, in bringing *The Ascendant* back into print and securing a relationship with Revelore Press to bring out issues on an annual basis. We are grateful to Alia, our authors and artists, and everyone who worked with us to make this issue possible.

We open with a contribution by Michael MacLafferty on the question of disability in astrology. We then move to an extended examination of the astrology behind the return of Wonder Woman; by none other than Wonder Bright, which weaves together the history and astrology of Wonder Woman's creation and reëmergence. From there, we encounter artist Grant Hanna's wandering pilgrims—a rich depiction of essential dignity per planet.

The next three pieces sharpen our technical toolkit: First we have Lars Panaro giving a concise consideration of the seven Hermetic Lots; we move on to learning how to use the prenatal syzygy and the Daimon to predict violent death according to Vettius Valens with Tania Daniels; and then Cassandra Tyndall takes us through the life of Madonna to demonstrate the technique of Firdaria.

Then we discover Gary P. Caton's new findings on the long cycle of Mars and Venus, a long-awaited companion to his contribution to volume one. Switching gears to a different long view, Estebon S. R. Duarte presents a scholarly piece on the history of astrological transmission from Mesopotamia to Greece. From Greece we hop over to India, where Freedom Cole reveals a more nuanced understanding of the practice of astrology on the subcontinent.

In our first issue, J. Lee Lehman scrutinized the potential

Image from Humour, Wit, & Satire of the Seventeenth Century, J. Ashton. L.P (London: Chatto & Windus, 1883), 178.

astrological markers of humanity's perilous relationship to the split atom. David Leskowitz brings attention to nuclear power again, through his exploration of how the trans-Neptunian object Berossus fits into the historical events and astrology. Pivoting ever so slightly, Kenneth D. Miller takes us through the incredible history of how Pluto got its significations.

Finally, we close the issue with a juxtaposition of new and old. Kent Bye returns to share his visions for astrology's future in 2025, and this is immediately followed by the first-ever English translation of a lecture given by philosopher Count Hermann Keyserling in Germany in 1910 about astrology and the human imagination. We end on this archival note firstly with the express wish to see more of you translating texts from relatively modern materials (not just Latin, Greek, and Arabic sources), but also to show how far we may or may not have come in the 108 years since that lecture was first delivered. After all, 108 marks the degrees of arc distance from the Sun when Saturn makes its stations—a celestial event occurring as we write this letter to you.

We are thrilled that authors, artists, and photographers from around the world contributed their work to this issue. Our contributors hail from Australia, Brazil, Bulgaria, Canada, Germany, Italy, Mexico, and the United States. A truly global effort.

On a technical note, please observe that the charts shown here depict degrees only. Since minutes are not shown, the degrees are not rounded up and you should be aware that if something reads 26° Aquarius, it indicates anyting between 26° 01' to 26° 59' Aquarius.

Welcome to the second issue of our journal, we hope you enjoy it.

Jennifer Zahrt, PHD,
Danny Larkin, AYA President
&
Nicholas Civitello

☿

Op-Ed: *A Reflection on*
Disability in Astrology

by Michael MacLafferty

DISABILITY IS A THEME that appears in astrology usually in reference to a hardship or mishap. For example, tuning in to one of my favorite podcasts, I was a bit taken aback by a guest saying that having a disabled child was one of "these very tragic experiences" that can happen within families.[1] It's not uncommon to portray disability as tragic, and to focus the narrative on the negative impacts on surrounding, non-disabled people. This is not a problem specific to astrology, but a reflection of views pervading the dominant culture. As a disabled person, I would like to see disability treated as an identity, intersecting with other types and levels of privilege. As a psychotherapist, I want to see disability destigmatized, to be recognized as a unique and valuable perspective in society, and for awareness to grow around the language that is used to describe it. As an astrologer, I want to see disability humanized and conceptualized as a multivalent archetype, not merely existing on a list of potential sour transits.

Disability is not a uniform or monolithic experience. Disability consists of an extremely diverse set of cultures. It includes differences of physicality, cognition, sensory processing, and psychological function; some are more readily apparent than others, and there are wide continuums within each. The connecting thread is that disability occurs when appropriate access is not provided by society (according to the social model of disability, in opposition to the historically predominant medical model, which views disability as an inherent problem within an individual body). I am physically disabled (diagnosed with cerebral palsy), and a wheelchair user, so my public access needs primarily revolve around wheelchair access and mobility. Here, I will be speaking very broadly about disability, only scratching the surface of this topic, and do not claim to speak for all disabled people. I am also white, cisgender, and heterosexual, which have also shaped my experience of disability, and conferred a certain amount of privilege, contributing to the opportunity to philosophize and critique the subject I am about to address.

Ableist Language

I think it is important to pay attention to the words we use as significations and interpretations, especially how they may belie histories of oppression, and/or reinforce ableist notions. Words like *crazy, invalid, mad, infirm, insane, crippled, idiot, maniac, lunatic,* and *moron* have been used by various state agencies in an attempt to exclude, isolate, institutionalize, and eradicate people with physical, developmental, and psychiatric disabilities in the US.[2] Many of these words are used casually today as pejoratives and expletives. Astrologers need to be aware of the bias that they are speaking or writing from, and acknowledge the privilege that comes with referencing groups of people they do not identify with.

Throughout his work, twentieth-century astrologer Reinhold Ebertin uses many significations that are problematic in contemporary terms.[3] Even though he wrote nearly eighty years ago, it is worth a modern critique because not only are many of the social ideas of his day still alive and well, but they have informed the way we understand planetary archetypes today.

The negative descriptors Ebertin very commonly used in relation to combinations of Neptune are *sensitivity, weakness,* and *illness*. I think this betrays a deeply ingrained belief about how the idea of strength is constructed and why it is so valued in society. The implication is that if one is overly sensitive then they are weak by nature, not capable of withstanding the demands of the world, eventually succumbing to some physical or psychic illness, thus impeding them from being a productive member of society. Here we see a sexist bias that values physical power and endurance (conflated with mental/emotional capacity), overlaying the capitalist ideal of deriving a person's value from their ability to produce.

What is needed is a new appreciation for sensitivity. Many modern astrologers do cast the sensitivity of the Moon and Neptune in a positive light,[4] highlighting enhanced access to intuition, creativity/inspiration, or psychic phenomena (and here there is a danger of objectifying or exotifying psychiatric disability). But what about people we deem "too sensitive"? This is a label often hurled at women (and people of color, and any other marginalized group that tries to speak to oppressive language) to excuse behavior that had a negative impact. If there is a strong dissonance, they might get labeled "crazy." What about the young boy who often cries at disappointment? What about the person who gets migraines from certain types scents or lights, or who needs certain conditions to have a calm nervous system? These are the people who would get slapped with Ebertin's label of "pathological sensitivity."[5] But what is pathology except a comparison to what we deem normal?

It also strikes me that Ebertin's negative significations are commonly moralistic. Here are some related to combinations of Neptune: *insane, mad ideas, unstable character, pathological tendencies, mental disturbance, weak constitution, mental or emotional illness, epilepsy*;[6] Venus/Mars/Saturn: *abnormal sex, polygamy/adultery*;[7] Venus/Neptune: *wrong ways of love, wrong or misdirected love sensations, sexual aberration, perversions*.[8] It has ever been the Western way to dominate and marginalize difference from an idealized "normal" by moralizing against it, and it is no coincidence to find supposed physical and mental defects juxtaposed with supposed character deficiency. It should be easy to see that the same reasons for applying a queer critical lens hold up for a disability-focused critique as well. The term "abnormal sex" could easily be applied to the pleasure of either group; disabled sex, inasmuch as it challenges heteronormative ideals, is perverse by definition!

Disability Signature

When I first became interested in exploring disability and astrology, I thought that a planetary signature might be found. After hearing Christopher Renstrom speak about the history of searching for "the gay signature,"[9] I was sure disability communities shared the mark of Uranus with queer culture.[10] What other bodies might be involved? Chiron? Saturn? When I looked to my own birthchart, I saw an exceptionally close Sun-Chiron conjunction, Uranus opposite Mercury/Venus/Chiron/Sun, Moon square Pluto, and a nearly unaspected Mars in Taurus. Undoubtedly the manifestation of disability in my life was an expression of these and other natal complexes. But there did not seem to be an obvious connection between my chart and those of other disabled folks that I could see. I was also inadvertently following a conventional line of thought about disability significations, which I will discuss below.

As I learned more about identity in the birthchart, I became more convinced that disability could not be divined from a chart any more than gender, race, socioeconomic status, sexual identity, or any other personal identifier, sometimes referred to as co-determining factors. Co-determining factors provide contextual elements for archetypal manifestation, and therefore are invaluable for making interpretations. Indeed, it is the extent to which we try to understand the factors outside our own experience that make us effective multicultural astrologers. The foundation of such an orientation is to not make assumptions or rush to conclusions about what a person's life circumstances mean to them, and to keep from assigning our own.

Chiron—More Wounded than Healer?

Chiron has become one of the most important celestial bodies in astrology outside of the standard planets and luminaries, and the one most closely relating to disability. Mythologically he is a centaur, mentor of Achilles, and extremely skilled in hunting and medicine. He becomes poisoned accidentally, and cannot heal himself, despite his great skill as a healer. He sacrifices his immortality (and physical form) in exchange for Prometheus' freedom, and is honored as a constellation in the sky. From a disability justice perspective, this myth is problematic, raising questions about the value of life with disability/illness, euthanasia, and life purpose being derived from serving/inspiring those not disabled.

Archetypally, Chiron is known as the Wounded Healer, which has associations with shamanic functions. Chiron symbolizes our deepest egoic wounds, where we often experience difficulty and shame. As we work through and attempt to heal our core issues, we gain wisdom and compassion that can then be of benefit to others.

Finding the cure in the cause is a psychospiritual principle I believe in. However, I find it interesting that we often cannot talk about the wound without immediately going to the "healing." There is a compulsion to get past pain, challenges, and vulnerability, and assign a positive meaning—which can be a constructive and profound spiritual process. But I think we need to be very careful as counselors when we make meaning of other people's suffering. Again, our preconceptions determine our interpretations, and if our bias causes us to speak about our client's life in a way that they do not identify with, we run the risk not only of being offensive, but of aggravating and reinforcing a wound that likely has a societal element to it.

Health and Wholeness

Since astrologers are often in the position of facilitating personal healing and transformation, what is also called for is a revision of our concepts of health and wholeness. These are ideas that are commonly the goal of any kind of healing or transformative process; integrating what has been fragmented, uniting what has been separated. It would be a mistake to think of disability as antithetical to this process. As I have already mentioned, it is common to conflate physical, mental, and spiritual states of being. Using myself as an example, some might consider a cure for cerebral palsy necessary for me to be healthy and whole. As far as I am concerned, I am already whole; I think of myself as physically healthy as the next person. What I seek to heal from emotionally and spiritually are the side effects of living in an ableist world. In fact I could be considered healthier in some ways, since I am not zealously attempting to attain medical or mainstream physical ideals.

It is also important that we do not confuse healing with

cure. As queer, disabled writer Eli Clare states, "Cure rides on the back of normal and natural. Insidious and pervasive, it impacts most of us. In response, we need neither a wholehearted acceptance nor an outright rejection of cure, but rather a broad-based grappling."[11] Anyone who has gone through any kind of recovery, healing, or transformation knows that you do not come out the other side the same as when you went in—a return to a previous or ideal state is not the goal. However, this idea is subversive coming from disabled people. Yet this is the very reason disability should not be eradicated: it holds a very important perspective for a world that is so concerned with materialism, productivity, and perfection.

Positivist Mentality

Another issue I wish to highlight is one that Chris Brennan has raised multiple times on *The Astrology Podcast*, which is, the danger of modern astrology to lean too far in the direction of free will and personal agency to determine the outcome of people's lives. The idea that every difficult transit or natal aspect can be handled or manifested gracefully, implies that when it isn't, the fault lies with the native. I point this out because on the one hand, able-bodied people love "inspirational" narratives of disability,[12] in which one bootstraps themselves into overcoming their circumstances—thereby negating any unpleasantness that might haunt the audience, and treat it as a passing phase. I have had people helpfully suggest that if I just tried hard enough, I could walk better—or in other words, be more normal. The other side of this coin is the idea that misfortune is deserved, perhaps even due to "karma." Nondisabled people always want to know, "what happened to you?" as if to ascertain the tragedy of it, and evaluate how well you are coping. Perhaps I will be seen as exceptional, making the most of my life *despite* disability, erasing the ways that disability has guided me where I am, as well as the great majority of my life that is quite normal and cliché.

To complicate things even further, there is a prevalent spiritual idea that those who are incarnated into more adverse circumstances are farther along in their soul's development or taking an accelerated path. The harder the life, the greater the spiritual lesson. I admit this is a notion that eases the discomfort that comes from witnessing the struggles of life, bolstering a sense of structure and fairness in the cosmos. However, I have to say that I think it can also be a way to place disabled people in the exceptional category, seeing them as extraordinary—anything but ordinary, over which the able-bodied have dominion.

All this is to say that disability is not something to be overcome on an individual level (as if that were possible), and to think so ignores the countless ways in which those complex circumstances shape one's character and outlook on life. It is also not the result of a divine punishment, nor is it necessarily a mundane foible. In Robert Hand's seminal *Planets in Transit*, he described several transits of Uranus with the potential for physical accident and injury, if handled incorrectly.[13]

In cases where disability has an onset, it can be located in time. Incurring an acute injury or trauma, receiving a medical diagnosis, or self-identifying as neurodivergent are all examples of major events that would have to be reflected in one's transits. But what you would look for as signifiers of those events (as well as natal elements) are completely determined by your beliefs about disability. If you believe disability commonly results from accidents or mismanaged energies, Hand's Uranus signifier may first come to mind. If you see becoming disabled primarily as the end of a life of freedom, then Saturn may be what you see. If you are afraid or uncomfortable with the idea of disability, then perhaps Pluto would be the signifier for you.

Seeing the Whole in the Fragment

As a society we need to change our concept of disability, and part of that process is changing how it fits into our cosmology. The tendency to associate disability with the malefic side of planets like Saturn and Pluto comes from the perspective of seeing disability as limitation and suffering. Except being disabled is not a perpetual state of suffering. Suffering can be involved though, especially as one confronts the expectations of society without the support to meet (or critique) them.

Each human experience contains all of the archetypes within it—this is the beauty of the holographic nature of existence. Like the Buddhist metaphor of Indra's Net, any piece of reality has every other aspect reflected within it. This is why it is difficult to reduce any experience to one archetype. For example anyone could agree that war is under the purview of Mars. But isn't Saturn present in the discipline of armies, Mercury in battle strategy, Jupiter waged in the name of a just or holy cause, Venus in acts of mercy and importance of appearance, etc.? Whatever broad archetype you begin with, the others come to light as you dig deeper and flesh out the actual phenomenon. Staying with a single archetype leads to pigeonholing and stereotypes.

Disability is no different. Yes, Saturn is embodied when I want to enter a building that only has stairs, but I invoke Jupiter when I speak to injustice and hope for a more equitable future. I encounter Pluto when I receive the projections of the shadow of society, as abnormal, pitiable, undesirable, or incapable. I channel Mars when I pursue my passions and face my challenges. I am Venusian when I exercise patience when I don't get my way, extend compassion for others who have their own life struggles, or find peace in a lover's touch that I do not take for granted. I mind-meld with Uranus when I encourage myself and others to redefine ideas of health and normalcy. All of these characteristics can be traced back to my birthchart, yet all of them have been shaped by living with a disability.

As I stated previously, I have an exact Sun-Chiron conjunction. Since Chiron is a disabled archetype, you could infer that combination has a lot to do with my identity as a disabled person. Also, since I see my "wounds" as more psychospiritual than physical, it has a lot to do with my identity as a therapist—which, in turn, is informed by my experience of being disabled. Uranus opposing my Mercury, Venus, and Sun/Chiron could be seen as a disruption of "normal" ways of relating and communicating. It is true that some people relate to disability in ways that can be jarring to me. Beyond that, Uranus in my chart is my feeling of not belonging to the mainstream, and my stolid rebelliousness. Pluto squaring my Moon relates to a deep and complicated relationship with my mother as my primary caregiver until adulthood, a deep sensitivity and tendency towards feeling shame (about being disabled and many other things), as well as the resulting opportunities for transformation which allow me to provide a strong container for my clients' emotions and not shy away from their shadowy parts.

My Mars in Taurus is also an interesting placement to explore; it seems a particularly apt analog for physical disability, Taurus being so carnal and Mars being the way we move through life. In my experience, patience is required for physical tasks. I often have to find my own way of doing things that works for me, and they get easier the more I practice. Slow determination is often most effective. Mars is in its detriment in Taurus, a debility—in other words, disabled. It is in a place of reduced access, and thus less able to express itself with ease. In order to do the same amount of work as a planet with the privilege of better access (in its domicile, exaltation, or a neutral sign) it must put in more effort, and sometimes be creative at finding ways of being effective. Because of that, a planet in detriment can end up being very skillful and self-aware with some work put into it. If it receives aspects from other planets, there is an interaction, perhaps an interdependence at play, so that it can benefit from the privilege of others, making a more cohesive and unique whole. So if one stops at the surface interpretation of a planet in debility being ill-placed and disadvantaged, they miss out on the potential benefits. In this way, disability has actually been inscribed into traditional astrological principles, and perhaps unsurprisingly, it can be seen with nuance, or simply as ill fate.

I hope that with what I have related here—through the example of my own chart and lived experience, as well as my reflections on our community and how it handles disability in our social spheres and in our personal cosmologies—we can understand with more nuance how disability weaves in and out of the archetypes and aspects, and start to apply more awareness when addressing these topics, both with our clients and in our daily lives.

Endnotes

1 *The Astrology Podcast*, episode 104, (April 17, 2017), produced by Chris Brennan, http://theastrologypodcast.com/2017/04/17/lynn-bell-astrology-family-dynamics.

2 "Disability History: Timeline," The National Consortium on Leadership and Disability for Youth, accessed March 22, 2018. http://www.ncld-youth.info/index.php?id=61. For example: "1907: Eugenic Sterilization Law Spreads Like Wildfire: Indiana becomes the first state to enact a eugenic sterilization law—for 'confirmed idiots, imbeciles and rapists'—in state institutions. The law spreads like wildfire and is enacted in 24 other states."

3 Reinhold Ebertin, *The Combination of Stellar Influences*, trans. Dr. Alfred G. Roosedale and Linda Kratzsch (1940; Repr., Tempe, AZ: AFA, 2004).

4 Though "lunacy" is a word I still hear used by contemporary astrologers to describe the "crazy energy" of a full Moon, as if Luna would approve of the way we treat those assigned her epithet.

5 Ebertin, *Combination of Stellar Influences*, 64.

6 Ibid., 64–98.

7 Ibid., 176.

8 Ibid., 188.

9 Christopher Renstrom, "The Problem of the Gay Signature: Unearthing the Queer Archetype in Astrological History and Culture" (presentation, Queer Astrology Conference, San Francisco, CA, March 21–22, 2015).

10 Michael MacLafferty, "Similar in Our Difference: A Call for Inter-Community Solidarity," Michael MacLafferty (blog), April 7, 2015, https://archetypal-wellness.com/2015/04/07/similar-in-our-difference-a-call-for-inter-community-solidarity.

11 Eli Clare, *Brilliant Imperfection: Grappling with Cure* (Durham, NC: Duke UP, 2017), quoted in Leah Lakshmi Piepzna-Samarasinha, "Disability is Not a Deficit and Other Truths in an Ableist World: A Review of Brilliant Imperfection: Grappling with Cure," *Bitch Media*, March 28, 2017. https://www.bitchmedia.org/article/disability-not-deficit-and-other-truths-ableist-world/review-brilliant-imperfection

12 Stella Young, "I'm Not Your Inspiration, Thank You Very Much," TEDxSydney, April 2014. https://www.ted.com/talks/stella_young_i_m_not_your_inspiration_thank_you_very_much.

13 Robert Hand, *Planets in Transit: Life Cycles for Living*, 2nd ed. (1976; Atglen, PA: Schiffer, 2001), 376–95.

MICHAEL MACLAFFERTY is an astrologer and a Registered Associate Marriage and Family Therapist* based in Oakland, CA. He has written about the intersections of psychology, disability, and esoterica on his blog and has contributed to *Psyched Magazine*. He has an increasing interest in working on Plutonic themes with clients, including childhood trauma and feelings of shame. You can find out more about his work and writing at www.archetypal-wellness.com *(IMF# 83155, supervised by Rawna Romero, MFC# 41466, at Grateful Heart Holistic Therapy Center.)

Image of the first issue of Ms Magazine *by Wonder Bright*

Wonder Woman *Returns:*

by Wonder Bright

WE OFTEN TALK ABOUT the Saturn return, when that planet returns to the same point in the sky that it occupied at your birth, but here I want to talk about the return of Wonder Woman, her history, and which planets herald her blockbuster return to earth just when we might need her most. What does it mean that she is back now, what themes does she bring with her, and what futures might it herald?

(Spoiler alert: they're *definitely female!*)

The 500-Year Cycle of Pluto and Neptune

Wonder Woman's creator, William Moulton Marston, was born May 9, 1893 with Pluto and Neptune scarcely a degree apart in Gemini. Richard Tarnas, in *Cosmos and Psyche*, observes that because this conjunction, which only happens every 500 years, is the longest of all the planetary cycles that the relative "historical and cultural phenomena are in certain respects the most profound and consequential."[1] The 1890's conjunction happened during the *fin de siècle*, that great cultural bloom of the last decades of the nineteenth century, an era marked by the utter assimilation of the Industrial Revolution and the subsequent dawn of geopolitics, with radical ramifications for gender and sexual parity.

Tarnas charts feminism by the path of Uranus/Pluto through the sky, and while the Uranus/Pluto opposition was in effect from 1896–1907, the first nation to give women the right to vote was New Zealand in 1893, the same year that Marston was born, when the conjunction of Pluto and Neptune was near exact. With the development of geopolitics in the same time period, a movement that looked at how the burgeoning technology of the day would change conquest, warfare, and mapping, it is hard not to read into the birth of Wonder Woman's creator the dawning of a new age, one marked by devastating new weaponry but also its opposite: a new call for peace and reconciliation and the inclusion of people long left out of the equation. Humanity's earliest understanding of ourselves as a global culture sparked the first World War, but that, in turn, called into question the need for war at all.

Marston created a heroine who explicitly did just this. Raised by a race of immortal women on an island hidden from mankind since the era of the Greek gods, Wonder Woman was born to love and from peace itself. Her moral compass is clear and unshakable, based on being raised within a climate of love and compassion, where transgression is met with justice, and cruelty is verboten. When our heroine encounters the world of mankind for the first time she is shocked by the violence that besets our nations. Her dismay is characterized time and again as a reflection and counter-point to the darkness of humanity's struggles. Through Wonder Woman's clear and compassionate gaze human cruelty and strife are seen as far from inevitable, altogether abhorrent, and ultimately unnecessary. Her compassionate heart, her extraordinary strength, her magic bracelets that deflect bullets, and her trusty Golden Lasso, which compels the truth from all those who seek to hide it, are all tools she uses in her fight for justice.

That we still commit actions that cause us to question the need for war is evidenced not only by the current polarized political climate, but by the return of Wonder Woman herself. In a truly canny moment of synchronicity the writers and director of the new film chose to place her new origin story during WWI, which goes against cannon because the first Wonder Woman was released July 18, 1942 during WWII, when the enemy was a little more obvious. However, the backdrop of WWI is where her story truly always began. Despite the bold, technicolor, optimistic strokes Wonder Woman is best painted with, these strokes inevitably mask her actual origin story—one marked by complexity, secrecy, technological upheaval, and collective doubt about the nature of mankind.

Marston, bless him, never met a problem he thought a woman couldn't solve. Buoyed by the extreme, if volatile, optimism described by a Jupiter/Uranus opposition in his chart, he crafted a heroine for this new age, one who could take on the troubles of the world and vanquish them with a snap of her lasso. Cheesy? Maybe, but if you think that is a valid criticism don't tell Patty Jenkins, the woman who directed the newest version of the story. Jenkins, who possesses Jupiter as the focal point of a T-square in her own chart (opposing Marston's Venus), has famously "banned" the word cheesy in her world. She says, "I wanted to tell a story about a hero who believes in love, who is filled with love, who believes in change and the betterment of mankind. I believe in it. It's terrible when it makes so many artists afraid to be sincere and truthful and emotional, and relegates them to the too-cool-for-school department. Art is supposed to bring beauty to the world."[2]

To truly understand Wonder Woman, you have to understand why painting in such broad jovial strokes, hiding the ugliness underneath, was necessary not only for her own survival, but for that of her creator, and arguably, for all the rest of us too.

The Future Was Always Female

"Frankly, Wonder Woman is psychological propaganda for how the new type of woman should, I believe, rule the world."
—William Moulton Marston
in a letter to Coulton Waugh, March 1945

William Moulton Marston was fascinated with Greek myths and embedded his heroine within them, casting her out of clay sparked to life by the Gods themselves, which can also be seen against the backdrop of the Pluto/Neptune cycle, as those two planets opposed one another during the Golden Age of Greece, and conjoined again at the close of it and the dawn of the Roman Empire and of the Hellenistic era. Jill Lepore, author of the fascinating *The Secret History of Wonder Woman* charts how Marston studied philosophy at Harvard in the heady early aughts of the twentieth century under the tutelage of a professor fully enamored of both Aristotle and early feminism. This professor, who was the faculty sponsor of the Harvard Men's League for Woman Suffrage, spoke passionately to his students about both Greek hedonism and intellectual pursuits and took pains to remind the young men in his classroom that women possessed the capacity for both as well, despite what was commonly thought.[3]

In addition, the feminism of Marston's young adulthood was colored by tales of Sappho and the Isle of Lesbos, both of which were used as mythological inspiration for notable fictions penned by early feminists, featuring lands populated only by women, Lepore reports.[4] Marston took all of this to heart. So much so that by the time he came to create Wonder Woman, thirty years later, a founding text for her character included the groundbreaking book published in 1920 by Margaret Sanger, *Woman and the New Race*. In this book, Sanger, who coined the term "birth control," declared that, "No woman can call herself free who does not own and control her body. No woman can call herself free until she can choose consciously whether she will or will not be a mother."[5]

> WE MUST SET MOTHERHOOD FREE. We must give the foreign and submerged mother knowledge that will enable her to prevent bringing to birth children she does not want. We know that in each of these submerged and semi-submerged elements of the population there are rich factors of racial culture. Motherhood is the channel through which these cultures flow. Motherhood, when free to choose the father, free to choose the time and the

number of children who shall result from the union, automatically works in wondrous ways. It refuses to bring forth weaklings; refuses to bring forth slaves; refuses to bear children who must live under the conditions described. It withholds the unfit, brings forth the fit; brings few children into homes where there is not sufficient to provide for them. Instinctively it avoids all those things which multiply racial handicaps. Under such circumstances we can hope that the "melting pot" will refine. We shall see that it will save the precious metals of racial culture, fused into an amalgam of physical perfection, mental strength, and spiritual progress. Such an American race, containing the best of all racial elements, could give to the world a vision and a leadership beyond our present imagination.[6]

Margaret Sanger was born September 14, 1879 with Mars and Pluto conjoined in the last degrees of Taurus and Venus at 6 degrees Libra. Her Saturn was in the 14th degree of Aries, so both her malefics ultimately report to her Venus (women) in the sign of the scales (justice). She was constitutionally unable to care about the feathers she ruffled along the way. Marston, born 14 years later, with Saturn rising on the horizon in Libra, was in a particular position to appreciate her fight for womankind, as Sanger's Venus in Libra conjoined his exalted Saturn there. In addition, her Mars/Pluto conjunction was just a few degrees away from his Venus in Taurus. His close relationship with a doting mother set him up for complete alignment with Sanger's fight for female liberation and the passion with which she undertook it.

So Wonder Woman was intentionally created as an avatar for a new breed of woman. A new breed of woman through which a new race would be born, an "American race," not limited by the colors of its skins, but liberated and enhanced by them and the histories they brought to the table. Women who would break free of the systemic constraint imposed upon them by endless cycles of reproduction and child-rearing and take over the world to remake it in loving and righteous order with government-sponsored daycare, family leave, and liberty and justice for all. And by all, she meant *all*.

Sadly and paradoxically, Sanger's reputation has been sullied in recent decades by accusations of a deadly racism, which, despite being soundly debunked,[7] persist. That these accusations stem from anti-abortion groups intent on discrediting reproductive rights activists seems not to have hampered the effectiveness of their campaign. In today's polarized political climate greater credibility is generally granted to cynics than optimists.

What's a Wonder Woman to do? In lieu of applying her magical lasso to those scurrilous liars, we must address their charges head on.

SANGER'S COMPLICATED CONNECTION TO EUGENICS

The main thrust of the complaint against Sanger is that she was a known supporter of the eugenics movement, a movement that promoted the use of scientific achievements to improve the human population through breeding techniques. After the Nazis promoted eugenics to such ill effect in WWII the movement was soundly denounced as deadly and nefarious. In Sanger's time, however, the movement passed for a widely accepted health philosophy that offered Sanger a strategic way to position birth control as a significant medical advance rather than a politically controversial feminist rhetoric.

Even then, Sanger found herself at odds with many of the edicts purported by eugenicists and often drew criticism from leaders of the movement.[8] Eugenicists as a whole were notably against birth control, promoting the idea that women needed to be at the mercy of their wombs in service to the stated intention of breeding an improved race of humans. Sanger argued that eugenicists missed the very thing which would allow this condition to occur, namely that "eugenics without Birth Control seems to us a house built upon the sands. It is at the mercy of the rising stream of the unfit. It cannot stand against the furious winds of economic pressure which have buffeted into partial or total helplessness a tremendous proportion of the human race. Only upon a free, self-determining motherhood can rest any unshakable structure of racial betterment."[9]

It is certainly true that Sanger aligned herself with certain ideals of the eugenics movement that do not fit with contemporary mores, however. Notably, "incentives for voluntary sterilization of people with untreatable, disabling, hereditary conditions, the adoption and enforcement of stringent regulations to prevent the immigration of the diseased and 'feebleminded' into the US, and placing so-called illiterates, paupers, unemployables, criminals, prostitutes, and dope-fiends on farms and open spaces as long as necessary for the strengthening and development of moral conduct."[10]

Furthermore, she seems to have suffered from certain classist assumptions that impoverished black people were unable to make "fit" choices about their own reproductive aims. She is often lambasted for having said, "The mass of Negroes particularly in the South still breed carelessly and disastrously, with the result that the increase among Negroes, even more than among whites, is from that portion of the population least intelligent and fit, and least able to rear children possibly." That this quote, while distinctly damning, was a quote she borrowed entirely from W. E. B. Debois, the prominent black activist, is generally left unacknowledged. However, that her views were shared by an educated black man does not alleviate the censure she is due for them.

So, was Margaret Sanger entirely exempt from the widely held racist ideology of her time? No. Definitely not. However, as journalist and reproductive justice activist Imani Gandy points out, "there's a difference between being a racist and making racist remarks. Margaret Sanger, without question, made a lot of racist remarks." Gandy asks, "But was she a capital-R racist?"[11]

All evidence points to the contrary, including, and perhaps most especially, Sanger's own words. As the paragraph quoted at the beginning of this article outlines, Sanger was vehemently in favor of a future we can only imagine, one where women were free of the economic hardships incurred by unwanted children. A future in which every child was desired, not out of obligation or duty, but because each child could be and hence *would* be cherished. In this miraculous future Sanger predicted that "such an American race, containing *the best of all racial elements*, could give to the world a vision and a leadership beyond our present imagination."

The hold up to this halcyon future? Gandy points to an interview Sanger gave to Earl Conrad for the *Chicago Defender* in 1945, where she states quite plainly, "the Negro's plight here is linked with that of the oppressed around the globe. The big answer, as I see it, is the education of the white man. The white man is the problem. It is the same as with the Nazis. We must change the white attitudes. That is where it lies."[12]

Far from being a Racist, capital-R, Sanger was actually a woman well ahead of her time, observing quite clearly how economic struggles had an impact on not only women, but their children, and how radically this had an impact on our cultures as a whole. That she has been maligned and mischaracterized so widely is an interesting testimony to her Taurus Mars in detriment conjoined Pluto as well as her Saturn in fall in Aries. Sadly we do not have her birth time, so we cannot see where in her chart those planets fall. However, we can but be grateful that she did not allow the criticisms and threats which beset her life's work to deter her, funneling her considerable drive into combating what mattered most to her: the liberation of womankind, and through us, all of the world's populations.

It's easy to see why Marston was so taken with her, and how he came to craft a heroine based on Sanger's idealism. In fact, Marston incorporated Sanger's philosophy into the creation of Wonder Woman so fully that when a new writer was brought onto the comic, she was given a copy of *Woman and the New Race*, and told that the slim tome would tell her everything about Wonder Woman she needed to know.

So is our technicolor heroine any more resilient to attack then the mortal woman so much of her character was based on? Let's find out.

The 12th House: What is Hidden Must Come Out

Of course we cannot talk about Wonder Woman without talking about her superpowers, and we can't talk about her superpowers without talking about her magic lasso, which she uses to bind people to get them to tell her the truth. The Truth then, for Wonder Woman, is part of the alchemical process of liberation, achieved through binding. This apparent contradiction is fascinating on several levels.

Let's start with the most obvious, which is that in order for the truth to be set free it must first be forced. This mirrors the ancient wisdom carried by the 12th house, the house of secrets, loss, and suffering. Of the twelve houses, which describe twelve areas of life, the 12th is traditionally considered the worst of the worst, and the area of life it describes the least desirable. Modern astrology hails it as the house of transformation, but generally transformation is not necessary if things aren't pretty crappy to begin with. But why? *Why* is the 12th house associated with secrets and sorrows? And what does it mean to transform those things?

A penetrating look at all the houses of an astrological chart reveals something very simple, yet almost always overlooked. The 12th house is only number twelve because it has just risen and will hence be the 12th and last house to rise again. Houses 1 through 6 are all below the horizon. We only have to consider the everyday experience of waking to understand the abrupt and even harsh change from below to above, from hidden to revealed, and from asleep to awake.

People with strong 12th house signatures carry something from their private, subterranean worlds into the inescapable prison of visibility. Of course we all have twelfth houses, we all have something to protect and shelter, but we are not all called to do so as a matter of survival the way people with strong 12th house signatures often are, with varying degrees of success. The trouble for such people is that they can't *not* see what they do, and after carrying the significations of their 12th house throughout the previous twelve hours the desire to share their experience is often characterized by both need and dread. Unearthing the buried is not always met with approval, after all.

We know that Willam Moulton Marston was never able to live out his truth; instead he lived with a massive secret most of his life. Despite being the inventor of the lie detector and the creator of a superheroine who wields truth like a weapon, the mores of his time (and even ours, for the most part) dictated absolute secrecy around his home-life. Marston lived a polyamorous life with one wife, a second live-in mistress, and at least one long-term lover invited into their home frequently. His mother knew about their arrangements, he apparently (from letters that still exist from her to him, Lepore reports) kept little from her. To the world at large, however, these arrangements, so far from commonplace in America in the early twentieth century, were kept entirely private.

This is reflected in his chart, with Mercury ruling both his 9th and 12th houses from Mercury in Aries in the 7th (His time of birth is revealed in the afterword of Lepore's book, where she quotes his loving mother's careful annotation of his birth time as 3:50 pm[13]). Marston's chart reflects his drive to ferret out the truth of others (Mercury in Aries in the 7th) whilst guarding his own secrets (Mercury ruling the 12th). Of course, his Pluto/Neptune conjunction is in Gemini, which is double bodied, and his Mars there, in mutual reception with his Mercury in the 7th only serves to underscore his desire for multiple partners and passion,

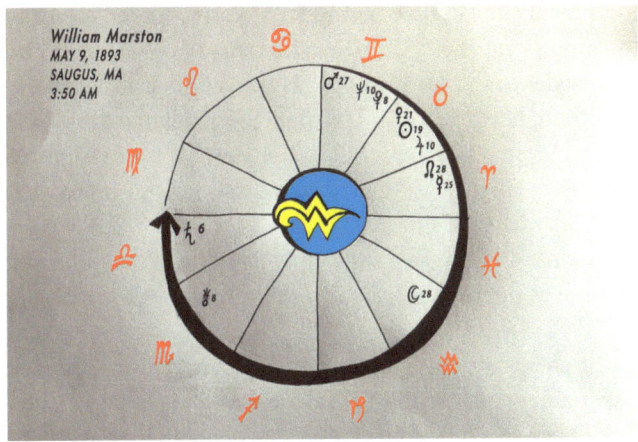

William Marston's chart drawn by Wonder Bright

both physical and mental, for each of them. That Pluto/Neptune conjunction, which is trine to Saturn (in the 12th house using quadrant houses) speaks to deep and grounded intuition regarding the cultural conditions of his time with a profound insight into what the future might bring forth from the changes afoot at the turn of the nineteenth to twentieth century.

Shame and the Context for Liberation

But what does Marston's need for secrecy tell us about Wonder Woman's desire to conquer it?

Well, first off, no one can speak more eloquently about the promised land than someone who has been there, and Marston certainly considered himself such a man. He was possessed not only of a strong bond with a devoted mother, but of intimate relationships with powerful women who adored him and children who grew up within a loving, if secretive household. His live-in lover was Olive Byrne, the niece of Margaret Sanger (a frequent visitor to their home), and an independent and strong thinker in her own right. His legal wife, Elizabeth Holloway Marston, was his teenage sweetheart and the breadwinner of the family, as well as his constant intellectual goad. Both women devoted considerable time and effort to Marston's research and ideas.

Marston could well be forgiven for thinking of women as superior to men. In his own life, this theme played out fairly consistently, as the women in his life protected him, sheltered him, and satisfied his desires on multiple fronts. This includes a wild and adventurous sex life that both sparked and supported an unusual philosophy about the importance of bondage and the release from it for living a full emotional life. Not only did Marston enjoy a polyamorous set-up with two live-in lovers, but the three were engaged for a number of years with a bondage sex club frequented by their fourth female lover, Marjorie Huntley, who stayed at their family home so often she had her own room.[14]

So, while Marston had secrets to keep, his secrets centered around a rich and rewarding personal life. This actually tells us quite a lot about the nature of the 12th house and secrets in general. Recall again, that houses 1 through 6 are all below the horizon; they are all hidden from view, and hence considered private (including the fifth house of sex). The 12th house, being the last house to rise again is actually the first house to emerge from this darkness, bringing it into the light. In other words, the private life is suddenly, with the full strength of dawn, brought into stark clarity, whether we are ready for it or not.

This is how the 12th house becomes the domain of secrets. People who have difficult 12th house signatures will be forced, whether by instinct or external pressure, to hide circumstances of their private life, or worse, some aspect of their actual nature. While the liberation of those bonds of secrecy may set them free they may also send them to prison, both real and metaphoric, as prison is also ruled by the 12th house.

And sometimes the secret *is the prison*. It cannot escape notice that even if Marston enjoyed his private life, the fact is he was forced to keep it secret. The repercussions for living publicly as a kinky polyamorous family are difficult to combat now, let alone a century ago. His children never knew about the secret lives their parents led, and there are multiple indications online that they dispute the events laid out in Lepore's very well documented book, despite having been the source of so much of the documentation themselves. The parents in this unconventional family thought deeply about their sexual lives and chronicled it thoroughly, yet could not, would not, share the stigma of their beliefs with their own children. That they did not get rid of the paper trail they left signals their own massive ambivalence.

The shame of living a life so beyond the bounds of his culture can't have been entirely shrugged off by Marston, try as he might. It is easy to read into his obsession with truth telling a righteous anger about the lie he found himself living, and the beliefs he possessed that perhaps made living that lie inevitable.

Marston was certainly preoccupied with the theme of ferreting out the truth. Graduating from Harvard with a PHD in psychology he left behind three notable legacies, each of which speak to his desire to bring what is hidden into public view. The first, while he was still an undergrad, was a systolic blood pressure test, a precursor to the modern-day lie detector. Ever the consummate showman, he publicized his experiments using the machine on young women for many years and often claimed credit for the invention, even after another inventor added measurements of heart rate, perspiration, and breath, developing it fully into the polygraph.

Marston also developed a theory he called DISC, which stood for "Dominance, Influence, Steadiness, and Compliance," phrases which are clearly and often explicitly linked to his experience with sex bondage. Writing about his theory in a book called *The Emotions of Normal People*, Marston's first paragraph is telling: "Are you a 'normal person'? Probably, for the most part, you are. Doubtless, however, you have occasional misgiving. Your 'sex-complexes', your emotional depressions, or your 'hidden fears' seem to you, at times, distinctly abnormal."[15]

While *The Emotions of Normal People* was published in the spring of 1928, with Saturn opposing his 9th house (publishing) Neptune/Pluto conjunction, it is arguable that the bulk of research for the book took place between October 25, 1925 and May 26, 1926, when Marston, three years past his Saturn return, went through an opposition of Saturn first to his Sun and then to his Venus (remember that his Saturn is rising in Libra). That was the year he and his lovers regularly met up at his paternal aunt's house, with a group totaling "about ten," for a series of sex parties that would "form all the basic principles" of the life Marston created with his unconventional family.[16] Importantly, "Sex parties" and "BDSM" were not terms at the time, and this was not how the group thought about their activities. These gatherings, which they called meetings, produced careful documentation of the discoveries and insights the group achieved through the exploration of bondage, submission, and control. The notes from these meetings were carefully collected and typed up by Huntley in 1943, who reportedly said about them, "The world isn't ready for this, and I have to destroy it."[17]

Marston's DISC theory was later developed by Walter V. Clarke, an industrial psychologist who used Marston's theories to create an assessment test, the decendant of which is still used widely today for training and development purposes in the workplace. Marston's book explaining his theory still remains in print, and the internet is threaded with praise for him along the lines of "perhaps Professor Marston's most enduring contribution to truth-seeking is the DISC Theory which reveals behavioral truths with profound effect on every-day people."[18]

However, of the three attempts to liberate people from secrets, it is arguably in Marston's fictional attempt that he succeeded the most. Wonder Woman's golden lasso, which she uses to *bind people in order to force the truth out of them*, is a marvelous narrative trick which succeeds largely by being so visual. Notably, it is also a means by which he could share his unorthodox views with his own children, as well as everyone else's. By operating in the world of story, truth can thus be set free. Here we can see a clear correlation between Marston's Saturn rising in Libra and the search for justice (Libra) through submission and dominance (Saturn rising in a Venus ruled sign) done in a visual manner (Saturn ruled by Venus in her own sign of Taurus).

But Marston could not escape the essential difficulties described by his 12th house. With Libra rising, Marston has Mercury ruling both his 9th and his 12th house by whole sign. With Mercury in the 7th in Aries conjunct the north node and in mutual reception and sextile Mars in the Gemini in the 9th, Marston has a clear signature for a compulsivity towards sexual impulses, as well as a need to explore (Mars) those impulses, possibly with multiple partners (Mars in a double bodied sign) and to understand and communicate those impulses (Mercury). Try as he might, the evidence is clear that he was never able to fully reconcile those needs with the cultural taboos against expressing them. More to the point, his needs arguably rose from the taboos themselves (Mercury ruling the 12th in mutual reception with Mars in the 8th). How much could Wonder Woman really liberate him, or any of us, from that inherited mantle of shame when the shame itself may even be part of the titillation?

So Marston used the lie detector and then Wonder Woman's golden lasso to trick the truth out of others, perhaps hoping to liberate them from the pain of their secrets, even while he maintained his own. Was he trying to prove to that his truth was more righteous than the culture that demanded he keep it secret?

We live in a period in which it's hard to imagine Marston being able to keep his secrets at all. Between corporate data mining for profit and government spying on private citizens courtesy of the NSA, secrecy has taken on a whole new meaning. That Wonder Woman should return to us now, in a time marked by the absolute blurring of privacy and secrecy is beguiling to say the least. It is tempting to read into that some message for us about what we might need to be set free from.

In a culture where shaming has become a national pastime, it is not hard to understand why the Marston household kept their family life a secret. They were likely right to do so. Even now, a hundred years later, his private life is considered shocking and suspect, the women he lived with assumed to be unwilling accomplices to his sexual proclivities, in spite of solid evidence to the contrary.

Despite the exacting research and its meticulous detail, at its core Jill Lepore's *The Secret History of Wonder Woman* contains a deep bias against Marston and a scarcely concealed delight in the attempt to shame him. Lepore saves her best turns of phrase for revealing public records of disdain for him, even though that disdain stems from people who may very well have been upset by his sexual appetites and bold statements about them. Her animosity may have

Close-up of Ms Magazine *courtesy of Wonder Bright*

driven her to research him as completely as she did, so I cannot fault her for it, but the most compelling moments of her research are never her arguments, but the source material she uses against her subject.

It is impossible to claim that he was a paragon of virtue or ever completely happy (can anyone be truly happy who is forced to live in secret?), but in my view the material documents Lepore uses against him do not actually vilify him the way she seems to assume they do.

Perhaps Wonder Woman is right to force the Truth only upon mortals who would use our secrets against us, shoving those villains into the very shackles they would seek to cuff us with. Maybe then they will confront the shame that drives them and, by so doing, release themselves of it.

The Neptune/Pluto Opening Sextile: The Story of Power, the Power of Story

Pluto was only discovered because Percival Lowell was attempting to find a planet that could account for certain anomalies observed in Neptune's orbit. These anomalies were later proven to be based on faulty data, but by using them Lowell calculated the planet he was looking for should show up inside a portion of the sky that Pluto was subsequently discovered traveling through. Pluto is, of course, on an order of magnitude several times smaller than the planet Lowell was looking for. Partly for this reason, its astronomical designation as a planet was contested and finally revoked less than a century after it was granted.

As a story of discovery, the illusory nature of Pluto's origin is a wonderful correlate to Neptune's notorious reputation as a glamour-casting magician. But the storytelling connections between these two planets go deeper than that. Astrologers like to relate the discovery of new celestial bodies and their meanings with events or technological breakthroughs that took place at the same time. In Neptune's case, it is generally observed that Neptune governs photography, a medium that deals in illusion, named officially only three years before Neptune's discovery. With Pluto the discovery of the neutron two years after the planet's discovery is commonly cited (and the smallness of Pluto gleefully approved as a correlate to the smallness of the atom and its parts). However, the roots of nuclear power go back to 1896, just three years after the last exact conjunction of Neptune and Pluto, and have partly to do with experiments using photographic plates.

It is even more interesting if you look at the cycles of these two planets in tandem over time. The way Neptune corresponds to media and the casting of glamours and Pluto to power describes the dance these two have engaged in for centuries. From the ancient Greeks to this very day the connection between rule and propaganda has been strong and sacrosanct, and the synodic cycle of these two planets describe it very well.

The correlations of the rise and fall of empires to the conjunctions and oppositions of Neptune and Pluto are numerous and well documented. What I want to draw your attention to here are the sextiles and trines between these two planets. Specifically to the opening sextile (following the conjunctions) and the closing trines (following the oppositions). The synodic cycle between these two bodies has a peculiar pattern that only reveals itself when you look to these aspects, commonly considered harmonious and less important.

However, observation of the cycle over time reveals something odd. Specifically, that of all the aspects these two planets make in their cycle, the conjunction, squares, opposition, sextiles and trines, it is only these two aspects, the opening sextile and closing trine, that last for longer than four or five years. If the duration of these two aspects were only a few years long, it would not be so noteworthy, but the fact is, the duration of these two aspects—and these two aspects only—consistently lasts over eighty years.

Using a one degree orb to examine this closely, it becomes immediately apparent that the "harmonious" opening sextile and the closing trine, actually oversee eras, such as the one we're in now, accompanied by strong cultural flux and crises wherein autocratic rule is both flexed and resisted. It is beyond the scope of this article to set this cycle against the backdrop of the entirety of Western civilization, however, this isn't needed in order to address the most striking things about our current timeline.

We are at the tail end of an opening sextile now and the roots to the last such cycle should not be far from our minds. After all, the last one saw the founding of the United States, and the seeds planted then are beginning to bear fruit. The last eighty-year "harmonious" cycle was the closing trine, taking place between 1702 and 1787. In short it covers the entirety of the American Revolution and the beginning stages of the French Revolution. Generally aligned with the Uranus/Pluto opposition that took place during the same decade, the French Revolution takes as its official start date 1789, just two years after the last exact aspect of the Neptune/Pluto closing trine. If that seems two years too late for inclusion, it is worth pointing out that the people who died in that war would have all possessed the closing trine in their own nativities.

Any American schoolchild learns the merits of these two revolutions. We are steeped in them from childhood as examples of our superiority as a culture that takes democracy, and *justice for all*, as its core and founding principle. We learn that the Golden Age of Greece (Pluto/Neptune opposition) brought to us the *idea* of democracy, to be fleshed out during the Renaissance (the conjunction), and the Scientific Revolution of the seventeenth century (opposition again). We learn that the American Revolution and the French Revolution are proof that Western civilization has triumphed over the hierarchal ideas used against the common man and been the cause of an egalitarian society that raises us all up.

The current opening sextile started in 1949, on the heels of the WWI and the overthrow of Nazi Germany. That win only served to cement national sentiment that the United States is the Land of the Free, against autocratic rule, and a benefit to all who live here.

The trouble is, all of this is a lie. The American Dream is just that. A dream. We have been told a story about who we are that clearly applies only to certain people in our culture. People who were not defeated in battle and their country and resources stripped from them, people who were not brought over here on slave ships and forced into labor for their oppressors, people who were not denied the right to vote on any of this until barely a century ago. We are told those events are all in the past, and we need to get over it, but anyone paying attention knows this is simply not true. The past does not die so easily.

Worse, the way in which the story of our time is told, is through mediums (a deregulated news industry that is not held account by fact, but only to stockholders) which are increasingly used against us. And by "us" I mean the commoners, the larger populace, the governed as opposed to the governing. And now, at the close of an opening sextile (the last exact aspect will be early in 2033), and the first Pluto return of the United States (exact in 2022) we find ourselves

Close-up of Ms Magazine *courtesy of Wonder Bright*

in new, yet remarkably familiar territory.

What is familiar is the way in which autocratic rule increases the distance between people with money and those without. The similarity between Donald Trump's love for gold and the gold-riddled excesses of Louis XIV, who reigned throughout the opposition of the seventeenth century, setting the stage for the populace to overthrow the monarchy in France at the closing trine, are obvious. What is not so obvious are the ways in which that distance is perpetuated currently. Louis XIV ruled through his superiority over his subjects. The story perpetuated by his court was that we must hold up the King in order to hold up France (the rest of us). Trump came to power through his remarkable capacity to convince people he's "just like us." If we work hard enough, we too can become millionaires and gild our homes with gold.

The underlying story is the same: one man with ultimate authority makes decisions that prioritize the comfort of the few to the detriment and struggle of the many. In both instances we are asked to live through the ruler. But the difference between living vicariously through a ruler we have no hope of becoming like and living vicariously through a ruler we are told we *could* become like if we only met certain "reasonable" conditions is actually vast. The former offers no hope whatsoever. The latter offers hope dangling like a carrot on a stick, always present, never forgotten, yet constantly at bay.

However, the populace of today, no longer divided merely by class, but by sex, gender, and the color of our skins, is wise to this hypocrisy. There are many people being told this story who are quite aware it does not apply to them. There are many more sympathetic to their plight. Those who know the wisdom behind Emma Lazurus' words, "until we are all free, none of us are free." Because although the American Dream may be a lie, may yet still be a dream, it is, perhaps, as a dream that its real worth may be determined. Without the dream, the lie bears no cruelty. And in the absence of looking at the lie, the worth of the dream cannot be measured.

The real story of Neptune and Pluto can now be observed over the course of centuries. Stories of power, its overthrow, of democratic experiments, of who, exactly, gets to benefit from those experiments, and who gets to write the history of them. But let us not forget the triple conjunction of the Axial Age and how it corresponds to the flowering of philosophic thought and the roots of democracy. This story is not over. This story, this dream, contains the nexus of the hope for a future where the dreams we have for our children may truly be met by all of them, independent of the station in life to which they are born.

It is into this peculiar thicket, where story and power meet, that we may rejoin William Marston and the creation of Wonder Woman for hints as to how we might begin to change the stories we tell ourselves.

The Pluto/Neptune Opening Sextile and Wonder Woman: Intersectional Feminism and Beyond

A lot of criticism has been leveled at the creators of the current Wonder Woman incarnation. The most important critique, in my opinion, is that there were no major, or even minor, black characters in the film. Why—Mikki Kendall, questions—was Hippolyta's consort and fellow ruler not a black woman, for instance, especially when it is part of the comic book series?[19] It is well documented that black people were a fairly significant part of the population during the Golden Age of Greece, and certainly by the Hellenis-

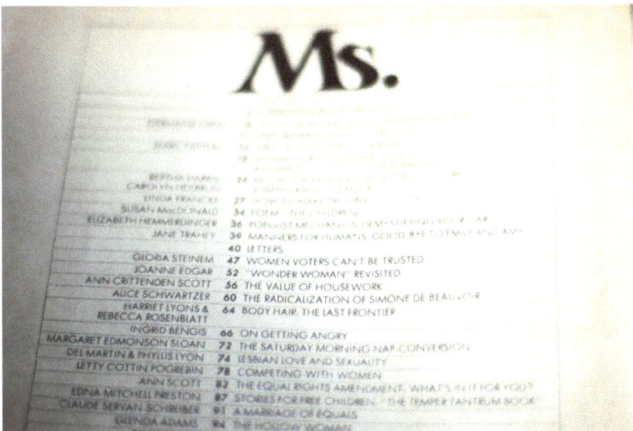
Close-up of Ms Magazine *courtesy of Wonder Bright*

tic era,²⁰ so why couldn't they be represented more fully as part of the ruling elite in Themiscyra? Diana's black tutor, who presumably had as great a reputation for education as Aristotle did for Alexander the Great, spends her only scene chasing after Diana as a child—a sight which echoes images of countless black mammys caring for white children over the decades. Why couldn't we see her educating a white child rather than running helplessly after her in a demonstration of that child's strength of will? And where was the black American soldier fighting alongside Wonder Woman in the scenes from WWI? It's a fact that black soldiers made up 13% of US fighters in that war, despite making up only 10% of the population at the time.²¹ That fact needs to be honored.

We live in an era where these sorts of call-outs are a constant goad. And while white people may chafe at the shame we experience when they occur, it is this very shame we need to embrace. We could view it as the binding Marston created as a metaphor through Wonder Woman's golden lasso. When Steve Trevor is bound with the lasso in one of the opening scenes of the film, we watch his resistance to telling the truth give way to the relief of being unburdened of it. This is a metaphor for the way in which being forced to tell the truth contains liberation. It is not experienced that way. On the contrary, it is painful to tell the truth, and sometimes hard to even discern what it is. But seeing it, owning it, and speaking it will set us free.

For white people the enemies of freedom during the American Revolution and the French Revolution were obvious. We overthrew the aristocracy, and we were free. The enemies are less obvious now because the real enemy resides inside us. Our inherited histories of racism and sexism are inflicting great evil upon all of us, and not only to the people who benefit directly from these delusions. When white people own the shame of our ancestry, and the inheritance of our privilege, it isn't only others we release from bondage, it is ourselves. The resistance we face towards that personal release is steep, but the rewards are profound. In the absence of facing our shame we can have no possibility of overthrowing it. This is the work of this opening Pluto/Neptune sextile. It is what is necessary as we move into the current epoch that began with the conjunction in the 1890's. The extent to which we deny ourselves this liberation lies in direct proportion to the extent to which we will have to revisit these themes again later. If studying history teaches us anything, surely it is this.

Feminism, like democracy or the American Dream, cannot exist so long as it only applies to the few. Arrogance felled the aristocrats, but it is hypocrisy that threatens us now. Intersectional feminism, a term coined by cultural theorist Kimberlé Shaw, is a philosophy that acknowledges the different ways that levels of societal oppression can intersect in one body. Being poor, being black, being a woman, being disabled, being gay or transgendered—any one of these things brings about certain conditions. Being born into several of them at once has an impact on your experience and your ability to pursue your inalienable right to happiness dramatically. Until we recognize this and address it as a culture we cannot overthrow it. And that will involve dealing with a great deal of shame.

Marston, a man whose greatest insights stemmed from sexual experiences he could not publicly claim, was in a particular position to appreciate how ruinous secrets and shame could be. As a psychologist he was keenly aware of the worth of self-examination and release from shame. He was not, however, immune to self-serving actions that underscored a genuine hypocrisy in his beliefs.

Marston's twin legacy to the Golden Lasso, after all, was the lie detector machine, which has not enjoyed the same noble narrative as its fictional counterpoint. The polygraph, a machine that measures heart rate, blood pressure, sweating, and breathing was designed to determine whether a subject is telling the truth, but has been proven many times over to be a failure in this regard. This is, of course, because those rubrics measure bodily responses that have less to do with lying than with nervousness. Worse still, those bodily responses can be manipulated both by the subject being tested, and the one doing the testing, depending on the training of the individuals in question. Results from lie detector tests have been banned from courtroom proceedings for this reason. They are simply undependable.

That does not stop the police, corporations, or the FBI from routinely using the polygraph as a form of intimidation and psychological profiling. Doug Williams, a former polygraph tech and internal affairs investigator calls the polygraph an "insidious Orwellian instrument of torture," and spent two years in prison for teaching people how to pass the test. He has devoted his life to educating people and fighting against its widespread use.²² Importantly, when 35% of the jailed population is black, but only 13% of the overall population is, it is difficult not to see in any technology used by law enforcement a weapon used against black people. In an attempt to do good, Marston had a hand in a very dark legacy indeed.

So Marston bequeathed to us twin legacies with strong 12th house and Neptune/Pluto themes; one with a strong moral compass, and one without. One which uses considerable power in the service of liberation and compassion, and one which uses power to keep others in abject servitude. Between the lie detector test and Wonder Woman's Golden Lasso, I know which one I would choose. Wonder Woman's great appeal lies in her ability to do the right thing. I trust her lasso to get at my Truth. I do not trust the man behind the polygraph machine.

That Marston literally *was* the man behind the polygraph machine did not stop him from inventing a woman who could transcend his own moral failings. That Wonder Woman's Golden Lasso is fictional should not dissuade us from embracing it. This is precisely where the strength of it lies. In the end Marston's great achievement was imagining someone better than he was or could ever be and gifting us with that imagination, too. If she isn't good enough yet, than we must keep imagining her. Recreating her in the image we need her to be. Using her example to create new and even better heroines.

In the comics Wonder Woman has a black sister named Nubia. When does she come out to play? This opening sextile better not end before she shows up, because we are ready and we have never needed her and her sisters more.

The Golden Lasso of Truth and the Importance of Storytelling

It remains to be observed that the current film incarnation of Wonder Woman was released June 2, 2017, with Venus conjoining Uranus in the 28th degree of Aries, closely conjoined Marston's Mercury in the 26th. His message to us is still bearing fruit.

Furthermore, his natal Jupiter/Uranus opposition was mirrored by a waning Jupiter/Uranus opposition—a contact that is connected to radical changes in technology and philo-

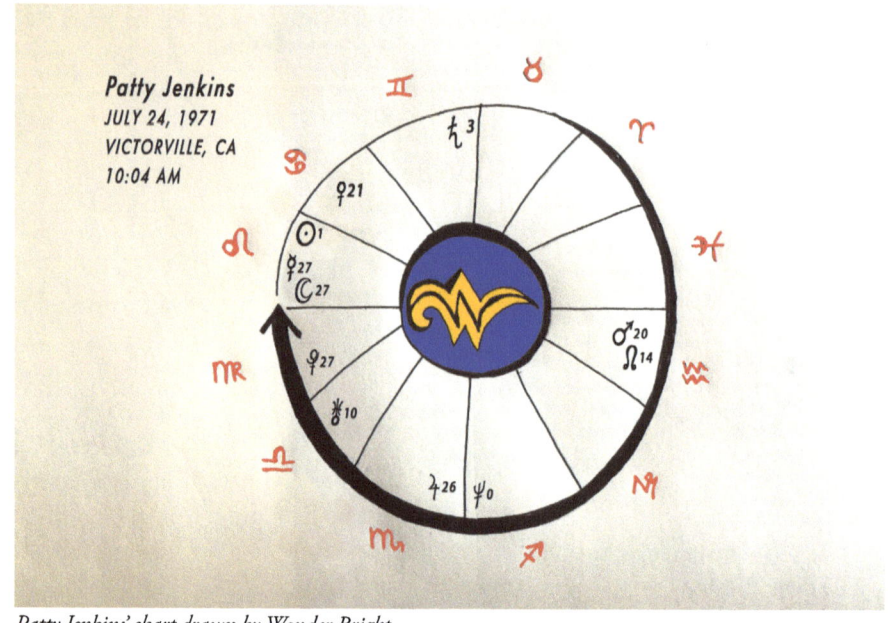

Patty Jenkins' chart drawn by Wonder Bright

sophical breakthroughs. That the film should be released directly on the heels of the powerful Venus in retrograde that followed the famous Women's March of 2017, and before Venus left Aries in her warrior goddess phase rising before the Sun, cannot be allowed to pass without comment. We have a president with Venus conjunct Saturn in detriment in his 12th house closing Planned Parenthood centers around the country. The astrological metaphors write themselves.

Patty Jenkins, the director who brought this story to the big screen, was born as Neptune approached its first opposition in our current Neptune/Pluto cycle (Neptune makes three orbits around the Sun, and Pluto two before they conjoin again in 2384 CE). Jenkins' Saturn is at 3 degrees Gemini opposing her Neptune and 5 degrees away from Marston's Pluto at 8 degrees.

She also carries a strong 12th house signature, but whereas Marston's appears dark and complicated, Jenkins' shows up …well, golden. She has a Leo (gold) 12th house with both the Sun, the Moon, (the lights) and the ruler of her chart, Mercury, inside it. Her private life seems to be just that, private, but she clearly has a strong drive for truth telling where others might balk. She wrote many times to Aileen Wuornos, one of the few female serial killers on record, in preparation for *Monster* in 2003. She sought to understand and give voice to the terribly tortured life that would create a woman who could kill seven men in cold blood. You would be hard pressed to find a film that explores 12th house themes with more compassion or clarity.

The 12th house is considered the worst of the bad houses, yet the word "transcendence" is always tacked onto it. Marston's life is a good example of why that might be so. The 12th house describes a condition of suffering that the native cannot get a handle on through obvious means because there is something about his or her circumstances that they are willfully ignorant of, blinded to, and often surprised by. Once alerted to his or her circumstances, however, and through considered thought and practice it is possible to alleviate ones suffering here and even to overcome it—even when this comes with mixed results.

Through Jenkins' Wonder Woman the viewer is forced to observe our world through someone innocent of the evil that we wreak upon one another. Through Wonder Woman's loss of innocence and grief over it we are invited to do grieve ourselves. We are given the opportunity for redemption and forgiveness just by observing the horrors and accepting both that they exist and that they do not have to. Wonder Woman is bowed by the realization, but not broken. She emerges stronger for having understood, finally, that the world of man needs her faith more than her innocence. This is the redemption promised by the 12th house, but rarely delivered.

That Wonder Woman and her Golden Lasso should arrive on the scene just months before the Harvey Weinstein scandal broke, and the subsequent #MeToo campaign that followed, is a genuinely fascinating synchronicity. The #MeToo campaign speaks to the power of storytelling in a world that has prioritized proof and material weight in order to combat injustice and unfairness. That those proofs have consistently been harder to deliver because of gender inequities has only worked in the favor of those in power. If storytelling alone can be seen to topple giants, then the concept of super heroes and the importance of Wonder Woman at the center of those constellations can also be seen to be important.

This period of time is remarkably unstable, as befitting an opening Neptune/Pluto sextile, and we are almost certainly heading into darker times ahead, if history is to be believed, let alone my Twitter feed. We need to take hope where we can, and stories deliver that like nothing else. Remember that it was not the opening sextile of Neptune and Pluto that brought down the aristocrats, it was people born during the generations whose nativities featured that aspect.

We may be closer to the world envisioned by Margaret Sanger than we think:

> The relentless efforts of reactionary authority to suppress the message of birth control and of voluntary motherhood are futile. The powers of reaction cannot now prevent the feminine spirit from breaking its bonds. When the last fetter falls the evils that have resulted from the suppression of woman's will to freedom will pass. *Child slavery, prostitution, feeble-mindedness, physical deterioration, hunger, oppression and war will disappear from the earth.*[23]

We owe it to future generations of storytellers to create this future. It is, after all, what Wonder Woman would do.

Endnotes

1 Richard Tarnas, *Cosmos and Psyche* (New York: Penguin, 2007), 417.

2 Cara Buckley, "The Woman Behind 'Wonder Woman'," *The New York Times*, accessed January 6, 2017 https://mobile.nytimes.com/2017/06/01/movies/wonder-woman-gal-gadot-patty-jenkins.html

3 Jill Lepore, *The Secret History of Wonder Woman* (New York: Vintage Books, 2015), 7–8.

4 Lepore, *The Secret History of Wonder Woman*, 22–23.

5 Margaret Sanger, *Woman and the New Race* (New York: Brentano's, 1920).

6 Ibid.

7 "Margaret Sanger and the African American Community," *Trust Black Women*, accessed March 1, 2018, https://www.trustblackwomen.org/2011-05-10-03-28-12/publications-a-articles/african-americans-and-abortion-articles/26-margaret-sanger-and-the-african-american-community-

8 Jean H. Baker, *Margaret Sanger; A Life of Passion* (New York: Farrar, Straus and Giroux, 2011), 164.

9 Margaret Sanger, "Birth Control and Racial Betterment," *Birth Control Review* (Feb. 1919); in Library of Congress Microfilm 131:0099B.

10 "Opposition Claims About Margaret Sanger," Planned Parenthood, accessed March 1, 2018, https://www.plannedparenthood.org/files/8013/9611/6937/Opposition_Claims_About_Margaret_Sanger.pdf, p. 3.

11 "How False Narratives of Margaret Sanger Are Being Used to Shame Black Women," *Rewire*, accessed March 1, 2018, https://rewire.news/article/2015/08/20/false-narratives-margaret-sanger-used-shame-black-women/

12 Earl Conrad, "On US Birth and Bias Control," *Chicago Defender* (Sep. 22, 1945): 11.

13 Lepore, *The Secret History of Wonder Woman*, 302.

14 Ibid., 117–21.

15 William Moulton Marston, *The Emotions of Normal People* (New York: Harcourt Brace, 1928) 1.

16 Lepore, *The Secret History of Wonder Woman*, 117–21.

17 Ibid., 377.

18 Coleen Kulkin, "Professor Marston: Creator of Wonder Woman & Father of DISC Theory," accessed March 3, 2018, https://blog.peoplekeys.com/professor-marston-creator-of-wonder-woman-father-of-disc-theory

19 Mikki Kendall, "Fiction, Research, Reality, More Research," accessed March 3, 2018, https://mikkikendall.com/2017/06/11/fiction-research-reality-more-research/

20 http://medievalpoc.tumblr.com/post/77597994529/hi-i-dont-know-if-this-is-too-early-for-you-but

21 https://armyhistory.org/fighting-for-respect-african-american-soldiers-in-wwi/

22 Drake Bennett, "Man Versus Machine: The True Story of an Ex-cop's War on Lie Detectors," *Bloomberg*, accessed March 2, 2018, https://www.bloomberg.com/graphics/2015-doug-williams-war-on-lie-detector/

23 Italics mine. See, Sanger, *Woman and the New Race*.

Wonder Bright is an astrologer, writer, and photographer living in Portland, Oregon. You can find her at www.starsofwonder.com

THE ASCENDANT

Grant Hanna, Jupiter (2017) Acrylagoache on wood 12"x12".

Pilgrims in the Sky: Envisioning the *Paths* of the Wandering Stars

by Grant Hanna

"A VEVE IS A MAP of the paths of a spirit." Sometime in late 2016 while listening to an occult podcast or reading through an esoteric blog post, I came upon this sentence; it struck me and I scribbled it down in my sketchbook. Now, I am not a practitioner of voudou so I don't know how accurately this summarizes the purpose of a veve, but I noticed the thought because of my own work with astrological talismans, which usually involves creating some kind of image in order to encapsulate the energy of a particular planetary spirit. As an illustrator, I approach astrology and astrological magic through the visual domain. I am especially interested in creating work that merges "pure" art with design to create something beautiful that also conveys technical data and works on the viewer both intellectually and spiritually to draw them closer to the essence of the planets and their associated forces.

The idea of a sigil as a map that has a level of interpretability and a link to data sets, as opposed to an Austin Osman Spare–style sigil whose meaning is obscure by design, stuck with me. I began to think of what granular data we have on the planets used in astrology versus their symbolic and mythic correspondences. The five-fold scheme of essential dignities—rulership, exaltation, triplicity, face and term—mapped out into sets of degrees governed by certain planets, seemed like a good starting point.

Most astrological magic and its associated images and symbols deal with planets in a particular sign or area of dignity—an image to be created while Saturn is in the second face of Libra, for example. These areas of dignity can be given a variety of names depending on astrological tradition—house, home, mansion. I wanted to create images that would take into account not just the palaces and refuges of the planets, but encompass their role as *planetes*, Greek "wanderers,"—pilgrims in the sky, moving along open roads from one situation to another.

The root of the English word "pilgrim" is the Latin *peregrinus*, which means "foreigner" and is used in astrology to describe a planet outside of its essential dignities. Peregrinus, broken down to its Latin root words, literally means "through a field." I was excited by this image of a planet as a traveler, carrying a walking stick and scrambling over a stile to get to the next field, wondering what they would find there—soft grassy ground? A swamp? A windswept moor?—and how each landscape would affect each planet in turn, as it provided me with a base for imaginal thinking about planetary powers while still remaining in the framework of traditional dignity doctrine (I have Mercury in Capricorn in the 7th…I like rules!).

My first round of planetary sigils were single-line drawings which traced the movement of each planet, starting in the sign and degree of their exaltation, along a circular path that represented the twelve signs, divided into seven concentric rings based on Lilly's point system of dignity and debility in *Christian Astrology*. When a planet was in a sign of rulership or exaltation (+5 or +4 points by Lilly's reckon-

Grant Hanna, Mars (2017) Acrylagoache on wood 12"x12".

ing), its line travelled to the outer ring. In a sign of detriment or fall, the line moved inward to a lower ring. Decans and terms were marked by crosses and diamonds. The resulting designs, with patterns of opposite high and lows for dignified and debilitated signs, resembled diagrams of the tumblers inside a combination lock, which I thought was appropriate for symbols that aspired to describe and unlock the sum total of each planet's path through the whole sky.

In 2017 I was invited to put together an art exhibition for Hauswitch Home+Healing in Salem, Massachusetts. Casting around for an idea, I found the path-sigils in my sketchbook and decided to develop them into larger pieces. More space meant more detail, and I went back to the idea of a planet as a wanderer travelling through a succession of landscapes more or less hospitable to its nature.

Looking at the essential nature of each planet (hot/dry for Mars, cold/moist for the Moon, etc.) paired with the nature of each sign gave me an idea of the how the planetary force might react in each environment. The lines of the planet's movements become more voluble in sympathetic signs. Each painting through the quality of linework and color gives an idea of the planet's essential nature. Cold, dry Saturn's path looks like a melancholy pie chart in wintry browns and blues; the Moon moves through the signs in a wash of waves and herbs brought forth by her generative nature, crowned by her twenty-eight-day cycle; and detail-oriented Mercury's path is a net of precisely calculated intertwining knotwork that unravels into a dizzy, tangled mess in Pisces, its sign of simultaneous detriment and fall.

Working with the dignities and debilities visually in this way led me to consider each planet's power in every single degree of the skies, much like Austin Coppock in *36 Faces: The History, Astrology and Magic of the Decans* (Three Hands Press, 2015), which I referred to numerous times while paint-

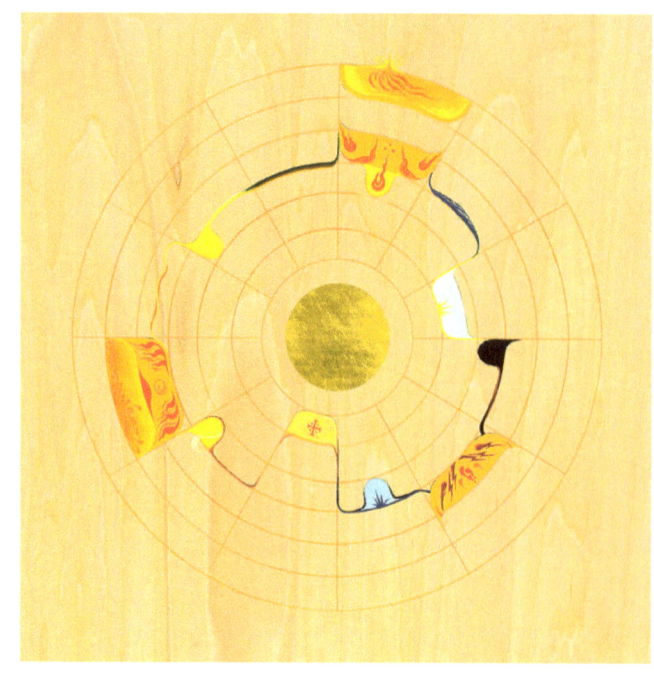
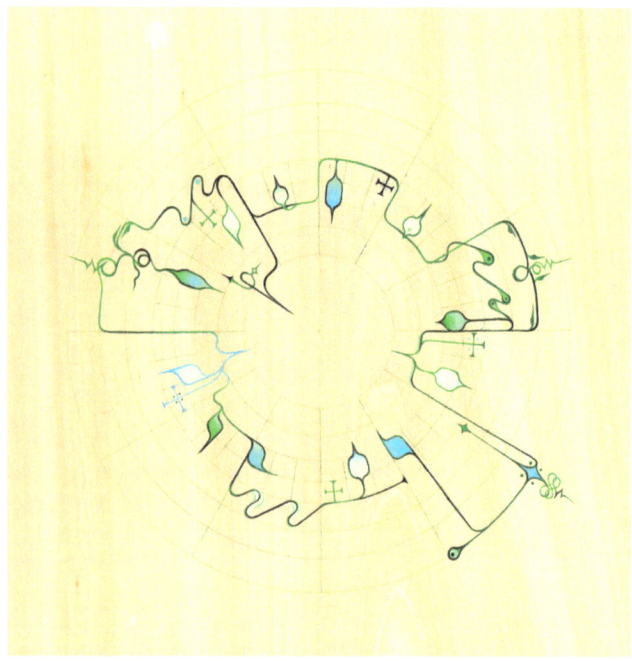
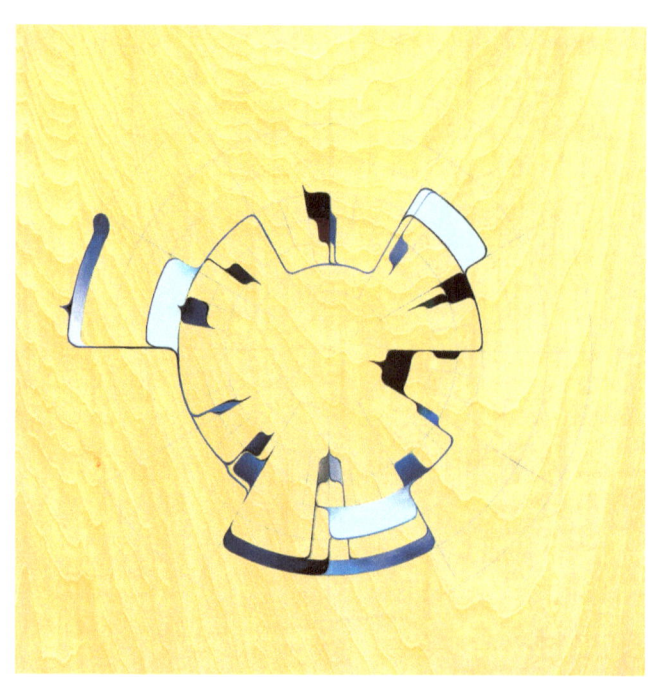

ing the seven planetary paths. For me the process opened up some new directions of inquiry into the nature of the planets, especially in my understanding of the malefics. Hot, dry, fiery, "male" Mars, for instance, had much more power in water signs than I had realized before, which gave me more clues to understand it as part of the nocturnal sect. I had always thought of Saturn as an extremely earthy planet, but its airy side (attested to in the Vedic tradition) came through strongly as I painted, which in turn got me reconsidering some of my ideas about Libra and Aquarius.

My visual exploration of the planets in their essential dignities not only honed my practical skills in assessing planetary strength in charts, but deepened my own internal connection to them. I feel I have a better understanding of each planet now at the close of the project—an understanding which, though rooted in traditional astrological theory, is personal to me and my relationship with the planetary forces. I encourage all astrologers to find creative ways to bring the planets to life, in addition to working directly from charts and research materials. Finding ways to vivify the cosmos within can only strengthen and deepen our understanding of the cosmos without.

☿

Grant Hanna, Mercury (2017) Acrylagoache on wood 12"x12"; facing page, in order from left to right, top to bottom: Moon, Sun, Venus, Saturn.

GRANT HANNA is an illustrator and traditional astrologer. He read about Aristotle's theory of the elements in the 8th grade and has been pursuing the idea through art, magic and astrology ever since. His current work focuses on astrological and ceremonial magic and ancient symbol systems. He strives to combine art and astrology as a portal for personal understanding, making talismanic pieces that are keyed to the energies of individual birth charts and moments in time. He lives in Massachusetts with a grey cat.

Mariana Palova, Sea Voice (2010)

Seven Reflections of Light
Commentary Upon the Seven *Hermetic Lots*
by Lars Panaro

The Cosmos is a play of light and shadow—subtlety and mystery weaving their way through the gross and tangible. In astrology light is bequeathed by the Sun, reflected by the Moon and transmuted by the five starry planets. Yet the shadows are cast in the mathematics of the Lots.

WHILE THIS IS AN ESSAY, it is also an evocation. Throughout the text I have departed from the usual rules of grammar and capitalized many a term in order to convey something beyond the word itself. The ideas discussed below will hopefully open the mind to new ways of thinking and stoke the fires of investigation which will lead those who heed its call to new methods of delineation and insight.

I also want to suggest, for those new to this area of study (ancient astrology), that things get very heady and academic at times and that it is important not to be overwhelmed by this. There are many endnotes here and if you find yourself becoming overwhelmed, feel free to ignore notes or skip over sections, and then return once you have digested the core of the article.

Lots: An Overview

Before the revival of the Hellenistic tradition, Lots (*Kleroi* in Greek) were known to the modern astrological world at large as Arabic Parts because ancient Greek sources on astrology were largely unknown or underutilized during the nineteenth- and twentieth-century revival of astrology in the west. The word *part* (from the Latin *pars*) was employed by medieval Latin astrologers who translated or quoted from Persian and Arabic-era source texts on astrology to speak about what the Hellenistic authors called Lots. We now know their origin lies in the Hellenistic world, not the Arabic-era one, and they originally carried the notion of *an allotment (or apportioning) of fate*.

The casting of Lots was often crudely employed for determining "who gets what" in an unclear situation. This, for example, occurs after Yeshua is crucified.[1] Yet it was and is much more than this. The casting of Lots was and still is a way to appeal to something higher, transcendent, or removed from our immediate human desires and thoughts, so as to determine what is real or True (whether we call it God's Will or "pure chance"). This happens when Christ's remaining eleven disciples attempt to fill the gap left by Judas.[2]

Through contemplation it occurred to me one day that while the planetary patterns of the chart display the broad strokes of the painting of life, Lots provide *insight* into the *ultimate outcome* of what is to unfold. They bring the planetary potentials into clearer focus, and in the case of the seven Hermetic Lots, symbolize the end of the story unfolding through each planet considered individually. Therefore in the astrological chart itself, these mathematically derived points, poetically referred to as Lots, can and do tell us much about the end result of a given matter.

Lots hint at the possibilities created by Providence (Divine Intervention). A person may be utterly fit and seemingly destined in every way to do something, yet apparent tragedy strikes, and suddenly their destiny is forever altered. So too a person may appear deserving over others when it comes to praise, fame, selection, etc., yet in casting their lots the direction of the wind or the angle at which they hit the ground reveal that there are other forces at work. There is always and forever something more than meets the eye, for, life is not a straight and narrow path, but a labyrinth of ineffable mystery and wonder.

This makes the Lots extremely important for holistic judgment as they steer us toward a hidden layer of fate—or pattern of consciousness—dwelling amidst the more surface factors of existence. They are even literally hidden within the mathematical relationship existing between the planets and the *horoskopos* (the ascendant).

Myth of Er[3]

This short chapter at the end of Plato's *Republic* sheds much light upon the concept of fate, free will, reincarnation, and the role of the Lots in all of this.

In the Myth of Er, Lots are cast to determine when those amongst the deceased (Souls), awaiting their moment of incarnation into a new life, shall *choose* their particular portion of fate. Plato illustrates how the Soul chooses both its Daimon (referred to here as *genius*),[4] to guide it in the life to come, and its *life* ("and the life which he chooses shall be his destiny").

Mortal souls, behold a new cycle of life and mortality. Your genius will not be allotted to you, but you will choose your genius; and let him who draws the first lot have the first choice, and the life which he chooses shall be his destiny. Virtue is free, and as a man honours or dishonours her he will have more or less of her; the responsibility is with the chooser—God is justified.

One set of circumstances and choices inevitably lead to perceivable and logical outcomes according to the Necessity (*Ananke*) that balance prevail as a basic law of The Cosmos. Therefore the planets, showing the beginning of a matter (circumstances and choices—a pattern of consciousness), find their conclusion in the pattern struck by the Lots. This myth drives home the point that Man is the author of his/her own fate and no one else, for "virtue is free... the responsibility is with the chooser—God is justified." The only piece of this whole process that appears to be fixed would be the initial casting of the Lots, which merely serves to focus one's choice based on the fact that there are other Souls present also required to make a choice. Yet upon one's turn to choose, the freedom to select a life amidst the remaining options stands wide open. The Lots focalize and cap the possibilities. By Necessity, each Soul's Lot and the ensuing choices that stand before it, must be in accordance with the principle "as above, so below," and therefore the Soul's past informs its present and future states, hence the Lots being derived from Lachesis' knee.[5]

After a statement concerning the Three Fates fixing destiny in place, almost rigidly so, and how each Soul is made to forget what it has just undergone before taking on the mantle of a new birth, Plato closes with this poetic and sound advice: "hold fast ever to the heavenly way and follow after justice and virtue always, considering that the soul is immortal and able to endure every sort of good and every sort of evil." This speaks to the latent potentiality of escape from the apparent rigidity life often seems to conform to ("unalterable fate") derived from *virtue* and *philosophy*. In fact this is taught in every Wisdom tradition throughout the world and therefore it comes as no surprise to find it in Plato as it is found in Buddha, Yeshua, and many more.

The Lots serve a very singular purpose in this myth—they fix the moment destiny can be chosen thus ensuring or enforcing Cosmic Harmony. This again points to their association with Providence which astrologically makes them quite profound for understanding the hidden realm of the tale of life.

The Seven Hermetic Lots

The seven Hermetic Lots are considered the "ascendants" of the seven planets.[6] They are:

- Fortune (Moon) *Asc + Moon - Sun*
- Spirit (Sun) *Asc + Sun - Moon*
- Victory (Jupiter) *Asc + Jupiter - Spirit*
- Eros (Venus) *Asc + Venus - Spirit*
- Nemesis (Saturn) *Asc + Fortune - Saturn*
- Boldness (Mars) *Asc + Fortune - Mars*
- Necessity (Mercury) *Asc + Fortune - Mercury*

What follows is a mixture of traditional meanings/ideas coupled and augmented with my own insights:

- Fortune (Moon) called Tyche in Greek, it tells the tale of fortune, a purely neutral principle in and of itself, qualified only by perspective. The Moon symbolizes the vital spirit, or pneuma, which deals with the subtle mechanisms necessary for life engrossed in the terrestrial sphere to grow and adapt itself for survival as an individualized consciousness. The Lot of Fortune becomes very important for charting modifications to our character based upon what life throws our way. It is of such importance that 2nd century astrologer Vettius Valens recommended reading the chart using the Lot of Fortune as an ascendant.[7]

- Spirit (Sun) called Daimon in Greek, it speaks to what connects us to the realm of pure spirit or *Nous* (symbolized by the Sun). *Nous* could be called Divine or Cosmic Mind and in Plotinus' Neo-Platonic philosophy is probably similar to what the Gnostics called Barbelo (or Luminous Forethought or Father-Mother)—the first emanation from the immutable reality called The One (Plotinus) or The Virgin Spirit (Gnostics) from which all else arises.[8] Thus ancient authors commonly describe this Lot as the native's truest highest intentions, detailing their relationship to God and concerning Divine inspiration. It speaks to how a person approaches or relates to Truth and what they do or contribute to the world because of a strong drive to realize something as a reflection of Truth, rather than fulfill some vital desire (Fortune/Moon).

- Victory (Jupiter) called Nike in Greek, it connotes victory, freedom, triumph, faith, and all things Jupiter. Nike was Zeus' charioteer against the Titans and even comforted him after Typhon stormed Olympus and all the other gods had fled during the war with the Titans. From this story it is apparent that Victory does not abandon those who choose Truth even in the face of apparent doom.

- Eros (Venus) Eros was Aphrodite's loyal yet discordant son who awakened the flame of desire within the hearts of men and women. This Lot shows attraction, longing, desire and eroticism, and therefore speaks about marriage and relationships in general. It also carries the connotation of friendship.

- Nemesis (Saturn) the Greek Deity called Nemesis "was the goddess of indignation against, and retribution for, evil deeds and *undeserved* good fortune. She was a personification of the resentment aroused in men by those who committed crimes with apparent impunity, or who had inordinate good fortune."[9] Therefore this Lot principally represents envy, jealousy, and the manner in which destruction is meted out for those times we transgress the Laws of The Cosmos. It also carries connotations of destruction, imprisonment, heaviness, and, in later commentaries, profundity and contemplation.

¶ BOLDNESS (MARS) (called *tharros* in Greek); there is no God associated with it, but the goddess Alke ("battle-strength, prowess, and courage") seems to be a good fit. This Lot depicts conflict, battle, wars, villainy and might, but more principally denotes the quality and degree of courage present in one's life and where/how it may manifest most markedly.

¶ NECESSITY (MERCURY) called Ananke in Greek, Goddess of "necessity, compulsion, and inevitability." This Lot principally shows the constrictive influence of our ideas and thoughts, especially those of a "compulsive" nature, which cut us off from discrimination and objectivity. It therefore speaks of impediments that keep one trapped in a point of view over a lucid and impersonal *viewing point*.

More Theoretical Commentary

These Lots open the portal to an individually unique dimension of the natal chart and the life of the person because they are calculated based on the Ascendant which changes rapidly throughout the day, unlike the planetary positions themselves. The planetary placements in a sign on a given day show things generally; the degree of the horoskopos focalizes this general meaning so that it becomes specific; finally the seven Hermetic Lots further refine the nature of planetary influences, as they reveal the mathematical relationship of planets to horoskopos.

These Lots are a focalized expression of the planets they correspond to, and can be used as alternate or secondary positions of said planets.[10] They show a more personal dimension of the planetary effects on a person's consciousness and thus within their life as a whole. In a sense they are the *reflections of the planets* and point toward the outcome of stellar influences being caged by the horoskopos as the Soul descends into matter.

Planets versus Lots

Below is a discussion of the Lots in relationship to the planets they represent with some brief examples. It is important that when using Lots that their testimony be considered within the context of the whole chart. This means that if the initial testimony looks one way, but the Lot tells a different story, then that initial testimony is altered or mitigated to a certain extent but not entirely effaced. In my experience the testimony of the Lots always augments the testimony of the other factors surrounding a given subject matter and is rarely, if ever, at odds with the rest of the judgment derived from planets and houses. While it is tempting to prioritize planets/houses over that of Lots (using the latter as a secondary level of testimony), recent experiences have lead me to believe that we should not underestimate them.

¶ SATURN REPRESENTS HOW DEFINITION IS CREATED IN OUR LIVES; HIS LOT SHOWS THE OFTEN TRAGIC RESULTS THAT ENSUE WHEN LIMITATIONS ABOUND.

In the chart of Indian revolutionary and mystic, Sri Aurobindo, this Lot is conjunct the MC, with its lord fallen in a dark house, illustrating both his imprisonment as a result of revolutionary activities and later silent retreat from the world for some twenty five years.

In civil rights leader Dr. Martin Luther King's chart this Lot is conjoined the South Node[11] highlighting a sharp rejection (or diminution) of the oppression and limitations prevalent in society for black Americans and making his life a focal point for such issues.

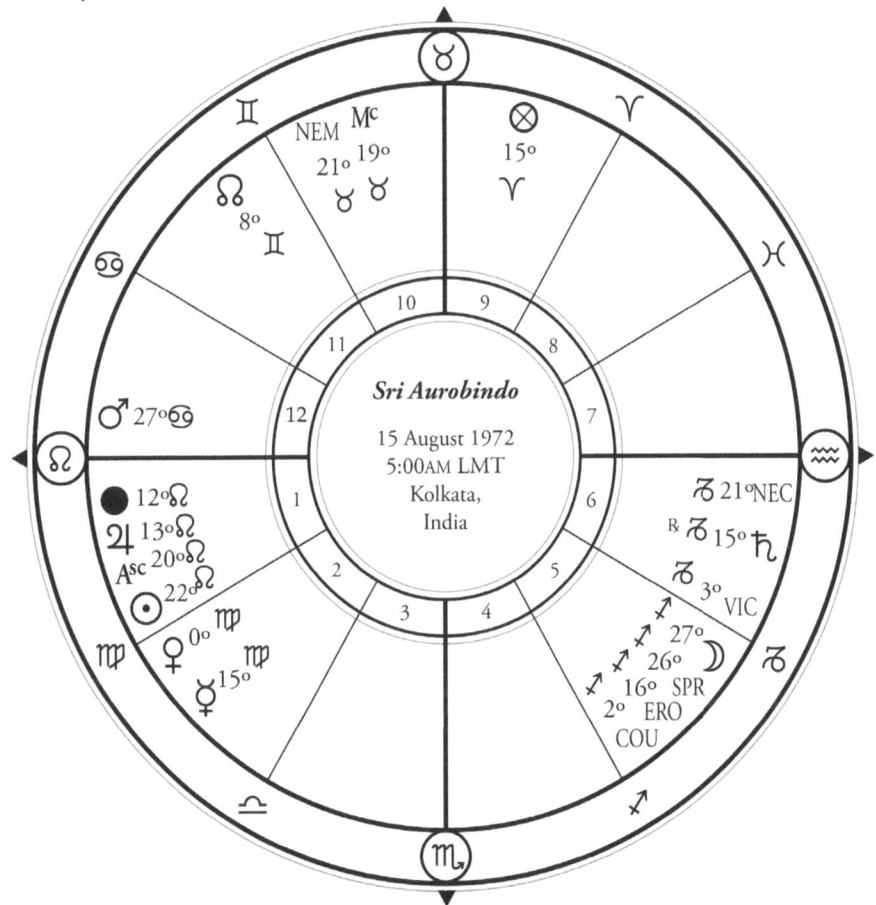

¶ Jupiter connects us to the greater whole, urging us toward higher, more selfless dimensions and his Lot shows the rewards so often reaped as a result.

Pope Francis' chart features this Lot in Pisces in the 9th house with Jupiter in exact sextile, a potent symbol of victory and blessings amidst religious institutions and faith in God. Jupiter is in a powerful mutual reception with Saturn and Mercury (for they exchange bounds), mitigating his otherwise weakened state (being in an angle and in close *antiscia*[12] with the Sun, whom Jupiter receives, also helps greatly).

Sri Aurobindo's chart features this Lot conjoined the Moon and Spirit by antiscia suggesting that spiritual aspiration (Jupiter) was joined with *intention* (Lot of Spirit) coupled with the influence of mind (Moon).[13] This Lot also resides in the 6th house and is co-present with Saturn, highlighting the Yogic insights gained during his imprisonment at the hands of his political enemies.

¶ Mars is the principle of action and initiative and his Lot describes the challenges or fears we are called to courageously overcome in order to triumph over the forces of inertia.

Muhammad Ali's chart features this Lot highly emphasized conjoined to Saturn in the 10th house, linked by antiscia to the Moon/Mercury and square to its Lord Venus (in mutual reception with Saturn). All these factors, when carefully tallied and understood, bring to life a person possessed of valour and courage, enough to conquer any obstacles present, something not otherwise obvious when considering Mars alone, which is occidental and peregrine. Mars squares Fortune and trines Spirit, which makes its influence very important, but this alone does not signify valor and courage, merely that martial circumstances are emphasized in the life.

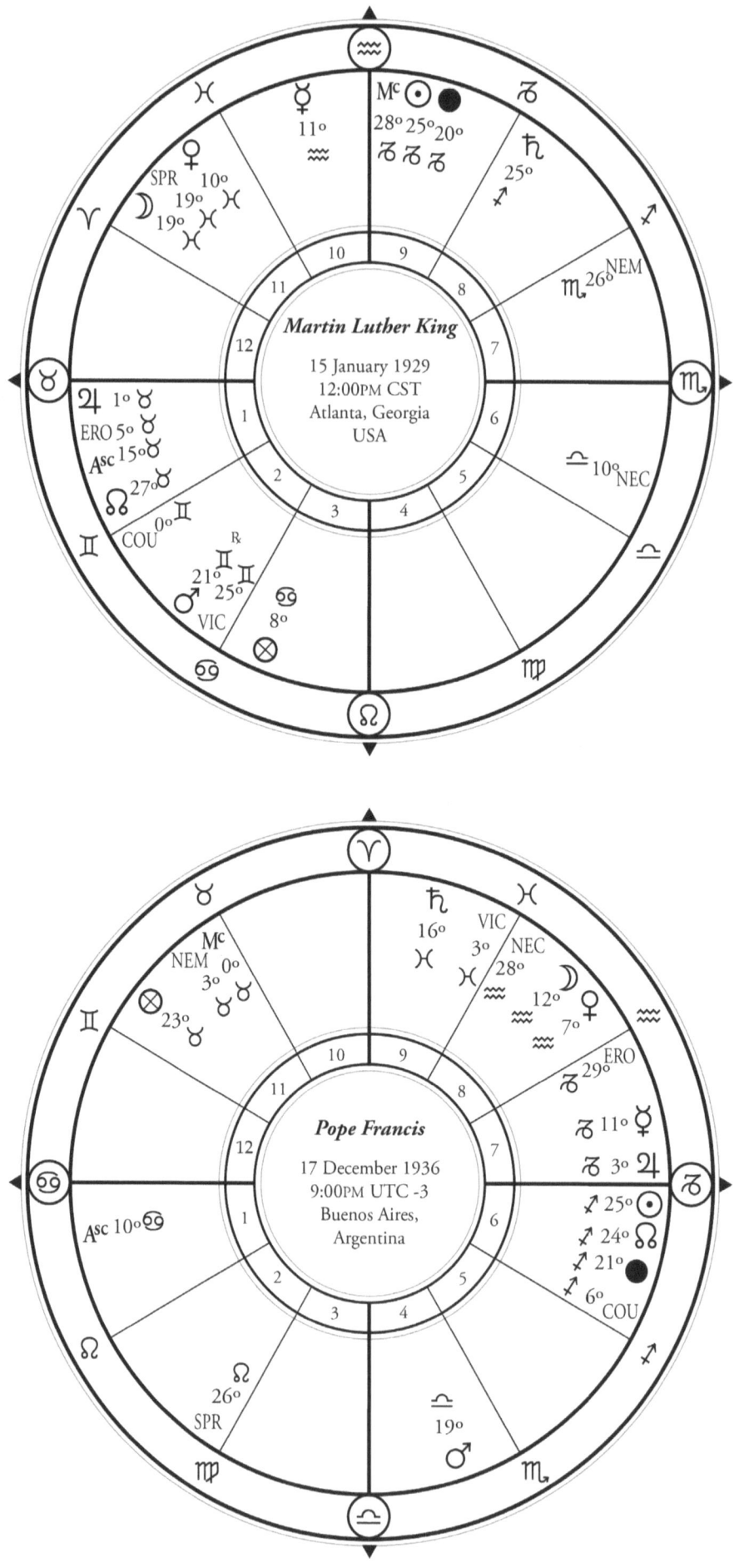

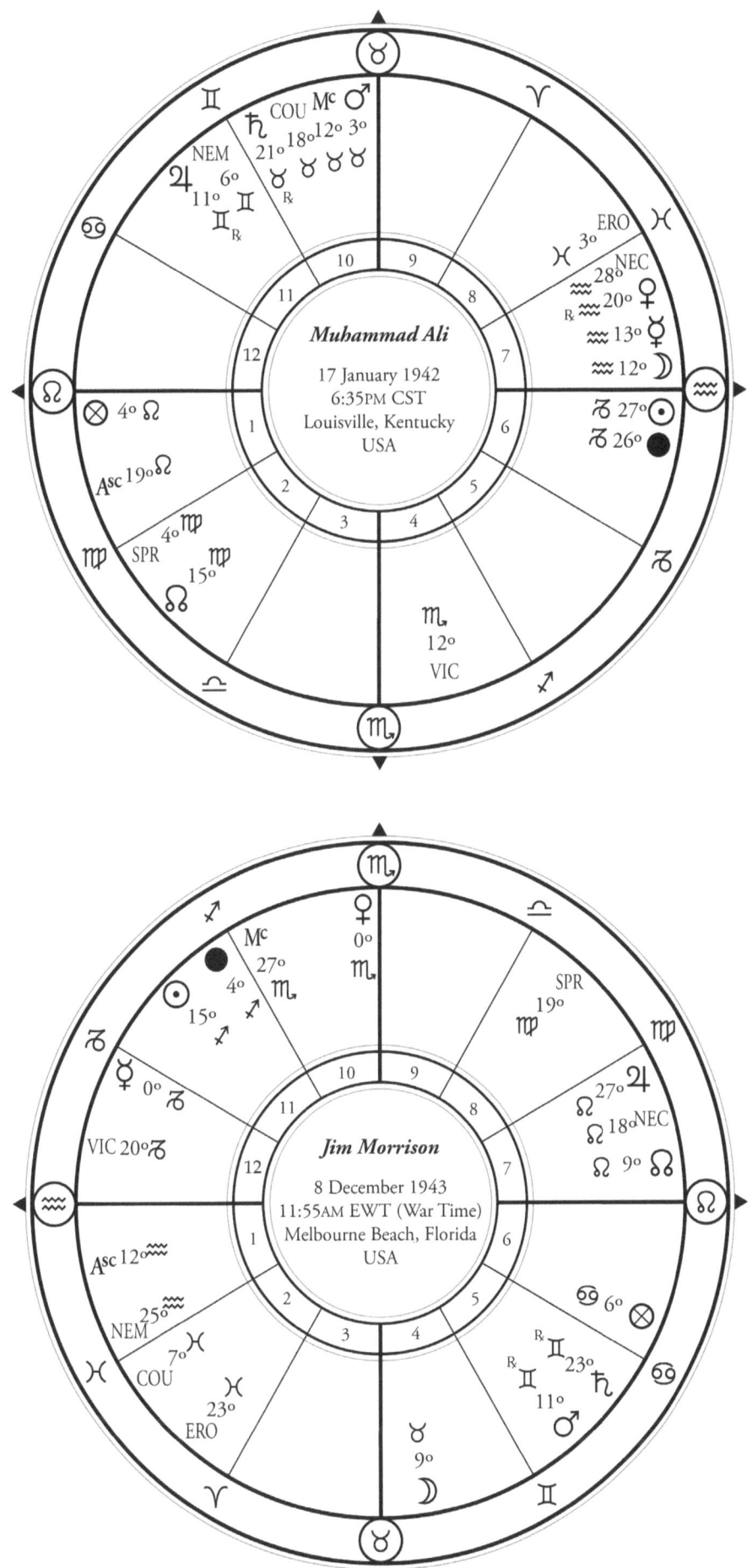

❡ Venus is the principle of attraction, drawing us toward that which we value or find pleasing; her Lot describes the results of such attraction—what is gained when beauty, as a means of self valuation, is pursued.

In Jim Morrison's chart this Lot is locked in an exact square to a retrograde Saturn, lord of the 1st and 12th houses, indicating that attraction to pleasure and beauty could be related to misery and suffering as well as being very unconventional. Afflictions to the 2nd house are common in charts of drug addicts (and people with eating disorders). The Lot of Eros, Saturn, and Venus herself, all reside in Martial bounds, while Venus is conjoined by antiscia to the Lot of Nemesis and opposed by Jupiter, further illustrating destruction and undoing through abundant pleasure seeking.

Elvis' chart features this Lot exactly conjoined the Ascendant, with its Lord in aversion in the 12th, speaking to his strong and often lewd sexual desires, sometimes involving underage women (as in the case of his first wife).

❡ Mercury is the intellectual faculty of discrimination and analysis. His Lot bequeaths insight into the potency of this discriminatory faculty and very often describes the cage that our ideas and belief systems close us in, and that which befalls us due to the ideas we espouse.

Returning to Dr. King's chart we find this Lot powerfully highlighted by virtue of a near exact antiscia conjunction with the Moon and Spirit. This also involves it in the square with Mars to the same two points. These factors are strong symbols for the power of ideas and speech and the types of mountains they can move—both heroically and tragically.

29

❡ The Moon draws us toward matter, and anchors our consciousness through association with some temporal, impermanent, sense of security and safety; thus the Lot of Fortune describes how such a strong attachment alters the very flow and contour of life.

In Elvis' chart this Lot is squared by its lord, Venus, in the 2nd house of *voice*, and trined by Saturn in Aquarius in the 3rd house (entertainment and arts, an interpretation which stems from the Indian tradition, and I find it a very useful way to utilize the 3rd house regardless of tradition). Venus sits with Spirit and Mercury, while Saturn sits with the Lot of Victory. This not only describes the great fortune that Elvis acquired through his music and film career, also, in terms of his character, stands in sharp contrast to Sagittarius rising with Jupiter in the 12th house. In fact, Elvis was deeply interested in occult philosophy, studying the likes of H.P. Blavatsky and Dane Rudhyar![14] The influences on Fortune (+ Lot of Eros on the Ascendant) show modifications to his character that lead to his successful, yet ultimately tragic, musical career—something in which an occultist may have had little to no interest.

❡ Finally the Sun is our Will[15] granted as a reflection of Truth and the intensity of our connection to It. Its Lot is the Solar Ray of Spirit shining in the darkness of matter and therefore describes how Truth (Sun) manifests in life and where it takes us . . .

Notable examples where Spirit is emphasized, displaying a life of great Spiritual potency, are Sri Aurobindo and Dr. King who both have their Moon conjoined this Lot.

Dane Rudhyar's chart also features this same link with the Moon, but through antiscia. The Lot of Spirit is exactly conjoined Saturn, ruler of the 2nd and 3rd houses, placed in the 12th house in Scorpio, while the Moon rules the 8th house and sits in the 3rd house (8th from the 8th[16]). These placements aptly describe Rudhyar's voluminous writings on occultism, whether astrology or otherwise, and paint a portrait of his great emphasis on how *crisis* can be a catalyst for spiritual growth. It is also fascinating that one of Rudhyar's most enduring contributions to astrology was his work with the *lunation cycle* and his emphasis on Cyclic Time (Moon and Saturn factors).

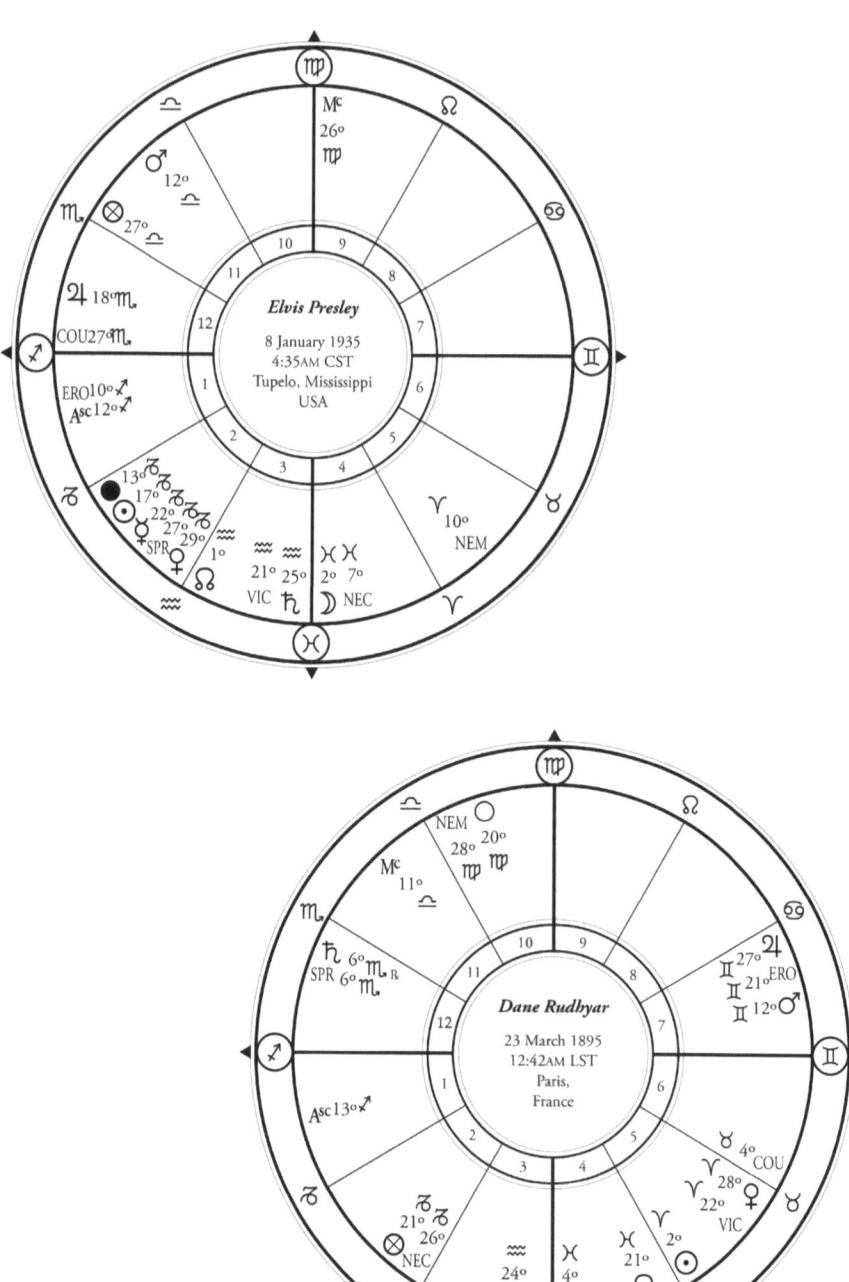

Key Considerations for Delineation

The most direct way to employ Lots in general (not just these seven) is to use them to find *confluence*, that is the repetition of a theme in a chart concerning a given factor or area of life. These seven Lots become emphasized when they are:

❡ Closely conjoined an angle

❡ Closely conjoined a planet

❡ In a house they share an affinity

with (Nemesis in the 12th or 8th house, Victory in the 9th or 11th house, etc.)

- In a sign/bound/face they share an affinity with
- Their lord or almuten[17] sits in a prominent position conjoined an angle or key planet, or the Lots of Fortune and Spirit
- They are aspected by their lord or almuten
- They are aspected by the planet they correspond to

These Lots are always useful for specific matters even if they are not heavily emphasized in the chart as explained above. My original opinion was that the Lots cannot logically be said to cast aspects (as they are non-luminous), but when they are conjoined a planet or point (including by antiscia) they co-mingle their significations with said planet or point. However after dipping into the world of Uranian-Symmetrical astrology I am weary to propose such limits. It seems that any powerful aspect between a planet and a Lot can appear as a co-mingling or association, not merely the planet actively influencing the Lot which remains passive. For example, a recent client's chart featured Sun in close square to Nemesis. The 2nd house Sun ruled the 4th place of property and dwelling place and it came out that the person had been deceived by the landlord (an individual possessing power—Sun) into paying more in rent for their apartment than was legal and was engaged in a legal dispute over this situation. Yet the Sun also appears to have a purifying influence upon Nemesis evidenced by this deception being brought to light in a way that extended beyond the native's direct involvement.

I have offered a mixture of traditional and modern commentary in my treatment of the Lots above. I want to make it clear that while I have perhaps focused on a more psychological approach that they are not to be restricted to this domain. It is very important to keep in mind the essential rules of ancient astrology and to be willing to let the chart speak without one's bias or desire to explain away what is shown (whether by pseudo-psychology, aggrandizement, or white-washing as is very often done). For example, Nemesis can often be a real kick in the teeth and may have very little to do with "how a person limits themselves," while Victory can literally appear as a person who wins more often than loses, etc. As an example, a chart of a friend features Leo rising with the 12th lord Moon exactly conjoined Nemesis, both very close to the angle; this person's mother was disturbingly malicious at times while they were growing up. Thus it would be foolish to assume that these Lots can only relate to the person's Psyche or that their effects stem from purely individual choice as we often understand it.

Another useful resource for better understanding how to use these Lots lies in the Indian text *Brihat Parashara Hora Shastra*.[18] There is a technique of calculating special non-luminous points called *Upa-Grahas*.[19] Slokas 61–70 in Chapter 3 (*Planetary Characteristics and Descriptions*) outline the basic calculation and provide some minor commentary. A later chapter (25) entitled *Effects of Non-Luminous Planets* outlines the effects of some of these Grahas through all twelve houses in specific detail. I highly recommend reading these chapters to gain insight into working with the Hermetic Lots, especially because each Upa-Graha corresponds to a particular Graha (including the nodes) and therefore they are very similar to the Hermetic Lots (notwithstanding some important differences). The most basic logic behind the delineations of these Upa-Grahas in the houses is the notion that the malefic ones do better in malefic houses while creating trouble in benefic houses and vice versa.[20] Therefore in the context of Hellenistic techniques and perspectives, the malefic Lots are likely to signify something auspicious when placed in malefic houses (3rd, 6th, 8th, 12th, and sometimes the 2nd) while benefic Lots perform best in benefic houses (1st, 2nd,* 4th, 5th, 7th, 9th, 10th, 11th) and vice versa. This is a simple yet effective way to begin working with them.

Finally I wish to mention a perspective found in Firmicus Maternus' *Mathesis*. The Lots are used to determine house topics in the sense that whatever sign the Lot falls in becomes the "house of ___."[21] Thus the location of the Lot of the father becomes the house of the father and so on for any other areas of life one casts a Lot for.[22] This is reminiscent of certain authors speaking of the Joys[23] of the planets as the house of that planet. Thus the 11th house is referred to as the house of Jupiter, the 6th house as the house of Mars and so on. Taking this a bit further, any house where we find Jupiter is going to become Jupiterian and the same for all other planets and houses. It is perhaps for this reason that many Jyotishis will look at a given house from a planet for a given topic, in addition to or sometimes in place of that house. Thus the 6th from Mars becomes important for accidents and misfortunes and its testimony is considered alongside the 6th house. For ancient authors it appears that the houses themselves are a foundational component in horoscopy rather than something always at the forefront of interpretation. Hence the house a Lot falls in becomes the first house for topics relative to that Lot and the actual house it falls in may not be fundamentally important. Taking the Lot of the father as the first house for the father one can derive a great deal of accurate information concerning the fate of the father and so on for other topics.

If we extend this idea to the Hermetic Lots we may find that the position of Nemesis becomes a place of contention, imprisonment, and deceit, similar to the 12th house. This also means the lord or almuten of that Lot becomes accidentally malefic, especially if other factors weigh in to make this so. Furthermore, borrowing from the Jyotishis, we may wish to look to the 12th house from Nemesis for losses, the 8th house for destruction, the 6th house for enslavement and so on. The 9th house may tell us something about the Divine purpose behind Nemesis' effects or symbolize the intervention of God upon such effects, etc. These are subtle and more advanced ways to utilize the Lots and I mention them mainly for completeness.

Commentary on Calculation

The Lots of the benefics, Venus and Jupiter, are derived from the mathematical relationship between those planets and the Lot of Spirit, while the Lots of the malefics (including Mercury) are derived from their relationship with Fortune.

This is not a "good versus bad" dichotomy. Instead it relies upon the notion that cruel and trying experiences are more the result of our terrestrial nature while true Good is derived from our relationship with God.

There is no reason one could not reverse the calculation for the Lots such that we take the relationship between the malefics and Spirit and the benefics and Fortune. The rationale for interpreting these might be that the benefic Lots show us the terrestrial shadow of Good, which is essentially fleeting and impermanent, while the malefic Lots hint at the trials and tribulations that contribute to the realization of Spiritual ideals.

Furthermore these Lot formulas could be cast from any one of the other three angles for insight into these three other quintessential dimensions of life. To make this simple all one need do is move in intervals of 90 degrees from a given Lot to find the positions relative to the MC/IC and move 180 degrees from the Lot to find it relative to the Descendant.

⁋ Eros and Necessity

A curious dilemma arises in that according to Valens the Lots of Eros and Necessity are calculated based upon the Lots of Fortune and Spirit, while Paulus gives those same two Lots as calculated based upon Venus and Spirit and Mercury and Fortune. In addition we find that the significations given are relatively similar, especially in later medieval texts. I have developed what I consider to be a very sound philosophical rationale for why there should be such a difference of calculation and how/when it becomes useful to work with both Lot calculations in a chart. To discuss this in depth would require another essay in and of itself, so for now I will just say that a careful reading of Valens' comments about these Lots points to the dichotomy of the Soul's desire (Eros) for incarnation and the results of its association with the non-luminous realm of Matter (Necessity). Eros expands upon Spirit while Necessity augments Fortune. Furthermore one of these Lots will always be the same as the Lot of Basis, which relates to the foundational strength of the entire Nativity and was used for predicting fame or preferement and status.[24]

Conclusion

The planets reflect the light of the Sun (as mirrors) and this light is further altered as it passes through the zodiacal signs (like a prism), and finally it shines upon and becomes associated with the non-luminous realm of matter in the houses. The Lots help to tie this whole process together and symbolically refer to the quality of this light's appearance in the world, for no matter the initial state of something there remains always the possibility of a reversal of fortune or a change in the flow.[25]

Confluence is the quintessential manner in which the chart speaks to us of the tangible components of life freed from what oft becomes a prison of astrological terminology. Confluence focuses the mind and opens the way to Intuition (*Nous*). Lots are a very powerful technique for finding confluence, one that should not be underestimated.

For those new to the Lots, or traditional methods in general, it may be tempting to write an interpretation for each Lot in each sign and house as is commonly done. As a contemplative exercise this could prove useful, but I must caution you against slavishly memorizing such ideas in an attempt to force the hand of delineation. The magic of astrology and all divinatory arts lies within the pattern of the Whole taken together with the moment one dares to look.

Symbolically speaking, an astrologer who is calculating the position of a Lot—something beyond the basic components of a horoscope—is indeed *casting Lots*, because once this is done, the doorway to knowledge portrayed by the chart is widened. Mystically, the Lots an astrologer chooses to investigate within the context of a reading are a direct reflection of the moment—the patterns of consciousness converging at that point in time/space. To venture down this line of thinking is to treat astrology in a more divinatory manner than is often done. Please enjoy playing with this technique and may the doors of awe stand open before you.

Glory To God Alone[26]

Endnotes

1 "And having crucified him they portioned out his garments, casting lots." Matthew 27:35, in David Hart Bentley, *The New Testament: A Translation* (New Haven: Yale UP, 2017).

2 "And praying, they said, "You Lord, knowing the hearts of all, show us which one of these two you have chosen to take a place in this ministry and apostolate, which Judas deserted for a place of his own. And they cast lots over them, and the lot fell to Matthias, and he was reckoned together with the eleven Apostles." The Acts of the Apostles 1:24–26, in Hart Bentley, *The New Testament*.

3 All quotes come from this version: https://www.thoughtco.com/the-myth-of-er-120332

4 There are many Daimones in Greek cosmology yet the most important one, which later came to be known as The Holy Guardian Angel, in medieval Christianity, represents what might be best described as a dominant quality of the

Soul which is always guiding us and leading us to the greatest good possible (see Robert Zoller's DMA course and the lesson about the Almuten Figuris).

5 Lachesis, one of the Three Fates (Moirai), is the sister of the past, and is the one said to oversee this process; the knees are related to Capricorn, the gate of death in Neoplatonic cosmology.

6 All Lot formulas given are day formulas, deriving from Paulus Alexandrinus, and the formulas reverse in night charts. For those wishing to investigate what classical authors had to say about these Lots, I recommend reading Valens, Paulus, Firmicus Maternus, Dorotheus, Al-Qabisi, Abu-Bakr, Bonatti, Ibn Ezra, and the list goes on. As one reads these older authors it will become apparent that they differ only slightly in their opinions. I also recommend having a look at this article (http://dlib.nyu.edu/awdl/isaw/isaw-papers/12/) discussing a horoscope dated to around 350 CE which showcases the Hermetic Lots according to Paulus' calculations and at the very least highlights how important they likely were for many astrologers.

7 For the importance afforded this Lot see section "3. The Lot of Fortune and its Houseruler", on pages 26–30 of Mark Riley's translation of *The Anthology* by Vettius Valens (http://www.csus.edu/indiv/r/rileymt/vettius%20valens%20entire.pdf). Also see page 34, the section entitled "The Lot of Fortune as the Ascendant" to learn more about this approach.

8 For more on this see: Bentley Layton, *The Gnostic Scriptures: Ancient Wisdom for the New Age* (New York: Doubleday Dell, 1987).

9 http://www.theoi.com/Daimon/Nemesis.html

10 In one of his lectures John Frawley proposed the idea that the Lots be treated as "super" versions of the planets they correlate to and indeed this is a great way to think about them.

11 See my essay on the nodes entitled "The Serpent of Reality"—a discussion of the nodes from an Advaita Vedanta perspective—in *IAM Magazine* (Jan/Feb 2018), the Immortelle Issue. I pull a lot from the Indian perspective when it comes to the nodes, and it has greatly expanded my ability to work with them. Ancient practitioners experimented with different techniques and perspectives all of the time and so should we. History, as we understand it today, is a very recent phenomenon and preservation of the past in a dead letter manner was not a common practice amidst civilizations before the eighteenh century. We should follow in the footsteps of the ancients and use what works in practice rather than slavishly adhere to some false notion or ideal of "tradition" and therefore, as a practicing astrologer, I find it impossible to see the nodes and think of them only as the Hellenistics did or as the Indians did. Instead, as I find great value in both perspectives, I inevitably use them together with great results.

12 Mirrored points relative to the solistial and equinoctial axes. See http://ambientastrology.com/antiscia/ for an overview of this technique, one that is vitally important for good delineation.

13 Aurobindo was first a revolutionary seeking *victory* against the British oppressors of India and later, in his Yogic work, sought Divine *victory* through his efforts to manifest in the world what he called The Supermind. In modern parlance the Moon is the lower mind, what the Stoics regarded as Psyche and what the Indian school of Samkhya would call Manas. Mercury is considered Logica Psyche, the higher mind, and what Samkhya would call Buddhi. In certain classical texts on astrology the Moon is referred to as the vegetative soul while Mercury is called the rational soul.

14 http://www.khaldea.com/rudhyar/astroarticles/secretelvis.shtml

15 I use this term (capitalized) in the sense that Rudhyar and Dr. Roberto Assagioli used it. See Assagioli's book *The Act of Will* for a more indepth look at this concept.

16 This comes from a powerful Jyotish technique called *Bhavat Bhavam*—again extraordinarily useful for delineation irrespective of tradition.

17 Almuten is a Latin transliteration of the Arabic term *al-mubtazz* meaning "victor." It is used to denote the planet having the strongest number of essential dignities over a given point (cusp, lot, or planet). An almuten has the most say over the matters signified by the point (or points) it rules over. In medieval astrology a weighted pointing system was created in which various levels of dignity were given more or less points, yet in Ptolemy's *Tetrabiblos* we find a system in which each dignity is afforded one point regardless of it being by domicile or bound etc. My own approach is largely derived from Ptolemy. I afford one point to the following: domicile, exaltation, bound, triplicity, decan, aspect (whole sign), and I afford more precedence to aspects within 3–5 degrees. There are various subtleties to employing this technique in a way that takes it out of a purely mechanistic realm, but this is another essay entirely. I have offered this brief explanation for those who wish to experiment with this approach.

18 The edition I reference is: *Brihat Parasara Hora Sastra of Maharshi Parasara*, translation, commentary, annotation and editing by R. Santhanam, (New Delhi: Ranjan Publications, 2014).

19 Graha is the sanskrit term for planet and means "seizer."

20 For example *Dhuma*, which is inauspicious and considered by some to be like Mars, is said to cause such effects: "If Dhuma is in the 3rd, the native will be intelligent, very bold, delighted, eloquent, and be endowed with men and wealth" (Sloka 4 of Chapter 25) versus "If Dhuma is in the 7th, the native will be penniless, be ever sensuous, skillful in going to others' females, and be always devoid of brilliance" (Sloka 8 of Chapter 25). In contrast *Chapa*, which is auspicious and considered by some to be like Venus, is said to cause such effects: "If Chapa is in the 7th, the native will be wealthy, endowed with all virtues, learned in sastras, religious, and agreeable" (Sloka 44 of Chapter 25) versus "If Chapa is in the 8th, the native will be interested in other's jobs, be cruel, interested in other's wives, and be defective limbed" (Sloka 45 of Chapter 25). If one investigates these slokas more then it will be seen that the basic logic described above about benefic-malefic associations between an Upa-Graha and a house will not always be so simple or straightforward. If anything this is a healthy reminder that there are always exceptions to every rule and very often the benefic-malefic dichotomy breaks down.

21 See Liber Septimus of *Ancient Astrology in Theory and Practice, Matheseos Libri VIII*, translated by Jean Rhys Bram, (Parkridge NJ: Noyes Press, 1975). The calculation of Lots as "houses" is scattered throughout this section. http://www.astrologiahumana.com/firmicusmaternustheoryandpractice.pdf

22 Firmicus also appears to have advocated for equal houses, and therefore if he was taking Lots to indicate houses he may well have been also casting equal house cusps from the very degree of that Lot instead of using a whole sign system. I believe that such techniques can be employed using whole sign or equal houses and that each offers something different in terms of the subtle information it can reveal.

23 http://theastrologydictionary.com/j/joys/

24 See Valens, *The Anthology*, trans. Riley, 38.

25 We see this most clearly through the mixture of essential and accidental dignity and especially through aspectual relationships—a planet in powerful/weak zodiacal state is made weak/strong by virtue of its angularity/cadency or by being aspected by a malefic/benefic.

26 This phrase closes out Abu Ali's text *On The Judgement of Nativities* and is an important reminder of something lost, especially in this day and age.

LARS PANARO is a guitarist turned astrologer and tarot reader. Toward the end of receiving a BFA in music with an emphasis on classical guitar and electric shredding, the gates of the esoteric burst open in the form of astrology, and he has been voraciously studying and practicing it ever since. For more information about his approach and services visit www.larspanaroastrology.com

Alison Tinker, Seventh Mansion of the Moon (2018)

ALISON TINKER graduated from the Rhode Island School of Design in 2008 and embarked on a career in illustration and web development. At the same time she was forming a deep interest in astrology. She was delighted to discover the artisanship of astrological talismans, which perfectly combine her love of art and astrology. In 2015 she began Christopher Warnock's Astrological Magic Course to learn more about the subject. In 2018 she joined AYA as a board member to become more involved in the astrological community. She lives and works in Richmond, Virginia.

Afflicted Syzygy and Daimon as Indicators of Violent Death According to Vettius Valens

by Tania Daniels

DEATH HAS ALWAYS BEEN a controversial subject in religious, philosophical or astrological circles. It was common for astrologers of the past to deal with it and to make precise prognostications about a native's life and death. Ancient masters mostly believed that there was a precise moment at which a native entered life, as well as a precise and thus forecastable moment at which the native was supposed to leave their physical body behind. They were sure that the birth chart revealed information about the "how" and the "when."

Over the last centuries, people dealt with death differently than we do now, and astrologers' clients were supposed to cope with certain information which the majority of today's astrologers would not even address, such as the possibility of a violent death. Many famous ancient astrologers worked for the royal court and one of their responsibilities was to protect the king, giving warning about possible accidents or conspiracy, suggesting alternative options, or, when things got really bad, they sometimes even suggested crowning a different person for a certain critical period, to ensure that the negative transits forecasted for the king would act upon that person and not the "real" king, who would take up his power only after these transits had passed.

Many ancient astrological texts deal with death. Vettius Valens (120–125 CE), author of the *Anthology*, is considered one of the originators of the length of life technique. He has a short chapter on violent death. However, this chapter is not a timing technique by itself, rather it shows how to look at a natal chart and quickly see whether a violent death is indicated. In this article, I will present this technique in depth, and show its validity on a series of seven charts of persons who suffered a violent death.[1]

In Book II, Valens gives precise instructions on how to recognize a violent death in a native's chart (emphasis mine):

> Now we will press on to consider violent deaths. When the ruler of the New or Full Moon at the nativity is turned away from its sign or is unfavorably situated, with a malefic in aspect, it indicates violent death. In the same way, if Mercury is in opposition to the Full Moon and has malefics in aspect, it brings a bad cause of death. If Saturn, Mars, or Mercury are located in the sign on the fortieth day, they indicate violent death. Likewise malefics in the Descendant or in the sign preceding the Descendant bring violent deaths or the onset of diseases and miserable deaths. The 8th Place from the Ascendant has the same influence on the cause of death; so does the 8th Place from the Lot of Fortune. It is necessary to examine the Lot and its ruler to see in which signs they are located, because the cause of death will be foretold by them: *the Moon (which is Fortune), when in conjunction with the Sun in Aries, suffers an eclipse or loss of light in the eighth sign, Scorpio. Therefore Scorpio is called its depression.*[2]

The passage I emphasize above did not make sense to me when I first read it. So I asked the Italian astrologer and philologist Lucia Bellizia for an alternative translation, which she made directly from the Greek of Pingree's critical edition into Italian. She translated the sentence as follows:

> It is thus necessary to observe the Lot of Fortune and its ruler, in which sign it falls; by these are shown the causes of the death, *because also in the cosmos, the Moon, which is Tyche, conjoined to the Sun in Aries in the eighth place, Scorpio, causes the eclipse and the subtraction of light, this is why (Scorpio) is called (the place of) its fall.*[3]

Valens thus simply means, that the 8th place from the Daimon shows the cause of death. He then continues and lists the pairs of signs that are in an 8th house relationship (Table 1). Therefore, the Daimon, the physical body, can possibly be destroyed in the 8th place from itself. Now let's look at these rules more in-depth.

As we can see from the translations, Valens is most concerned about the *syzygy*. The term *syzygy* describes the position of the prenatal New or Full Moon, depending on the lunar phase when the native was born. If a person is born closer to a New Moon than to a Full Moon, his or her sygygy is a New Moon. If he or she is born closer to a Full moon, than the sygyzy is a Full Moon.

The position of the syzygy and its ruler was given a great deal of importance by Hellenistic astrologers. This is because the Moon is the natural significator of the native's body, similar to the ASC ruler or the ruler of the Lot of Fortune (also called Daimon or Lot of the Moon). We can consider the prenatal Moon as the jar which is going to be filled with the Sun's spirit during birth, therefore, the prenatal Moon needs helpful aspects in order to guarantee good health and luck to the still unborn child. When the ruler of the syzygy was in an angular house (especially the first and the tenth), and thus strongly placed, the native would have good fortune in life. Hephaistion of Thebes, fifth-century author of *Apotelesamatics*, writes:

Daimon in	Destroyed in	Death by
Aries	Scorpio	Mars destroys himself: suicide, accomplices in crime, bandits, murderers, death by animal attacks, fire, collapsing buildings, bleeding, attacks.
Taurus	Sagittarius	Venus is destroyed by Jupiter. Death by luxurious living, stuffing with food, alcohol, sex, strokes while asleep or while relaxing. No distressing cause of death, unless configuration with malefic.
Gemini	Capricorn	Mercury is destroyed by Saturn. Death by black bile, painful cramps or harmed in damp places by beasts or by crawling things. Condemnation to death, imprisoning, suffocation. Attacks by bandits or enemies.
Cancer	Aquarius	The Moon is destroyed by Saturn. Death by dampness or internal complaints from pains of the spleen and stomach, from vomiting fluids. Death on the sea, rivers, from chills, attacks of beasts or crawling things. Illness such as elephantiasis, jaundice, lunacy, poisoning, long imprisonment, and chronic fevers. Women die from pains in the breast, cancer, infirmities of the genitals or the womb, suffocation and abortion.
Leo	Pisces	The Sun is destroyed by Jupiter. Heart attacks, complaints in the liver. They are at risk in wet places or from moist complaints, falls, the ague, accidents in the bath, treachery of women.
Virgo	Aries	Mercury is destroyed by Mars. A death by attacks of enemies or bandits, burns, collapsing buildings, blindness, imprisonment, the wrath of noblemen, from captivity, falls from animals or high places, crushing of limbs, animal attacks. Women die from collapsed uterus, abortions, hemorrhages, consumption.
Libra	Taurus	Venus is destroyed by herself. Suicide by poisoned drinks, snakebite, through self-starvation, excessive intercourse, excision of the uvula, drowning or by mutilation, blindness, or paralysis. Attacked by females or fall from high places or from animals.
Scorpio	Gemini	Mars is destroyed by Mercury. Death by knife cuts to the genitals or the rump, from strangury, festering sores, choking, crawling things, violence, wars, attacks by bandits, assaults of pirates, by fire, impaling, attacks of beasts and crawling things.
Sagittarius	Cancer	Jupiter is destroyed by the Moon. Death from disorders of the spleen, liver, stomach, from vomiting fluids or blood, falls from animals, attacks of ravenous beasts, collapsing buildings, shipwreck, wet places. They die from lunacy, blindness, feebleness.
Capricorn	Leo	Saturn is destroyed by the Sun. Death by heart attacks, fractures, accidents in the bath or from burns, through the wrath of kings and noblemen, by impaling, injuries from animals, falls from high places.
Aquarius	Virgo	Saturn is destroyed by Mercury. They die by wasting of the vitals, dropsy, elephantiasis, jaundice, fever, sword slashes, dysentery, treachery of women.
Pisces	Libra	Jupiter is destroyed by Venus. Death from moist complaints, poisoning, painful fluxes or cramps, complaints of the genitals or liver, sciatica, attacks of beasts and crawling things.

Table 1

For no small power occurs with the prenatal conjunction whenever it chances to be upon a pivot, especially the Horoscopos and the Midheaven.[4]

Valens says similarly:

> If the sign of the New or Full Moon or the ruler of this sign happens to be in the Ascendant or at the MC, the native will be fortunate.[5]

However, if the ruler of the syzygy did not aspect its own sign and was configured with malefics, this was considered a bad omen regarding the native's life: the malefics would threaten life at some point.

Nevertheless, the syzygy is only one issue factor to check; the other is Mercury. Mercury can either act in a positive manner or as a malefic, depending on which planet he is associated with:

> Mercury will make everything capricious in outcome and quite disturbed. Even more, it causes those having this star in malefic signs or degrees to become even worse.[6]

When he thus opposes the syzygy and is configured with the malefics, he transfers their light to the syzygy and diminishes its power.

> Saturn, Mars, and Mercury cause crime, treachery, judgments, and alarms. Men go into debts and expenses for the sake of scriptures or mystic lore, and they suffer no ordinary tribulations and ruin. In other cases, these stars make men keen and intelligent in business, leading a varied life, maligned by some because of violent and illegal activities. Occasionally they become involved in toilsome and dangerous business and fall into poverty. Then they blame their own Fortune, blaspheme the gods, and become oath breakers and atheists. If the stars are not in their proper domicile, they bring criminal charges and imprisonment.[7]

In order to understand why the fortieth day of birth is so important, we have to consider that this time is associated with the concept of renewal. According to the Talmud, it takes forty days for an embryo to be formed in its mother's womb, and forty weeks to be born. This may also refer to the time a baby needs to learn to suckle and regain weight after its initial loss during the first few days after birth.

After forty days, the Moon has made a complete revolution around the zodiac plus 160° (calculating its average speed with 13° per day): this is what Valens refers to in his passage in *Anthology* Book I, 15K, *about the third, seventh and fortieth days of the Moon*. Rather than counting degrees as, he says, his colleagues do, Valens seems to consider the opposition of the Moon to his own sign in the birth chart when he says:

> The third, seventh, and fortieth days of the Moon as follows: assume the Moon is in Scorpio 7°; the third day will be in Sagittarius 7°. [It is necessary to investigate the day in this way. Sagittarius 7° has become the third day.] In the nativity chart the seventh will be found in square, at Aquarius 7°. The fortieth will be at Taurus 7°. (Some add 160° to the Moon's position at birth and count off this amount from the Moon's sign. Others add to the Moon's position at birth on the third and seventh and fortieth days, then after calculating, they interpret the Moon at those places).[8]

Both Mercury and the Moon are associated with the human brain. While the Moon rules over instinctive intelligence, Mercury rules the rational mind. When Mercury is configured with the malefics, the rational mind could potentially be harmed or uninhibited. Therefore, when Mercury is opposed to Saturn, the brain might show dysfunctional disorder or might not be fully developed. Mars in opposition could show some damage to the brain (as for example the consequences of an unsuccessful abortion or similar). However, since the sentence in Valens' passage is not very clear, my interpretation is that he is asking to check if malefics are in the sign of the sygyzy Moon after forty days. However, Valens himself does not apply this rule in his examples charts very thoroughly.

According to Valens, the Lots, especially the Daimon (Lot of Fortune) are as important as the syzygy. This is because Fortune is associated with the body and physical well-being of the native, similar to the ASC and its ruler, or the Moon, which also describes the physical shape of a person. In fact, Valens derives places from the position of Daimon in order to identify particularly strong or weak places.[9] Many of his techniques are based on the houses derived from the Daimon. Following this logic, in the 8th place from Fortune, the Daimon is "eclipsed" and loses its life-light. It is thus necessary to examine the position of the Lot of Fortune and its ruler in order to determine which sign they are in because the manner of death is foretold by them.

Generally speaking, it seems from Valens' example charts, that he uses the sygyzy to establish whether the chart warns of a violent death and uses the Daimon to define the cause of death.

In summary, here are the indicators of violent death in a natal chart according to Valens:

¶ The ruler of the NM/FM is turned away from its sign or is unfavorably situated with an aspect to a malefic

¶ Mercury is in opposition to the sygyzy[10] and is configured with malefics

¶ Mars, Saturn or Mercury are located in the sign of the sygyzy[11] on the fortieth day

¶ There are malefics in the DSC or the sign preceding (6th house)

¶ Malefics are in the 8th place from the ASC

¶ Malefics are in the 8th place from the place of the Lot of Fortune.

We will now apply Valens' rules to modern nativities.

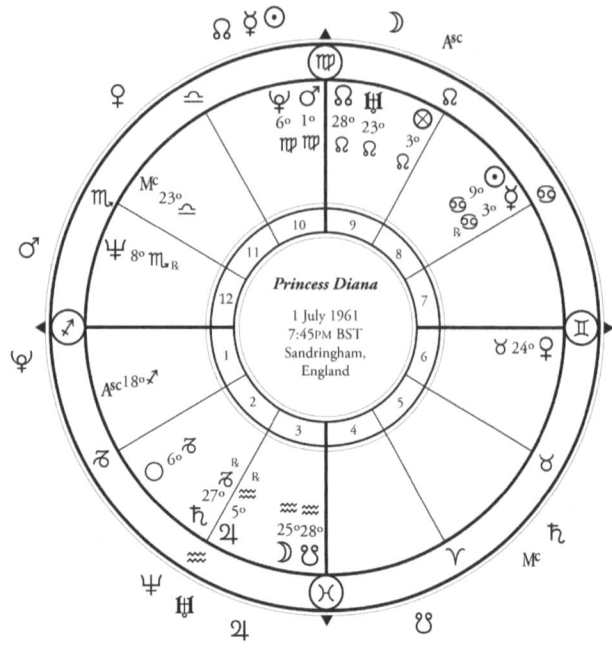
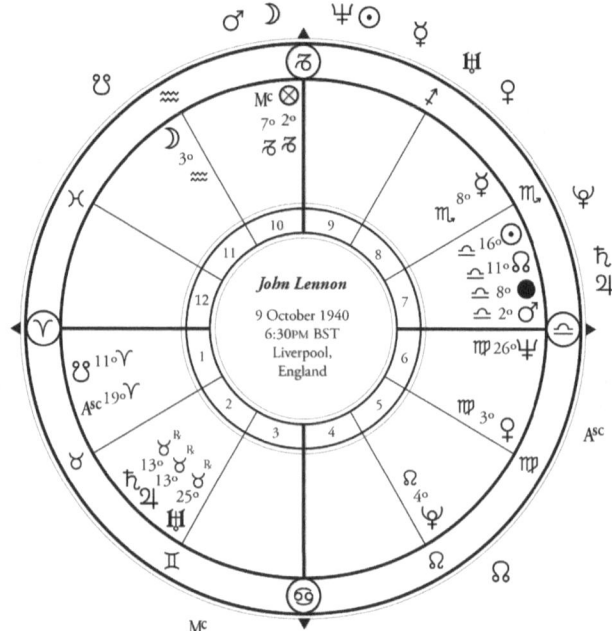

❧ Diana, Princess of Wales

Diana, Princess of Wales, died in a car accident on August 31, 1997 together with her lover Dodi Fayed and the driver Henri Paul, while her bodyguard Trevor Rees-Jones survived.

❧ Diana was born prior to a Full Moon with the Moon at 6° 33' of Capricorn, thus ruler of her sygyzy is a malefic. Saturn is retrograde but in his own domicile and trined by Venus. (The position of the sygyzy is trines a Mars/Pluto conjunction, if we want to consider the outers).[12]

❧ The position of the sygyzy is opposed by peregrine Mercury, whose next aspect is a sextile to Mars, the malefic out of sect[13] (and conjunct Pluto).

❧ On the fortieth day after Diana's birth, Saturn was in the sign of the sygyzy (chart not shown).

❧ There are no malefics in the DSC or the sign preceding.

❧ There are no malefics in the 8th house.

❧ Fortune is in Leo and thus its dispositor, the *Sun, is destroyed by Jupiter*, ruler of the 8th place from the Daimon.

Diana died during a Jupiter return, and in a 1st place[14] profection year. Her profected ASC ruler was Jupiter (the exaltation ruler of her 8th house), who was exactly opposing transiting Moon (L8) over her 9th house (foreign country). The 8th place from the Lot of Fortune is the radical 4th place, ruled by Jupiter. The 4th place describes places below the earth. Diana died in a tunnel under Paris, which ran alongside, but not below the river Seine. Aquarius is the sign of the water pourer, associated with water but not a water sign. Jupiter is in a human sign in Diana's 3rd house, which describes cars, but also reporters, who were chasing her at the moment of her death.

❧

❧ John Lennon

John Lennon was born prior to a New Moon at 10°08' Libra and the ruler of his sygyzy is Venus. She is turned away from her own sign (Libra), in a cadent house, in her fall, and trines and receives Saturn, the malefic out of sect.

❧ Mercury is not in the opposition of the sygyzy.

❧ On the fortieth day after Lennon's birth, Mars is in the sign of the sygyzy (chart not shown).

❧ The malefic out of sect, Mars, is on the DSC opposing his own sign.

❧ Mercury is in the 8th place, opposing Saturn.

❧ Fortune is in Capricorn and thus ruled by Saturn. Fortune is exactly square Mars, who opposes the ASC (Life). The 8th place from Fortune is in Leo, ruled by the Sun in his fall, opposing the ASC.

Saturn is destroyed by the Sun. Transiting Saturn is conjunct the sygyzy and applying natal Sun. Lennon's profected ASC ruler was the Sun. The luminary (destroyer) is in the 9th house (US, foreign country) exactly conjunct transiting Mars (1st house ruler, Life) by antiscia. Transiting Moon is conjunct Daimon and makes a trine to natal Venus (the 8th place ruler from Daimon and squares natal Mars). Transiting Daimon is in the 8th place from its natal position.

Can the death by shooting being seen? The 8th house is ruled by Mars, natural ruler of guns. He is in the 7th of open enemies (Lennon did superficially know his killer). The 8th place from Fortune is in Leo, a fire sign and natural significator of the heart, where he was shot.

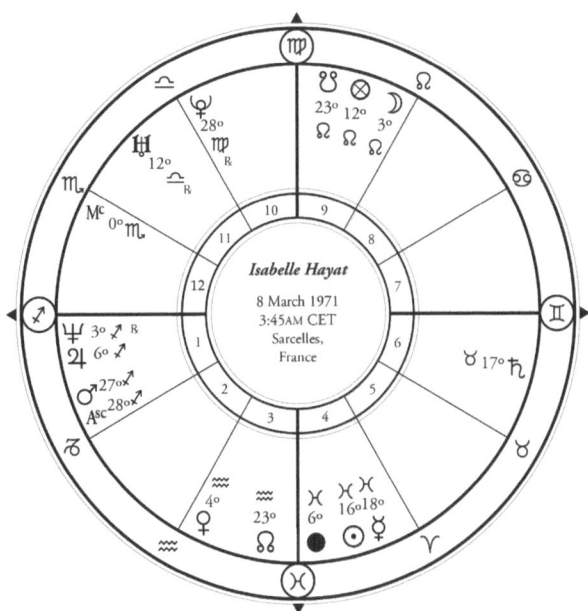
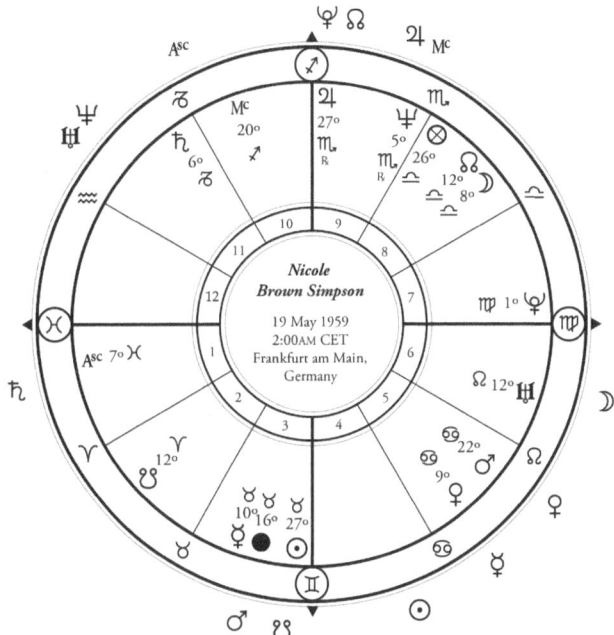

❡ Isabelle Hayat

French infant, who died in the maternity ward of the Clinique Alexis Carrel in Sarcelles. On 13 March 1971 at around 11:45 PM, a fire broke out in the maternity ward where 32 babies were asleep.

❡ The baby was born following a sygyzy in Pisces, thus its ruler is Jupiter, who also rules the ASC.

❡ Mercury is not opposed to the sygyzy, but in the sign of the sygyzy, combust and configured with both malefics.

❡ The baby lived less than forty days.

❡ There are no malefics on the angles, but Saturn is in the 6th place.

❡ The ruler of the 8th place has no malefics, but its ruler is turned away.

❡ Daimon is in Leo, together with the Sun and the South Node. The 8th place from Daimon (Pisces) is the sign of the sygyzy, and Jupiter is the destroyer. Jupiter exactly squares the sygyzy. The chart is overall fiery. Jupiter is in his own domicile, triplicity, and angular. The Moon trines him from Leo.

In this case, given the infant's age, if we want to look at profections, we need to use days instead of years. Annual profection can be done on a daily basis, using one sign for each 2.5 days or 12° every day. The baby died six days after it was born, so the profected ASC is in Aquarius, opposing the Moon (ruler 8th house) and Daimon.

❡ Nicole Brown Simpson

Nicole Brown Simpson was the ex-wife of the former football star O. J. Simpson; she and her friend Ronald Lyle Goldman were murdered together on 13 June 1994.

❡ Nicole was born following a sygyzy in Taurus, whose ruler is Venus in Cancer, exactly opposed by Saturn. Mars is in the same sign as Venus.

❡ Mercury is in the sign of the sygyzy, configured with both malefics.

❡ On the fortieth day after her birth, Mercury was not configured with the malefics (chart not shown).

❡ There are no classical malefics in the 7th or 6th place, but Pluto is angular.

❡ The 8th place has no malefics.

❡ Daimon is in the radical 8th place together with the Moon, who squares Venus and Mars in the 5th place. The 8th from Daimon is the sign of the sygyzy, ruled by Venus. Valens says:

Venus is destroyed by herself. Suicide by poisoned drinks, snakebite, through self-starvation, excessive intercourse, excision of the uvula, drowning or by mutilation, blindness, or paralysis.

Nicole was in a 12th house profection year and the profected ASC was in Aquarius. Transiting Saturn was in her 1st house, trining natal Venus. Transiting Venus was conjunct her natal Mars.

She was mutilated, with her head nearly being severed from her body. Jealously was a suggested motive; her ex-husband was accused of the murder but found "not guilty." Mercury, ruler of the 7th place, is exactly conjunct Venus, the destroyer, and opposed her profected ASC ruler.

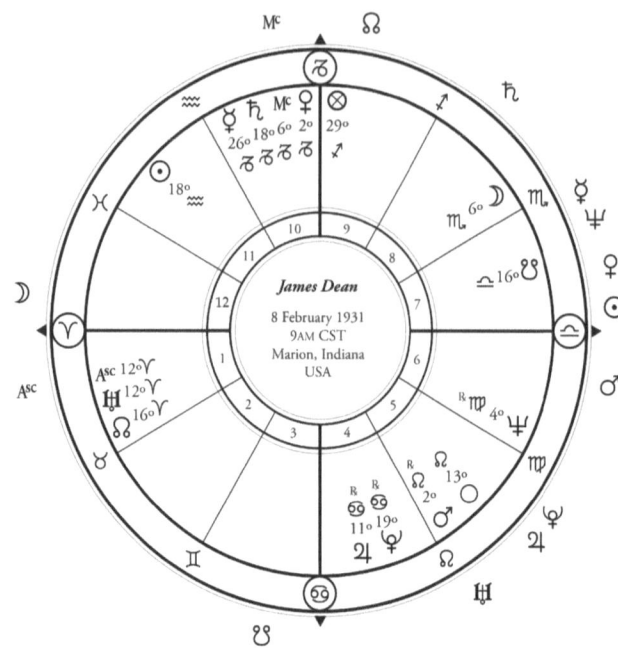
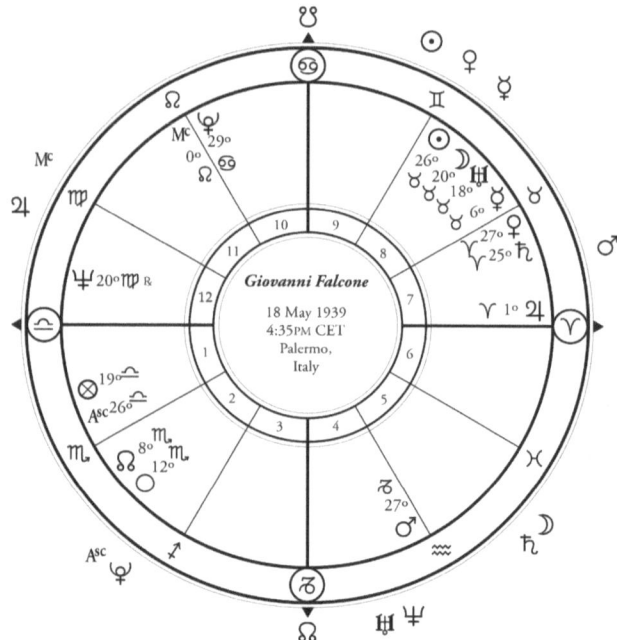

☽ James Dean

James Dean was a famous American actor, who died in a car crash at age 24.

- He was born after a Full Moon with the Moon in Leo, so the ruler of his sygyzy is the Sun. Mars, the malefic out of sect and ruler of the 1st and of the 8th place, is in the same sign.
- Mercury is turned away.
- On the fortieth day after Dean's birth, Mercury is not opposing the sygyzy, but it is trining Mars with reception (chart not shown).
- There are no malefics on the DSC or the 6th house.
- The Moon is in the 8th place, squaring the sygyzy and Mars.
- Daimon is in the 8th place, Mars makes only a whole sign trine. The 8th place from Daimon is Cancer:

Jupiter is destroyed by the Moon. Death from disorders of the spleen, liver, stomach, from vomiting fluids or blood, falls from animals, attacks of ravenous beasts, collapsing buildings, shipwreck, wet places. They die from lunacy, blindness, feebleness.

He had seen the other car in front of him but was convinced it would turn around, so he did not take his foot off the gas pedal. Maybe this is also a kind of (judgmental) blindness? The transiting Moon (destroyer) was exactly opposing Dean's natal Mars (1st house ruler), which, at age 24 was also his profection ruler.

☽ Giovanni Falcone

Giovanni Falcone was a famous Italian judge and a member of the anti-Mafia pool. He was assassinated by the Sicilian Mafia on 23 May 1992 by a car bomb.

- Falcone was born after a Full Moon, with the Moon at 12°17' Scorpio. Its ruler is thus exalted Mars, the malefic out of sect. He is not turned away, but makes a square to Saturn, who is exactly opposing the ASC from his fall.
- Mercury is conjunct the South Node and opposes the Moon during the syzygy.
- On the fortieth day after Falcone's birth, Mercury was squaring angular Saturn (chart not shown).
- Saturn is in the 7th place.
- The 8th place in Falcone's chart falls in Taurus. Its ruler Venus is in aversion to her own sign. The Moon (general ruler of the body) is in this place, combust.
- The ruler of Fortune in Falcone's chart is detrimental Venus, conjunct Saturn, both opposing the ASC. The 8th place from Daimon is the radical 8th place in Taurus, ruled by Venus, and thus *Venus is destroyed by herself.*

Mercury is in the 8th place. It rules the 12th place, associated with hidden organizations such as the mafia. The Sun is also here, it was his profession as a judge (ruler MC) that brought him to the attention of the mafia bosses.

Venus, the destroyer, is in a fire sign, exactly squaring Mars, natural significator of bombs. The bomb was hidden at the entrance to the highway, under the pavement. When the bomb exploded it caused a huge chasm, and Falcone's and two other cars were destroyed. Mars is in the 4th house in an earth sign and disposits of Venus.

Exalted transiting Venus was exactly conjunct Falcone's Sun. His profected ASC was in the 6th house in Pisces, Venus' exaltation and ruled by Jupiter, who is in the 7th house, together with Venus (whole sign aspect). Transiting Moon transfers light from Saturn (ruler of his 4th house of grave) to Venus, ruler of his 8th of death.

¶ Woman who died in a car accident

The woman, walking down the road to the bus stop, had stopped at the traffic light. It was early in the morning, streets were empty but she waited patiently for the green light. When it came, she was hit by a car and died several hours later from brain damage.

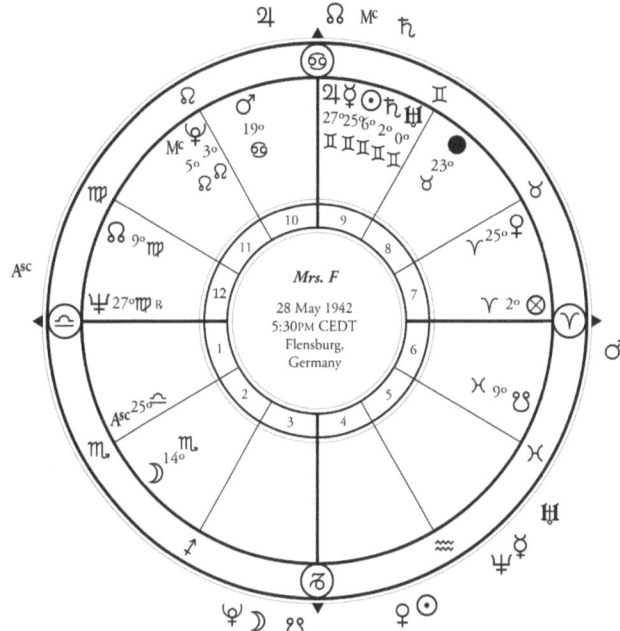

- ¶ The native was born following a New Moon at 23°45' Taurus in the 8th house. The ruler of the sygyzy is Venus, in her detriment opposing the first house of Life. She is in aversion to her sign in which the New Moon occurs. She squares Mars, her dispositor.

- ¶ Mercury is not configured with the New Moon and is linked to Saturn only by a separating whole sign aspect.

- ¶ On the fortieth day. Mercury is conjunct Jupiter and is linked to Saturn only by a separating whole sign conjunction.

- ¶ There are no malefic planets either in the descendant nor the 6th house, but the South Node is there.

- ¶ Daimon is in in the 7th house in Aries, ruled by Mars. It is exactly sextiled by Saturn.

The 8th place from Daimon is Scorpio:

Mars destroys himself: Suicide, accomplices in crime, bandits, murderers, death by animal attacks, fire, collapsing buildings, bleeding, attacks.

The Moon (physical body) is in the 8th place from Daimon, closely trined by Mars, the malefic out of sect, her dispositor and destroyer. Also the ASC is squared by Mars, with mutual reception by domicile.

It is worth noticing that Mars is in the 10th place. The woman was going to work, when she was hit (Mars) by a car. Her profected ASC was in the 12th house and its ruler Mercury squared the Moon in the 8th place from Daimon, while the destroyer Mars was in exact opposition to transiting Venus (1st and 8th house ruler).

Conclusion

As we can see from the example charts, when the ruler of the 8th from Daimon is in the place of the sygyzy, or in the sign of the Daimon, it is a strong indication of a violent death. As an area of further study, there seems to be a strong connection between the 8th place ruler from Daimon and the profections. I did not find the rule of the fortieth day very useful in any of the example charts, however, difficulties are already indicated by the rulers of the sygyzy and the Daimon being turned away from their signs.

Tania Daniels holds a degree in business administration. She became interested in astrology in 1998 after having read an astrological analysis of Leonardo da Vinci's *Last Supper*. She finished her training in psychological astrology in 2002 in Berlin at the DAV and was introduced to traditional astrology in 2009. She holds the STA Horary Diploma (mastercourse) and gained her certificate in Hellenistic Astrology from Chris Brennan. She has also enrolled in Robert Zoller's Medieval Astrology Course. Tania currently teaches the Qualifiying Horary Practitioners course for German-speaking students. Her numerous articles have been published in English, Italian, German, and Turkish. She lives in Italy.

Endnotes

1 All chart data was gathered from astro.com, A or AA rating, only nr. 4 is personal with AA data.

2 Vettius Valens, *Anthology*, Book II, trans. Riley, 55. Available online: http://www.csus.edu/indiv/r/rileymt/vettius%20valens%20entire.pdf

3 "Occorre pertanto osservare la sorte e il suo signore, in quale segno cade; in essi saranno mostrate le cause delle morti, poiché anche nel cosmo la Luna, che è Tyche, congiunta al Sole in Ariete, nell'ottavo segno, lo Scorpione, causa l'eclissi e la sottrazione della luce; perciò (lo Scorpione) viene detto (luogo della) sua caduta." (The English translation above is mine). Vettii Valentis, *Antiocheni Anthologiarum Libri Novem*, ed. D. Pingree, (Leipzig: Tuebner, 1986).

4 Hephaistio of Thebes, *Apotelesmatics*, Book II, Schmidt trans., 53.

5 Valens, *Anthology*, Book II, 38.

6 Ibid., 2.

7 Ibid., 20.

8 Ibid., 33.

9 Chris Brennan, *Hellenistic Astrology: The Study of Fate and Fortune* (Denver, CO: Amor Fati, 2017), 518ff.

10 Valens only has "Full Moon" here, but since the paragraph is about sygyzys, I suppose he is referring to either (prenatal) Full *or* New Moon.

11 Valens only has "Moon."

12 Hellenistic astrologers did not know about the outer planets (Uranus, Neptune, Pluto). Many modern traditional astrologers do not use them either. I personally consider them, when they are angular or in conjunction to any of the seven traditional planets. I will put these planetary contacts into brackets, as they are are a modern interpolation.

13 Sect refers to whether a chart is a "day" chart or a "night" chart, depending on the position of the Sun. The luminary of the day sect is the Sun attended by the greater benefic and malefic (Sun, Jupiter, Saturn); the luminary of the night sect is the Moon attended by the lesser benefic and malefic (Moon, Venus, Mars). Mercury may belong to either sect depending on certain conditions.

14 Hellenistic astrologers devided the zodiac in twelve segments of 30° each. They start with the ASC at 0° of a given sign and each sign is called "place" in order to distinguish these segments from quadrant houses which can start at any given degree and whose segments are called "houses."

Mariana Palova, Elusive Nature (2016)

Mariana Palova (Jalisco, 1990). She is a Mexican writer, designer, and artist. Mrs. Palova has a degree in graphic design. She is an enthusiastic alchemist, lover of nature, mysticism, occult arts, and folk music. She has been writing since she was thirteen, but she started creating works of art at seventeen and her visual work has been presented in more than seventy exhibitions in Mexico, United States, South America, Asia, and Europe, as well as printed in various art books and collections around the world. In 2015, she decided to take a step outside of her artistic career to focus on her dream of becoming a writer. In 2016, her career and work were honored at the Autonomous University of Aguascalientes, being recognized as one of the most representative artists of the state. Three months after self-publication, *The Nation of the Beasts*, its first literary saga, was acquired in 2017 by a publisher in Los Angeles for translation and publication in English.

Medieval Timelords in Modern Life
The Firdaria Through the Life and Career of Madonna
by Cassandra Tyndall

Cause we're only here to love
Like there's no tomorrow
So let's live each moment like our time is only borrowed
—Madonna, "Borrowed Time," *Rebel Heart*, 2015

MADONNA IS KNOWN for her love of astrology. Throughout her 35-year career, she has referenced time in her lyrics on numerous occasions. It is unlikely that she is familiar with the firdaria, the medieval time-lord system that divides a person's life up into "chapters of time." Whether she is singing about time moving fast, slow, or standing still, the life and times of Madonna makes a fascinating study of this traditional technique.

The resurrection of traditional astrology in recent years has brought a wealth of new knowledge to our ancient craft. One of the lesser known techniques, the firdaria, derives from the medieval period. Like the daily dance of the Sun and Moon, a similar dance occurs in our lives and is guided by the Chaldean order of planets. Medieval astrologer Al Buruni, (1029 CE) states that the "years of a man's life are divided into certain periods"—or time.[1] Differing from transits or progressions, the firdaria involves dividing time into planetary periods. While this technique would have been primarily used for mundane predictions, its symbolism can be applied to our modern life.

As with all time-lord systems, the firdaria allots one of the seven traditional planets as a ruler over a certain period of time. These differing periods throughout life can be compared to a chapter in a book. Assuming that we are fortunate enough to live for an entire human lifespan, we will all go through a Mars chapter, where we may have the confidence to take more risks in life or assert ourselves in a way previously unseen. Similarly, we may all go through a Jupiter chapter, where the quest for meaning and purpose in life may dominate the flavor of that time. And so on.

This article seeks neither to discuss nor debate the intentions of our astrological forebears regarding the technique, rather the purpose of this article is to give insight into this simple yet practical tool. After seeing it in action, I invite you to consider the firdaria as a worthy addition to your astrological toolkit.

What is the Firdar?

The first known use of the firdaria system dates back to 787–886 CE by Abu Ma'shar and is witnessing renaissance today with contemporary astrologers who favor ancient techniques.

The firdaria is a system where one or two of the seven traditional planets hold rulership over a natives' life at a given time. As a prognostic method of medieval astrology, this series of divisions creates an outline of a person's life. One planet has a long period of rulership (the chronacrator) and the other planet (sub-planet) has a shorter period. In contrast with other predictive astrological tools, the firdaria offers specific dates for the beginning and end points of planetary periods.

> Each of the seven stars, and the Ascending and Descending Nodes, has certain determinate times, and each star administers to the native in accordance with its proper firdar. The firdar of the Sun, then, is 10 years; of Aphrodite, 8; of Hermes, 13; of the Moon, 9; of Kronos, 11; of Zeus, 12; of Ares, 7; of the Ascending Node, 3; of the Descending Node, 2—altogether,

Day Chart	Night Chart
Sun 10 years	Moon 9 years
Venus 8 years	Saturn 11 years
Mercury 13 years	Jupiter 12 years
Moon 9 years	Mars 7 years
Saturn 11 years	Sun 10 years
Jupiter 12 years	Venus 8 years
Mars 7 years	Mercury 13 years
North Node 3 years	North Node 3 years
South Node 2 years	South Node 2 years

> they are 75. In the case of a diurnal nativity, then, the Sun takes the governorship of the first firdar, whether it should be present, then Aphrodite, then Hermes, then the Moon, then Kronos, in accordance with the order of their zones. In the case of nocturnal nativities, the Moon takes the first firdar, then Kronos, then Zeus, then Ares, in accordance with the prior order.[2]

The word *firdaria* is the plural for *firdar* and comes to us from Persian astrology. Firdar has the same etymological origin as the Greek word for "period." "The years of the alfidar" as Ibn Ezra refers to them are a Persian concept, in which planetary periods are irregularly divided up into years which each period being ruled by a planet, luminary, or the nodal axis.[3] The quality of each firdar is determined by the quality and condition of the ruling planet in the natal chart. Astrologer and scholar Rob Hand relates that,

> as a consequence, when a planet becomes either a short or long period ruler, the issues that it has rulership over become

heightened in significance and brought to the fore. When there is a period in which two planets which are in aspect with each other become rulers, one short and the other long period rulers—the issues indicated by the aspect come especially important.[4]

Thus, for interpretation of how a period will be experienced, and what may be experienced during that period, we need to pay attention to the quality and condition of the ruling planet for clues.

The Firdaria Pattern

The planetary rulers of each firdaria period are determined according to the Chaldean order of planets, which are arranged in ascending order of speed. Here we must pay attention to whether the chart in question is a night or day chart, as this will determine a variation in which planetary ruler we begin with. A diurnal (day) chart begins with the Sun and a nocturnal chart (night) begins with the Moon.

Once we come to the end of the Chaldean order, there are another two periods that are the same in both day and night charts. The North Node takes over for three years and the South Node for two years. The placement of the Nodes in the firdaria pattern is controversial due to an ambiguity between the translations of Abu Ma'shar and Bonatti that I will not go into here. This total of nine periods equals 75 years; if the life in question is longer, then the sequence starts again.

Generally speaking, the planets in rulership of a firdar will be a prominent theme for that given time. If someone is in a Saturn firdar, they will experience challenges, yet it will be necessary for them to overcome them and to find solutions. The Mars period is a time of self-assertion and desire to prove oneself. Increased energy needs to be positively spent, or it can become destructive. Taking the meaning of the planet and considering its essential and accidental dignity will describe the native's life experience during the period of the firdar.

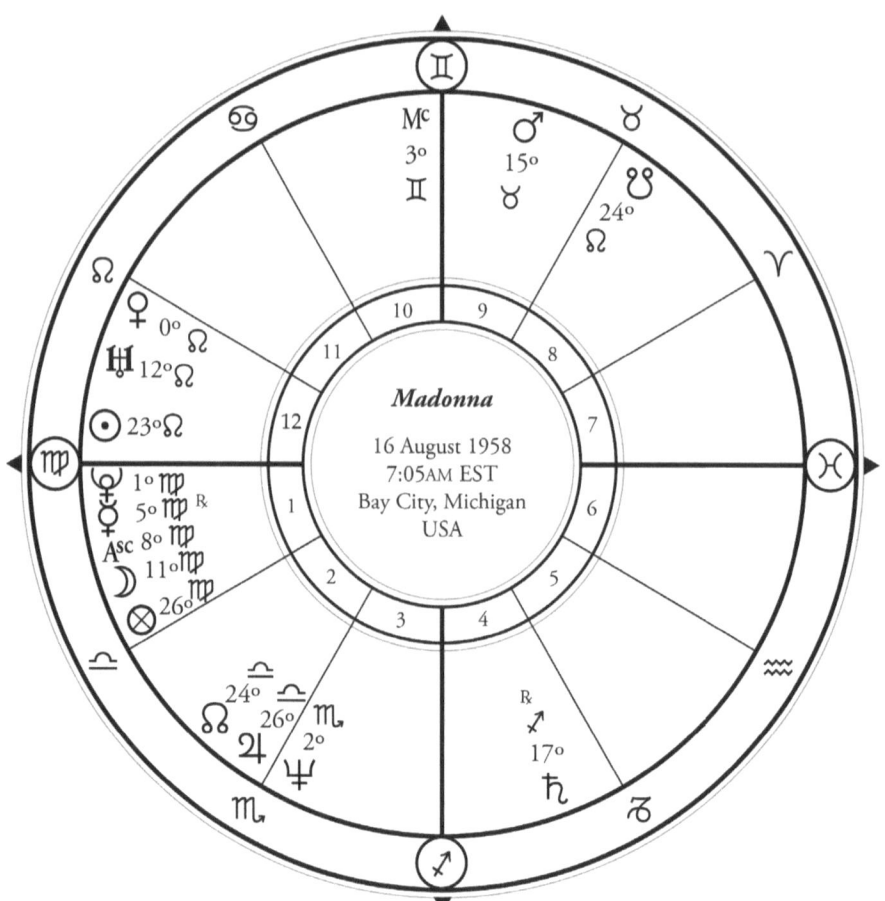

A Few Points to Consider

When the chronocrator (major ruler) changes (for example, from Venus to Mercury), it will spend the first stage of its rulership solo—being completely in charge. Due to its initial phase as a solo ruler, it will bring extra prominence to the meaning of that planet in its allotted period of time. Thus to the native, a change of the major planetary rulership in firdaria is as equal in importance as their secondary progressed Sun changing signs. What is particularly remarkable about the major planetary ruler changing signs, however, is that it occurs more frequently than the progressed Sun sign change. It offers us a new way to mark major shifts in peoples' lives.

When the major ruler is then joined by a sub-ruler, it is akin to a change in tempo or key. The major planet is still at the helm, but the beat may be syncopated, depending on the nature of the sub-ruler. For example, if Mars is at the helm, the beat may be fast or loud, but when Saturn joins as a sub-ruler, the bass kicks in and the tempo slows down. This may show up as obstacles to overcome, a reduction of energy, or a test to see how badly one wants to achieve a certain objective. We need to consult the specific natal chart to determine how this will be likely to manifest.

When a natal aspect is emphasised in the firdaria, the themes of the planets involved will dominate the experience for the indicated length of time, as allocated by the firdaria period.

There will be firdaria periods that will not necessarily be life changing or particularly eventful, especially if the planets involved do not "speak" volumes in the natal chart. Conversely, the volume on a quiet planet may be turned all the way up to ten (or eleven!), and may bring challenge and difficulty for the native or possibly, an immensely welcome shift in fortune.

Firdar	Date / Age		Firdar	Date / Age
☉	16 Aug 1958 0.0		♃	15 Aug 2009 51.0
☉/♀	20 Jan 1960 1.4		♃/♂	3 May 2011 52.7
☉/☿	24 Jun 1961 2.9		♃/☉	18 Jan 2013 54.4
☉/☽	28 Nov 1962 4.3		♃/♀	7 Oct 2014 56.1
☉/♄	3 May 1964 5.7		♃/☿	24 Jun 2016 57.9
☉/♃	7 Oct 1965 7.1		♃/☽	12 Mar 2018 59.6
☉/♂	12 Mar 1967 8.6		♃/♄	28 Nov 2019 61.3
♀	15 Aug 1968 10.0		♂	15 Aug 2021 63.0
♀/☿	7 Oct 1969 11.1		♂/☉	15 Aug 2022 64.0
♀/☽	28 Nov 1970 12.3		♂/♀	16 Aug 2023 65.0
♀/♄	19 Jan 1972 13.4		♂/☿	15 Aug 2024 66.0
♀/♃	12 Mar 1973 14.6		♂/☽	15 Aug 2025 67.0
♀/♂	3 May 1974 15.7		♂/♄	15 Aug 2026 68.0
♀/☉	25 June 1975 16.9		♂/♃	16 Aug 2027 69.0
☿	15 Aug 1976 18.0		☊	15 Aug 2028 70.0
☿/☽	24 Jun 1978 19.9		♃☊	15 Aug 2031 73.0
☿/♄	3 May 1980 21.7		☉	15 Aug 2033 75.0
☿/♃	12 Mar 1982 23.6		☉/♀	19 Jan 2035 76.4
☿/♂	19 Jan 1984 25.4		☉/☿	24 Jun 2036 77.9
☿/☉	28 Nov 1985 27.3		☉/☽	27 Nov 2037 79.3
☿/♀	7 Oct 1987 29.1		☉/♄	3 May 2039 80.7
☽	15 Aug 1989 31.0		☉/♃	6 Oct 2040 82.1
☽/♄	28 Nov 1990 32.3		☉/♂	12 Mar 2042 83.6
☽/♃	12 Mar 1992 33.6		♀	15 Aug 2043 85.0
☽/♂	24 Jun 1993 34.9		♀/☿	6 Oct 2044 86.1
☽/☉	7 Oct 1994 36.1		♀/☽	27 Nov 2045 87.3
☽/♀	19 Jan 1996 37.4		♀/♄	19 Jan 2047 88.4
☽/☿	3 May 1997 38.7		♀/♃	11 Mar 2048 89.6
♄	15 Aug 1998 40.0		♀/♂	2 May 2049 90.7
♄/♃	11 Mar 2000 41.6		♀/☉	24 Jun 2050 91.9
♄/♂	6 Oct 2001 43.1		☿	15 Aug 2051 93.0
♄/☉	3 May 2003 44.7		☿/☽	24 Jun 2053 94.9
♄/♀	27 Nov 2004 46.3		☿/♄	3 May 2055 96.7
♄/☿	24 Jun 2006 47.9		☿/♃	11 Mar 2057 98.6
♄/☽	19 Jan 2008 49.4		☿/♂	19 Jan 2059 100.4

Case Study: Madonna and the Firdaria

For over thirty-five years, with barely a pause to catch her breath, Madonna has dominated the popular music industry. An entire rainforest could be harvested just to print a compendium of her oeuvre, her re-inventions, and her personal life. Though Madonna uses the theme of time in many of her songs, it is doubtful that she is aware of the cycle of time as governed by the Chaldean order of planets—the firdaria.

Madonna provides an excellent case study of firdaria. Here I outline how firdaria periods play out in her childhood and the early portion of her career, and I have also included some other major periods as her life and career have evolved. To demonstrate how I personally use the firdaria in my consultation work, I have also overlaid and integrated other astrological techniques, but have intentionally omitted excess details for ease of reading and to keep the focus on the firdaria itself. I sincerely hope this offers you suitable entrée to the topic, and allows you to explore this system and apply it in your practice.

¶ The Sun Firdar

With her diurnal chart (16 August 1958 7:05 AM Bay City, Michigan), Madonna's firdaria begins with the Sun, doubly important because Madonna is a Leo.

Madonna's firdaria changed to Sun/Venus not long after her first birthday. It has been said that Madonna's mother did not discipline her, and she was able to express herself freely. Madonna—who carries her mother's name—was adored by her and could do no wrong in her eyes. As a young child, Madonna's mother encouraged music and dance and generally let her children be free spirits.

December 1 1963: While Madonna was in a Sun/Moon period, her mother loses her battle with breast cancer. At the time transiting Pluto was close to Madonna's Moon (which conjoins her ascendant); she is quoted as saying that after her mother's death she "felt invisible."

During the Sun/Saturn period and the aftermath of the loss of her mother, Madonna's father went through several housekeepers and eventually married one of them.

At this time Madonna's natal Saturn in Sagittarius in the 4th house turned direct by secondary progression, and she entered a Sun/Jupiter period. Stepmother Joan came from a different religious background to that of the Ciccone clan. It has been said that she ran the household like a "drill sergeant" making Saturn's presence dominant in Madonna's life now—a stark contrast from the all-love and no-discipline approach of her biological mother.

In the book *Goddess: Inside Madonna* by Barbara Victor, Madonna's stepmother is quoted as saying: "God knows how these kids would have grown up if I was not their mother. At least I am organized and have my feet on the ground so they get a good dose of reality."[3] At this time Madonna also had to take responsibility of her younger siblings and a strict Catholic upbringing was forced upon her. This firdaria sequence activated the natal

Sun/Saturn trine. To this day, Madonna is renowned for her discipline.

In 1966, Madonna took her first holy communion. At this time, she was in a Sun/Jupiter firdar and her secondary progressed Sun changed from Leo to Virgo, entering the first whole sign house. Around a year later, she was confirmed and added the name Veronica to her birth name. Here, we can see a doubling of themes around a shift in her identity, hinging particularly on her religiosity. The Sun/Jupiter sextile in the natal chart had been activated. Religious symbolism in Madonna's work has been a mainstay feature. In her personal life, she has always been devoted to spiritual and religious growth.

¶ The Venus Firdar

In 1968, Madonna entered a major Venus period. Her family moved to a wealthier area of Michigan and her step-mother legally adopted Madonna and her siblings. By secondary progression, her progressed Venus conjoined her natal Uranus. Madonna began to experiment with what she will eventually become famous for—shock value—and did what she could to stand out to win her father's attention.

In 1971, during a Venus/Moon period, Madonna convinced her father to let her begin ballet classes. Her secondary progressed Sun in conjoined natal Mercury, the ruler of her ascendant and midheaven. Despite her Sun, by progression, no longer occupying the sign of its rulership, it is now empowered or goaded by its new position in the first house.

At age fourteen, and in her Venus/Jupiter period, Madonna met Christopher Flynn, a gay dance teacher who became one of her biggest champions and inspired her to become a professional dancer. Flynn not only fulfills the Jupiterian influence, he also took her to the gay clubs in Michigan and taught her about art and culture, symbolizing both Venus and Jupiter themes active at that time in her life.

¶ The Mercury Firdar

In the fall of 1976, Madonna began her Mercury period and enrolled at the University of Michigan after being awarded a dance scholarship. By the time she entered her Mercury/Moon period, frustrated with a lack of progress at university, she moved to New York to find fame and fortune as a dancer.

While in her Mercury/Saturn period, Madonna learned to play drums and guitar in an abandoned synagogue in Queens (natal Saturn in Sagittarius in the 4th), where she also lived with her older musician boyfriend. Here she mastered skills that would develop her career as a musician and entertainer.

In November 1982, just a few months after Madonna's secondary progressed Venus entered Virgo and her 1st house, she signed a record deal with Sire Records, a division of Warner Brothers. At this time, she was in her Mercury/Jupiter period, and she received the largest sum of money she had ever been given. Her secondary progressed midheaven also made an exact trine to her natal Jupiter in the 2nd house, sealing her fate for a massive career and bank balance!

In 1984 Madonna began her Mercury/Mars period. By now, all her Leo planets, including her natal Mercury retrograde—her ascendant and midheaven ruler—had progressed into Virgo and the 1st house. This was the year Madonna's star truly rose and she became a household name. During this firdar, she met and married Sean Penn. The marriage was marred by aggression and violence. The media described them as "the poison Penns." Due to Madonna's work commitments, there were long periods of separation—the domain of Mars.

¶ The Moon Firdar

As her Mercury period drew to a close, Madonna filed for divorce. Despite a tumultuous marriage, her star continued to rise. By 1989 and in her Moon firdar, she released the album *Like a Prayer*, dedicated to her mother. The Moon in Madonna's chart is conjoined the ascendant and it was the most auto-biographical and personal album she had ever recorded. Even though the album was released and gained popularity by the time Saturn was in Capricorn, its creation was during her Saturn return in Sagittarius in her fourth house. Its themes included religion, death, the endings of things, and her family.

Note that before someone begins a new major firdar period, due to its sim-

> *"...Time goes by so slowly for those who wait and those who run seem to have all the fun."*
> —"Love Song," 1989 & "Hung Up," 2005

ilarity to the secondary progressed Sun changing signs, it will more often than not, denote periods of endings, before new beginnings can occur. This was the case with Madonna.

In 1992, Madonna's secondary progressed Mercury had come to conjoin her Moon. As the ascendant and the Moon both represent the body, by this time, there literally wasn't a piece of Madonna's body we hadn't seen—or so we thought! She was at the height of her popularity, pushing every boundary and blazing new trails. In October of the same year, just when we thought she couldn't push any more limits or generate more shock value, she released her controversial *Sex* book.[6]

I rarely consider progressions from Jupiter and Saturn unless they are at the beginning or end of a sign at birth. At the time Madonna released this book, her secondary progressed Jupiter had conjoined her natal Neptune in Scorpio. She defended her work by proclaiming it was about her sexual fantasies. Her Moon had progressed to conjoin her natal Saturn, and the bubble of fame and popularity seemingly popped. The aftermath of that firdar led Madonna into a somber period of isolation and self-doubt, all too fitting for when the Moon and Saturn connect. Nevertheless, as Madonna had self-funded the entire book project, she made a very handsome profit out of her sexual fantasies with her natal Jupiter in the second.

After the darkest phase in her career, Madonna emerged triumphant with the release of *Evita* during her Moon/Venus phase. In order to play the role, she learned how to sing (Venus) differently than she ever had before. Her popularity began to rise again, and her image also softened under the influence of the feminine planets.

Via secondary progression, Madonna's Mars had changed signs and entered the tenth house. Her public and professional motivations were undergoing a major shift in direction. Madonna had her first child in October that year, just one month before her Sun progressed into Libra.

¶ The Saturn Firdar

In 1998, Madonna emerged with a new look, a new album, and explored mystical and occult philosophies while transiting Saturn, lord of her firdar, was in her eighth house. She released a dark and haunting song called "Frozen."

By the time she entered the Jupiter sub-period, she moved overseas and married Guy Ritchie as transiting Saturn entered her ninth. She had a second child.

By 2008, in a Saturn/Moon firdar, transiting Saturn conjoined Madonna's Moon/ASC, and Madonna and Guy divorced. Reflecting on the marriage, Madonna says that she felt "incarcerated," typifying Saturn's associations with prisons. Once again, we see an ending before we see a beginning. For Madonna, her two marriages ended just prior to a new major firdar period.

¶ The Jupiter Firdar

Back in her adopted hometown of New York, Madonna continued touring, and in 2011 her first feature film *W.E.* is released.

In 2016, during her Mercury sub-period, she moved to Portugal to support the career aspirations of her adopted son. Her first Mercury/Jupiter period in her early twenties was when her own career dreams started to come true.

As I write this in February 2018, Madonna is just a few weeks from beginning her Jupiter/Moon period. She has recently posted topless selfies on her Instagram account that have caused a lot of age-related criticism. Significantly, the repetition of themes here resonates with her Moon/Jupiter period, when she released the *Sex* book.

Concluding Thoughts

As you can see through the example of Madonna, firdaria offers us a clear way to describe the various chapters, or in her case, songs, of her life and career. By applying the significations of one or two planets, a distinct tone or thread can highlight the thrust of life at a given time.

Astrological techniques rarely stand alone, and the firdaria is no exception. It can only suggest what may possibly unfold from the natal chart. Unless you are looking at a chart where the native is entering a change in the major firdar period, which in and of itself can speak volumes, this technique tends to serve as a useful tool to support other commonly used astrological techniques.

Now that you have a sense of how firdaria works, I invite you explore the themes of your own personal firdar, and to discover how the Chaldean order of planets sets the beat and volume in your own life.

Endnotes

1 Darrelyn Gunzburg, *Life After Grief: An Astrological Guide to Dealing With Loss* (Bournemouth: Wessex Astrologer, 2004).

2 Abu Ma'shar, *On Solar Revolutions*, part 2, trans. Robert Schmidt (Cumberland, MD: The Phaser Foundation, 1999), 42.

3 Abraham ibn Ezra, *The Beginning of Wisdom*, trans. Raphael Levy, (Baltimore, MD: The Johns Hopkins UP, 1939).

4 http://www.arhatmedia.com/firdar2.htm

5 Barbara Victor, *Goddess: Inside Madonna* (New York: Harper Collins, 2001), 131.

6 Madonna, with Steven Meisel, Fabien Baron, Glenn O'Brien, *Sex* (New York: Warner Books, 1992).

Hailing from Australia, Cassandra Tyndall brings the ancient wisdom of astrology and applies it to modern life. With over twelve years in private practice, she combines consulting, writing and teaching. Known for her passion, honesty and insight, her aim is to make astrology accessible, available, and easy to understand. Cassandra is the former President of the Young Astrologers Association (Australia) and national board member for the Federation of Australian Astrologers (FAA). When Cassandra doesn't have her head in the stars, you can find her in the gym or with her young son.

Cosmos and Chaos:
Perpetual Tides *of the* Venus-Mars Epoch
An Astro-historiographical Documentary Essay, Part II
by Gary P Caton

> "A twofold tale I shall tell: at one time it grew to be one alone out of many, at another again it grew apart to be many out of one.
> ...and these things never cease their continual exchange, now through Love all coming together into one,
> now again each carried apart by the hatred of Strife."
> – Empedocles of Acragas, Greek pre-Socratic philosopher, 5th century BCE[1]

IN PART ONE OF THIS ESSAY I discussed the approximately 300-year cycle in the pattern of Venus-Mars conjunctions. This larger period splits into two smaller unequal periods, each showing phenomenological agreement with the archetypal nature of Venus or Mars. I then examined impressive similarities between the historical trends within any of these periods and the archetypal nature of the corresponding planet, as well as notable similarities throughout history, with periods of the same nature showing similar trends again and again.

A cyclical model of history is far from new and certainly not peculiar to astrologers.[2] Nearly everyone has heard of the concept of historic recurrence via the aphorism that "history repeats itself." But if we tend to see the nature of reality as inherently consistent or unchanging, is it any wonder that we see the same ideas springing up repeatedly throughout our history? It seems possible that ontogeny, the development of the cultural organism, recapitulates ontology, our ideas about the nature of existence.

From my exploration of the Venus-Mars epoch in part one of this essay, an aspect of reality emerges that seems to be consistent, repetitive, and self-perpetuating. And yet, the experience of change itself also seems to be fundamental to the nature of existence. Ontology seeks to clarify and explain these differences. Does anything ever really change? How do we account for change? Are all changes simply the experience of cyclical forces? By necessity, any ontological model has to find a way to answer these questions. A spectrum of divergent ontological models seek to provide answers to these questions.

In our Western heritage, Parmenides was among the first to delineate an ontological model. Born in the sixth century BCE in the Greek city of Elea, Parmenides became known as the founder of the Eleatic school of philosophy. Parmenides' model of the universe is very radical, in that it is divorced from sensory experience and utilizes pure reason or abstract argument. Strictly interpreted, fundamental to the Parmenidean model is the concept of a single unifying force underlying the entire Universe. This has become known as the Monad or simply Being.

Parmenides tells us that when classifying existence we have basically three choices, either something is (it exists), it is not (it does not exist), or it both is and is not (both exists and does not exist). Parmenides argues that if something is not (does not exist) then we have no way of knowing it, and thus throws out both the categories of not being and simultaneous being and not being. By saying "nothing comes from nothing," Parmenides argues that anything which can be said to exist could not have come from nothing, and therefore existence must be eternal, uniform, and immutable. In fact, for some interpreters of Parmenides, it seems change does not exist at all—it is an illusion. Everything that can be apprehended is but one part of a single entity—Being. Parmenides tells us that Being is changeless, timeless, and uniform—and so is seen to take the shape of a sphere.[3]

Less strictly interpreted, Being can be seen to refer to the essence of any one thing that exists. That which is intelligible to us, in its essence, is eternal and imperishable, while the *perception* of it, as a phenomenon, is disordered and changing. Parmenides' model has become known as Eleatic Monism, and counterintuitive as it may at first seem, this way of thinking is foundational for much of Western philosophy and science. Think of the law of conservation of energy in physics, which states that energy cannot be created or destroyed, but only change form. What would happen if we were to apply something like this law to our historiography? Well, if nothing is created or destroyed but existence only changes form, then the Being-ness that is Rome has no beginning or end. Thus, we might see various empires or nations making claims to be the "third Rome," for example. In fact the use of the *"translatio imperii"* concept, which

Elodie St-Onge-Aubut, Moving Skies (Venus and Mars, January 7, 2017)

claims continuity with the Roman Empire to legitimize political power, became widespread. Beyond the examples of the German and Russian empires we saw in the first part of this essay, the French, British, and even Americans have also used it to justify their growing power.[4]

In other words, the abstract nature of Parmenides' static model can be seen to be reflected in relatively static ideological fixtures of history, which often shows us very persistent ideas or abstract forms. An example is the idea and/or form of Empire itself. Empires are by nature syncretic, that is, they are typically coalesced out of diverse ethnic, national, cultural, and/or religious components. *"At one time it grew to be one alone out of many."*

Empires have existed as far back as we know, from the Akkadian Empire of Sargon the Great in the 24th century BCE, arguably right up until the present day. Taken in the philosophical context described above, the enigmatic statement on the Great Seal of the Unites States, *E Pluribus Unum*—"out of many, one"—can be taken to be a statement of intention toward Empire. Interestingly, if we go back to Sargon we also see what becomes a prototypical story of a male child of low birth who is placed in a basket upon a river and then miraculously goes on to become king. This story is later repeated with Romulus, the founder of Rome and again with Moses, the Judeo-Christian patriarch.[5] It seems that, indeed, some things never change.

In opposition to static Monism, where a single unique and unchanging Being stands behind nature, lies the pluralistic concept of Becoming, which implies a universal flux of various primary constituents. In the sixth century BCE, Heraclitus of Ephesus posited that nothing in this world is constant—except change itself. Becoming assumes a "changing to" and a "moving toward," and Heraclitus saw the nature of existence as something like a river, perpetually moving and flowing. This flow was also characterized by a series of transformations or "turnings of fire," with "ever-living fire" as the primary element, "kindling in measures and being quenched in measures." The transformation of the elements proceeds from fire to water to earth, giving us a similar image to the river—which remains the same river, despite its ever-changing material contents.

Heraclitus also posited a unity of opposites, and that all beings are characterized by pairs of contrary properties in a state of constant flux. Thus, when Heraclitus tells us that "strife is justice," he is not promoting a nihilistic view, but rather suggesting that strife begets or *becomes* justice—just as night becomes day. Conflict is a precondition of life, for if some things do not die, then others cannot be born. Thus by forming a system, contraries are the same, much like the Taoist yin/yang—pairs such as alive-dead, waking-sleeping, young-old all exist within us as the same, regardless of the apparent manifestation of only one polarity in any given moment. "For these things having changed around are those, and those in turn having changed around are these."[6]

Heraclitus' concept of Becoming also survives up until the present day via philosophers such as Nietzsche.[7] Because it is a model which more closely reflects the flux of everyday sensory reality, we might see Becoming reflected in a more "boots on the ground" type of historiography. For instance the time lapse maps of territorial boundaries which have become popular on the internet reflect the flowing nature of Heraclitus' model.[8] Like a river whose waters change in volume, clarity, and so on over time and yet still remains the same river, we can see the dynamic flux of various boundaries and/or national identities flowing over time through a particular area while the ethnic identity of the people inhabiting the region remains relatively the same. *"At another (Time) again it grew apart, to be many out of one."*

So, do we take the Parmenidean view that the nature of existence is constant and all change an illusion? Or do we take the Heraclitian view that change is the only constant? Is it possible that we can see both truths operative, each within their own distinct socio-cultural and/or historical milieu? It seems that perhaps we can, via Empedocles, who transforms this either/or dichotomy into a both/and view of existence that also happens to be remarkably proto-astrological.

During the fifth century BCE, Empedocles was a physician, philosopher and poet active in the democratic politics of his native city of Acragas in Sicily. Empedocles' poetic philosophy ingeniously blends the static permanence of Parmenides and the dynamic flux of Heraclitus. He was the first to propose what we call today the four elements of fire, earth, air, and water. Together, these four "roots" are like the Parmenidean monad—timeless, uniform, and unchanging. Upon these four changeless elements move two cosmological forces: Love and Strife. Love brings the four elements together, and Strife drives them apart. Just as painters create endlessly wondrous artwork from just three primary colors, the various combinations that result from this alchemical mixing and separating of the four elements forms everything in the World. For Empedocles, existence is both static and unchanging, via the four elements, and yet also in constant flux, via the forces of Love and Strife.[9]

Empedocles' model is proto-astrological not just because we find here the foundation of the four elements theory, but in the waxing and waning of the forces of Love and Strife, reflecting the three primary cycles of astrology—daily, monthly, and yearly—which oscillate between light and dark. Furthermore, Empedocles goes so far as to equate the four elements with both natural phenomena (Sun, Earth, sky, and sea, in fragment 22) and also with various Greek deities, thus giving us the classic above/below parallel. Empedocles identifies Zeus, Hera, Dis (Hades/Pluto), and Nestis (Persephone) with the four elements (fragment 6). He also clearly identifies Aphrodite with Love (fragment 17).[10] Given this, it seems relatively certain, at least to some classic scholars that Strife is Ares or Mars.[11] Thus, there seems to be a parallel between Empedocles' cosmos of alternating Love/Strife and the Venus-Mars epoch with its alternating periods of consistent/erratic interactions.

The connection between Homer's Ares/Aphrodite and Empedocles' Strife/Love was noted as early as the first century CE. It was also noted then that Harmonia was born of the union of Ares and Aphrodite, so that when these two lovers are together, harmony is created.[12] Moreover, if we choose to extend this apt metaphor, we should note that there are six children of Aphrodite and Ares: Eros, Anteros, Harmonia, Phobos, Demos, and Adrestia. It might be instructive to attempt to fit these children into our historiography, after a little review.

From the associations of the two planets and forces with the two sub-periods of the Venus-Mars epoch, we can then easily assign their children, simply by joining them with the parent whom they most resemble. Because the 200-year period is defined by regular and consistent interactions, this is the time when the children who are most archetypally similar to their mother Venus should emerge and come to the fore in our historiography. These are Eros (associated with intimate love and the arts), Anteros (requited love, or love returned) and Harmonia (harmony, accord). Conversely, the 100-year period is defined by the largest separation (940 days) between Venus and Mars, and so this is the time when the children of this pair who are most archetypally similar to their father, Ares, should tend to emerge and dominate the scene. I am speaking here of Phobus (fear), Deimos (terror), and Adrestia (revenge).

For instance, the last time the Venus-Mars cycle extended to its maximum duration of approximately 940 days (which happens only once or twice every 300 years) was from May 10, 2002 until December 5, 2004. This maximum separation of the two planets marks the height of the Mars period, when the children of Mars should be dominant. It is a rather dramatic synchronicity that America found itself deeply engaged in a vengeful "global war on terrorism" at that point in time. On a more symbolic (and perhaps Freudian) level, George W. Bush first described this war as a "crusade."[13] We will soon see how this remark then also brings in a diachronic historical pattern, in that the First Crusade also happened during the height of a Mars period—and more specifically, close to another instance of this relatively rare ~940-day maximum extension of the Venus-Mars cycle, which takes place only every 300 years.

As we resume our historiography, we will look for additional meso-cosmic parallels to Empedocles' cosmological model. It seems that just as Love and Strife alternately mix and separate the four elements in the Empedoclean cosmology, the Venus and Mars periods alternately mix and separate the meme-stuff of a culture over the course of the 300-

year Venus-Mars epoch. *"And these things never cease their continual exchange, now through Love all coming together into one, now again each carried apart by the hatred of Strife."*

SYNCHRONIC PATTERNS

♀♀♀

¶ ERA OF THE TENTH-CENTURY RENAISSANCE
(VENUS PERIOD ~845–1044)

We enter another Venus period, defined by the regular and consistent repetition of the 77-month Venus-Mars cycle for 32 iterations. Symbolically, this period is associated with Eros (intimate love and the arts), Anteros (requited love, or love returned) and Harmonia (harmony, accord). It is synchronic that we find here the first of a series of periods which have come to be described by historians via the term "Renaissance." The term renaissance was originally confined to the Italian Renaissance (of a later Venus period), but many historians have now recognized the existence of medieval renaissances. Since the word renaissance implies a re-birth of some kind, immediately we can see a connection with the past, and a renewal of the classical ideals of Antiquity. This unity with the past and constancy of expression is also reflective of the Parmenidean concept of an eternal and unchanging Being behind all material manifestations.

In the West, the period begins with the reign of Alfred the Great, who defended his kingdom against the Viking attempts at conquest, and whose reputation has been that of a learned and merciful man who encouraged education and improved his kingdom's legal system, military structure, and his people's quality of life. This is followed in central and southern Europe with the Ottonian Renaissance that accompanied the reigns of the first three Holy Roman Emperors of the Ottonian dynasty. Otto I inspired renewed faith in Empire, creating a period of heightened cultural and artistic fervor. Ottonian patronage of arts and architecture, illuminated manuscripts, spiritual and political ideology were all revived in order to confirm a source of legitimized power linked from Constantine and Justinian.

In the East, this period is characterized by what became known as the Macedonian Renaissance of the Byzantine Empire. Basil I, the founder of the Macedonian Dynasty of Byzantine rulers, regained control over Crete and Cyprus and held back Bulgarian advances into his territory. His dynasty was then able to maintain a period of peace under which economics, philosophy, art, and culture could thrive. Macedonian art featured classical styles in mosaics, sculptures and more realistic paintings of people and is seen by some to have had a strong influence on early Italian Renaissance (twelfth-century) artists such as Cimabue and Giotto (of the subsequent Venus period).

♂♂♂

¶ ERA OF THE FIRST CRUSADE
(MARS PERIOD ~1048–1143)

In part one, we outlined the previous Mars period which saw the children of Ares manifesting through Charlemagne's holy war to convert the Saxons. In an impressive diachronic pattern, this Mars period culminates in the establishment of the *institution* of holy wars, via the Siege of Jerusalem and the First Crusade. Another synchronic pattern during this period is the Norman conquest of England, and the subsequent brutal harrying of the north by William the Conqueror. We can see something of a diachronic pattern here as well, because William is the descendant of Viking raiders who first appeared on the shores of Britain during the previous Mars period.

Politically, we can see the divisive and separative powers of Mars in the East-West schism of the Church. Just as the Roman Empire had been previously divided east-west, the Church would now suffer the same fate. In 1054 mutual excommunications began a centuries-long process that eventually became a complete schism. The Church split along theological, political, and geographic/linguistic lines, and the fundamental breach has never been healed.

Another synchronic pattern of political nature is known as the Investiture Controversy. This was essentially a struggle between Emperor and Pope to decide who controlled the political power of investiture, or appointment of church officials, and indeed the office of Emperor itself. Pope Leo III had crowned Charlemagne, and in 1075 Pope Gregory VII claimed for the papacy the sole power to depose an Emperor. Essentially Gregory was claiming ultimate authority through the sole universal power of God, a power which was in previous centuries seen to be held by the Emperor. This resulted in nearly fifty years of civil war in Germany, with the Emperor appointing various anti-popes and succeeding Popes trying to diminish imperial power by stirring up revolt in Germany. All the dynamic flux between opposing forces during this period is reminiscent of the Heraclitean model, wherein conflict is a precondition of life.

♀♀♀

¶ TWELFTH-CENTURY RENAISSANCE ERA
(VENUS PERIOD ~1144–1342)

The next Venus period returns us to another period which is often characterized by historians using the term renaissance. In many ways, the Renaissance of the twelfth century is the most extensive of the medieval renaissances. Encompassing socio-political, economic, and intellectual transformations, this period is now seen to have formed the foundation for the later advances during the Italian Renaissance and Scientific Revolution (a good portion of both occur during the subsequent Venus period). Particularly, this period sees the flourishing of Romanesque and Gothic architecture, the establishment of the first medieval universities, and Latin translations of Greek classics coming from the East. This period also sees the spread of Christian humanism, which culminates with Petrarch's "Ascent of Mt. Ventoux." Dante's classic, *The Divine Comedy* was also published toward the end of this period.

Another synchronic pattern during this period is the establishment in the east of the Mongol Empire and subsequent *Pax Mongolica*, or Mongol Peace, which was characterized by the re-establishment of the ancient land-based Silk Road and new maritime versions. This further resulted in what is now seen as the first world trade system, with a series of inter-connected trade routes linking Europe, Asia, and Africa. Many of the cities participating in the thirteenth-century world trade system grew rapidly in size. This is the period of Marco Polo's famous journeys to China, the chronicles of which would become an inspiration to explorers like Christopher Columbus during the subsequent Venus period—establishing a diachronic pattern between the current and coming Empires.

♂♂♂

¶ Hundred Years War Era
(Mars period ~1347–1442)

In 1345, Edward III of England failed to pay all his war debts to his Italian creditors, contributing to a widespread banking collapse. England was fighting a war on two fronts, with both Scotland and France, and Edward's response was to refuse to pay homage to the French King Philip VI and instead lay claim to the French throne himself. This was the seed of a long-term series of conflicts between England and France, with each side drawing many allies into the fighting. Later historians invented the term "Hundred Years' War" as a periodization to encompass these and other inter-related European conflicts, actually lasting from 1337 to 1453. This construction becomes the longest military conflict in history—one that happens to coincide quite closely with this hundred-year Mars period. This is the very definition of a synchronic pattern.

At the beginning of this period also came the Black Death, or bubonic plague, which is thought to have been transported from Asia by Mongols on the Silk Road. The Black Death wiped out an estimated one quarter to one third of Europe's population and had widespread implications to further European history. The resulting labor shortage increased wages, and as Europe's devastated population once again began to grow, this created a new demand for products and services—resulting in a growing class of bankers, merchants, and skilled artisans. Additionally, the aforementioned banking collapse opened the way for the Medici to rise to prominence in Florence. Thus, many of the developments during this Mars period can be seen as crucial preconditions for the ensuing Italian Renaissance of the subsequent Venus period.

Once again the Mars period brings to mind Heraclitus, and the ideas of Becoming, dynamic flux, and unity of opposites. Dead/alive is an inseparable pair. Conflict between these opposites is a precondition of life, for if some things do not die, then others cannot be born. Like the classic river analogy of Heraclitus, the Silk Road carried both the harmonizing and life-giving forces of trade during the Venus period as well as the destructive currents of war and plague during the Mars period. Going further, we can see another vivid example of the Empedoclean model, as the forces of Strife during this Mars period eventually give way once again to the forces of Love and Harmony during the ensuing Venus period.

♀♀♀

¶ Italian Renaissance Era
(Venus period ~1443–1647)

The beginning of this period sees the forces of Strife still active. The Ottomans conquered Constantinople in the spring of 1453, successfully employing the relatively new technologies of cannon and gunpowder—which would proliferate and diversify considerably in the ensuing period. The conquest of Constantinople transformed the Ottoman state into an empire, and the economic and social stability attained at the height of the Empire's power during the sixteenth and seventeenth centuries has become known as the *Pax Ottomana*.

At the same time that the Ottomans were establishing an Empire in the East, Spain and Portugal were establishing the first New World empires. Accompanied by the Spanish Golden Age of flourishing arts and literature, Spain also achieved a political stability in Europe known as the *Pax Hispanica*—evincing a developing diachronic pattern. Historians dubbed one of the early Venus periods (studied in part one of this article) the *Pax Romana*, or Roman Peace. In later Venus periods we see the *Pax Mongolica* and then the synchronic *Pax Ottomana* and *Pax Hispanica* of this period. All of these periods of peace are also attended by flourishing cultural developments or "renaissances,"—both of which are classic associations of Venus.

After the Fall of Constantinople, the resulting flight of intellectuals—particularly to Italy—helped to fuel the coming Renaissance. Coming into currency in the nineteenth century, the word *renaissance* means "rebirth" in French, and the era is well known for the renewed interest in the culture of classical antiquity. Much of the focus was on translating and studying classic works from Latin and Greek. However, unlike previous classical revivals (which we have seen are also now referred to with the term renaissance) the Gutenberg Revolution facilitated the spread of these classical ideas on an unprecedented level.

Around 1450, Johannes Gutenberg invented an improved movable type mechanical printing system. By 1500 thousands of printing presses were in operation in Europe producing millions of books. This contributed greatly to the burgeoning Scientific Revolution, which in turn was significantly aided, ironically—by astrologers. Regiomontanus, (the latinized name of Johannes Müller von Königsberg) was an astrologer, scholar, printer/publisher and classic "renaissance man."[14]

In Nürnberg, in 1474 Regiomontanus compiled and published one of the earliest printed tabulations of the day-to-day positions of the heavenly bodies, the *Ephemerides*. These ephemerides were very popular and were used by the great navigators of the oceans who opened up the world at the end of the fifteenth century. Famously, Columbus is supposed to have used them to awe and manipulate the indigenous people in the Americas by "predicting" a lunar eclipse.[15]

Regiomontanus completed his teacher Peuerbach's half-finished epitome, or abridgment, of Ptolemy's *Almagest* in 1462, and was one of the first to notice inconsistencies in the Ptolemaic model and provide alternatives.[16] First printed in 1496 as *Epytoma in Almagestum Ptolomei*, it was later used by such greats as Copernicus in the height of this period.[17] *De revolutionibus orbium coelestium* (*On the Revolutions of the Heavenly Spheres*) first printed in 1543, is the seminal work on the heliocentric theory of planetary motion by Nicolaus Copernicus, which would eventually displace the Ptolemaic model as the standard model of the universe. Galileo's observations of Venus and Jupiter late in this period (1610) brought resolution to the many inconsistencies observed by the young Regiomontanus a century and a half earlier,[18] and effectively served as proof for the Copernican heliocentric model. The astronomical revolution of this period is capped by Kepler's laws of planetary motion, published in 1609 and 1619 respectively.[19]

The dominant memes established during this Venus period form a new kind of hegemony, an intellectual one. This period can be seen as essentially inaugurating science as an institution. The belief in this institution gradually becomes a new kind of secular creed for a New World. Some call this new creed scientism.[20] The full expression of this new creed will only be realized during the next Venus period.

☾☾☾

⁋ Era of General Crisis
(Mars period ~1648–1741)

In the mid-seventeenth century we enter a period that is seen by many historians to be one of a generalized or widespread crisis. In the New World this was the Golden Age of Piracy. In old Europe, economic contractions, wars, political insurgencies, revolts, secessions, and the like were quite common and widespread during this period. Various authors have framed the primary engine of this widespread change and the resulting transition from early-modern to late-modern eras of history as being primarily economic (Hobsbawm), socio-political (Trevor-Roper), cultural-intellectual (Rabb) or even climatological in nature.[21]

And yet, even though it is clear to many this era was one of global crisis, there remain intriguing anomalies. At the same time that much of Europe and the rest of the world were experiencing revolutions, droughts, famines, invasions, wars, and regicides, in the Netherlands we see the Dutch Golden Age or "Dutch Miracle"—a transformation from mere possession of the Holy Roman Empire to one of the foremost maritime and economic powers in the world. This has caused many historians to be wary, if not condemning of, even the most obvious of generalizations regarding this period. Victims of the reductionist and positivist tendencies of Scientism, historians have largely come to deny these broad patterns and bury themselves in the intellectual safety of specialty areas—divorced from philosophical and metaphysical concepts to the degree that they seem to no longer be able to see the forest for the trees.

For those who have the audacity to embrace their philosophical and meta-physical sensibilities, the Dutch Miracle is not a problem, but rather "the exception that proves (the existence of) the rule." Moreover, just as the Dark half of the Yin/Yang contains a small seed of Light within it, the Dutch Golden Age can be seen as the "seed" of the coming Enlightenment and Modernity—struggling to rise out of the darkness and chaos of the General Crisis. For instance, Jonathan Israel sees the Dutch philosopher Spinoza and "Spinozism" as the "intellectual backbone" of what he calls the "Radical Enlightenment," which, with its predilection for religious skepticism and republican government, leads on to the modern liberal-democratic state.[22]

This kind of thinking should come as no surprise to astrologers, since they are not chained to scientism. Indeed Dane Rudhyar, one of the leading astrologers of the previous century, tells us that it is always in times of great crisis that the seed for a new culture-cycle is formed.[23] In this fashion, we can see here the seed of the so-called "Great Divergence," which enabled Europe and Western civilization to separate and move ahead of the rest of the world, and was as much philosophical in nature as economic.

⁋ The Greater Divergence: From Ptolemy's Sphere to Kepler's Ellipse

In fact, when we look with whole-seeing eyes through the lens of the Venus-Mars epoch, we can see that the Light of the previous Venus period, which is now known as the Renaissance, also contained within it the Dark seed of chaos which then flowered during this Mars period. The "above" astronomical revolution of the preceding Venus period now finds its "below" counterpart in the seminal 1687 publication of Newton's law of universal gravitation, the *Principia*. This work becomes a major historical milestone and demarcation point, not just in the history of science but for the entire history of Western civilization because it can be seen as formalizing the split between the Ptolemaic and Copernican views of the universe.

Far from being flat, the universe was envisioned as spherical all the way back to Anaximander in the sixth century BCE. Plato's student Aristotle codified this view into a series of nested spheres in the fourth century BCE. Ptolemy later merged this philosophical universe of nested spheres with the mathematical knowledge of planetary motion passed down from millennia of observations by Mesopotamian astrologers, and later, Hipparchus. By employing eccentrics and epicycles, Ptolemy's geometrical model of *planetary hypotheses* achieved greater mathematical detail and predictive accuracy than ever before. The Ptolemaic geocentric system served as the primary world-view for 1500 years.

In the Aristotelian/Ptolemaic universe, the earth is at the center, and is the natural place of all heavy material bodies (in which the earth element predominates). Around the earth are successive lighter spheres containing the elements of water, air, and fire. The spheres of this "sub-lunar" region are seen as imperfect and the place where all change (or Becoming) happens. The heavenly spheres beyond the sublunary region, which contain the seven visible planets (in the Chaldean order), are seen as perfect and unchanging—i.e., in, or approaching, the realm of Being.

The enormous intellectual and technological advances by Renaissance astronomers began to expose serious problems with this idea of unchanging heavens. In particular, both the Nova of 1572 and subsequent Great Comet of 1577 were observed, carefully examined, measured and written about by Tycho Brahe. Given Brahe's reputation as a nobleman and meticulous observer and maker of instruments, his observations were key in establishing that these phenomena took place above the sublunary spheres, and thus the heavens were not immutable, as Aristotle had argued. Further, comets were not only in the heavens (that is, above the sub-lunary sphere), they moved through the heavens in a non-spherical manner. Thus, the idea of celestial spheres was thrown into question, and the seed for a new view of the universe was planted.[24]

With Brahe's accurate measurements, his student Kepler was able to establish that planets actually move in elliptical orbits (rather than circular or spherical) around the Sun. Thus Brahe and Kepler together crippled the age-old dichotomy between the corrupt and ever changing sub-lunary world and the perfect and immutable heavens. This created a hospitable environment for the widespread acceptance of the heliocentric planetary arrangement proposed by Copernicus in 1543. Ultimately, Newton's 1687 elucidation of gravitational principles in his *Principia* dealt the final blow to the Ptolemaic world-view.

According to Newton's theory of universal gravitation, all matter attracts other matter. If comets are made of matter, then they are attracted to the Sun just as the planets are, and so must also move about it. The abandonment of the idea of celestial spheres has enormous philosophical implications. Remember, Parmenides envisioned Being as perfect and immutable, and thus the universe as a sphere. Yet it seems there are no such things as spherical orbits in our heavenly realms. Does this mean that Being is the "empty fiction" Nietzsche proclaims it to be?[25]

Ironically, the material certainties of motion and gravity achieved by science during the Era of General Crisis cast a long shadow of doubt upon the very philosophical traditions that made them possible. That a comet would help catalyze a process which ultimately dealt a fatal blow to the Ptolemaic system, is of course also deeply ironic given the so called "superstition" around comets being harbingers of great change. With the Earth now most definitely spinning about the Sun, humanity collectively lost our center, and in many ways we are still reeling from this division. Science has separated us from our foundational philosophies, and yet offered us no real replacement. As Nietzsche put it, "Since Copernicus, man seems to have got himself on an inclined plane—now he is slipping faster and faster away from the center into—what? into nothingness? into a '*penetrating* sense of his nothingness'?"[26] Properly understood, it is really no surprise that philosophical "nothingness" arises from a true understanding of Kepler's first law. The Sun is decidedly not at the center of an elliptical orbit, but rather resides at one of two foci. And what do we find at the other foci, but nothing? It seems we have yet to find the philosophical antidote to this nothingness.

♀♀♀

¶ Era of Great Powers (Venus period ~1742–1946)

At the start of a new Venus era—with its steady repetition of the 77-month Venus-Mars cycle—celestial observers reported an extremely unusual phenomenon. A new comet had appeared in late 1743 and by March 1744 had brightened considerably and developed a spectacular tail. Observers in the southern hemisphere reported the tail length as long as 90 degrees—that is, reaching from the horizon all the way up to the middle of the sky. For a few days, in the early morning hours the Great Comet of 1744 could be seen displaying a fan of six separate tails above the horizon. Astronomers now call these "synchronic bands" and while other comets have displayed multiple tails on occasion, the sixfold tail of the 1744 comet was unique. The phenomenon remains a puzzle to astronomers. As an astrologer, that this Great Comet—unique amongst all Great Comets ever known—appears at the beginning of a 200-year era seems worthy of special attention. The number six could have some kind of special meaning for the coming era, and we should remain alert for it as our historiography continues.

The idea of a "balance of power"—that that no single state should be allowed an inordinate amount of power over its neighbors—becomes increasingly important during this era. A classic example of this "balance of power" idea was Old Europe, which was seen as a community or system of inter-related states. It was believed to be the interest, the right, and indeed the duty of every European power to interfere, even by force of arms, when any of the members were infringed upon by any other member of the community. This principle formed the basis of the coalitions against both Louis XIV and later Napoleon.

The term "great power" then originates during the post-Napoleonic era. In 1815, the Congress of Vienna was the first occasion in history where, on a continental scale, national representatives came together to formulate treaties. The Congress of Vienna consisted of the five "great powers" of Europe: the Austrian Empire, France, Prussia, Russia, and Great Britain. These five "Great Powers" of the time then formed the "Concert of Europe," which claimed the right to joint enforcement of the postwar treaties, and at times of crisis any of the member countries could propose a conference. Thus, the Concert of Europe serves as a model for later international organizations formed during this period such as the League of Nations in 1919 and the United Nations in 1945.

Like the Venus periods that have come before, this Venus period also saw the formation of an Empire. With the aid of new technologies, the steamship, and the telegraph, Great Britain controlled most of the key maritime trade routes and enjoyed mostly unchallenged sea power. The British Empire becomes the global hegemon of this Venus period. The ensuing *Pax Britannica* saw relative peace in Europe and the World during the "Imperial Century" (1815–1914). The Pax Brittanica was concurrent with the prosperous Victorian era in Britain, which had parallels in the Belle Epoque of France and the Gilded Age in the United States. These also form a diachronic pattern with the various "renaissances" which accompanied the *Pax* or "great peace" of previous Venus periods.

In terms of international relations, the British Empire uses the balance of power concept to adopt the role of "global police." Thus, the period following the Congress of Vienna marks a major shift in the application of the balance of power concept, so that this period is defined by the integration of most of the entire world's nations into a single balance-of-power system. By the twentieth century the "great powers" have grown by three. The "eight nation alliance" consisted of Austria-Hungary, France, Germany, Italy, Japan, Russia, the United Kingdom, and the United States. To put down the Boxer Rebellion, troops of these eight nations invaded and occupied Beijing on August 14, 1900.

After World War I, the "great powers" are reduced back to five in number, with the "big three" of France, United Kingdom, and the United States wielding noticeably more power and influence on the proceedings and outcome of the Treaty of Versailles than Italy or Japan. The end of World War II saw the United States, United Kingdom, and Russia emerge as the primary victors. At the end of this Venus period, these three are joined by China and France in the group of five countries allotted permanent seats in the United Nations Security Council. Eventually these five are also considered to be accepted "nuclear-weapon states" under the terms of the Nuclear Non-Proliferation Treaty.

As mentioned previously, often there are no hard edges in history, but rather the Mars-Venus eras gradually flow one into another and also contain small seeds of one another inside themselves. In previous eras, we have seen the intrusion of Mars forces spilling over into the beginning of a Venus period. In this case, near the end of a Venus period we see the early arrival of Mars in the form of two related World Wars. And yet, we can still see the ultimate effects of Venus in that the outcome of WWII was decisive and served to create a hegemony for the US, since it was the only victorious country to survive with its infrastructure intact. Venus periods can still contain wars, but their ultimate effect is to unite, whereas the effect of war in Mars periods is much more divisive.

Nevertheless, for most of this period we see a world politically dominated by five "great powers." As an odd number, five is inherently unstable. Because it does not divide equally, five lends itself to a lopsided 3–2 format where the three dominates. This is elucidated clearly in a famous quote by Otto von Bismarck: "All politics reduces itself to this formula: try to be one of three, as long as the World is governed by the unstable equilibrium of five great powers."[27] We are left to wonder what the world may have looked like if the number of countries formally recognized as "great powers" had ever become an even six in number, matching the number of tails on the Great Comet of 1744 which appeared at the beginning of this period. Perhaps a more balanced six-nation Venusian hegemony would have been much harder for Mars to break down.

♂♂♂

¶ Era of Cold Wars
(Mars period ~1947–2040)

Politically, this era can thus far be seen as a series of covert struggles between the Great Powers to break free from the former five-nation balance of power and become Super Powers. By the 1950s the main contenders were the US and USSR, with bids to control the new balance of power resulting in the NATO and Warsaw Pact coalitions. The fall of the Berlin Wall and break-up of the Soviet Union in the early 1990s marked the apparent end of the "Cold War." The US seemingly became the main contender for Super Power status. However, at this time China

Elodie St-Onge-Aubut, Mars and Venus in Pisces (January 7, 2017)

began to restructure its industrial sector, bringing foreign investments which resulted in an economic boom that appears to put China on course for becoming the world's largest economy before the end of this period. The arrival of foreign terrorism in the US in the early 2000s sparked an enormous response by both sides in what has now become a global "War on Terror." This along with a severe global economic contraction has seemed to relevel the playing field somewhat. Recent tensions between the US and Russia have caused some to wonder if we are seeing a resumption of the Cold War. The balance of power is very much up in the air.

Socially, the break-up of hegemony that is often noticeable during the Mars periods can be seen in changing ideas about relationships and marriage and the move away from the nuclear family as the main social unit. In the US, legislation limiting discrimination based on color, gender, and sexual preference have advanced minority interests and also seemed to put the straight/white/male hegemony in question for the first time. While there is still much progress to be made in these areas, it appears that the disruptive forces of the Mars period can also yield positive social reforms.

At the same time, the War on Drugs has resulted in booming prison populations in the US, with wide racial disparities in arrests, prosecutions, and sentencing. In addition to the rise to prominence of the Military-Industrial complex, we have seen the creation of a Prison-Industrial complex during this period. Some see the domestic effect of the Prison-Industrial complex as the creation of a kind of permanent underclass. One must wonder then if the Military-Industrial complex and Prison-Industrial complex together have created a kind of international underclass. Drug cartels have become a significant disruptive force for many Latin American countries including US's immediate neighbor, Mexico. There has even been some official discussion of the possibility of Mexico becoming a failed state, and the huge national security implications that would entail. Could this become the perfect excuse for the eventual absorption of the Mexican state into the US? Could a more positive outcome result from the formation of an "American Union" during the next Venus period, compared to the chaos, which currently besets the European Union, formed in a disruptive Mars period?

Going back to part one of this essay, we will remember that the crisis of the Roman Republic began with the assassination of two brothers who were political reformers. Thus the Gracchi could be seen to form a diachronic pattern with the Kennedy brothers of the current Mars period. Given that the Gracchi marked the beginning of the transition from Republic to Empire, this begs other questions: Were the military style police reactions to the Occupy movement and the Ferguson, MO protests only the beginning of the American version of Sulla's purges? Are we then awaiting an "American Caesar" to finally cross a metaphorical Rubicon? Or have we already seen this metaphorical crossing in Obama's claim of the authority to assassinate and indefinitely detain American citizens without a trial and/or Trump's attacks on immigration and various government institutions? It seems particularly difficult to look ahead with clarity during a disruptive Mars period, at least with regard to specifics, and yet it is crystal clear that we are indeed in a period of intense socio-political chaos and division—as my model predicts.

As during previous Mars periods, we can definitely observe a general trend of the Heraclitean concepts of perpetual flux and conflict between opposites coming to the fore. Decolonization has seen the dismantling of the previous eras Empires, and increasing fluidity in boundaries and national identities. It is also interesting that none of the major international conflicts since the beginning of this period have come to clear resolution. The Korean War, the Cold War, the Vietnam War, the War on Drugs, and now the War on Terror have all resulted in extended conflicts with no clear-cut victor or new balance of power emerging. This actually makes sense when viewed in terms of the dynamic of the Venus-Mars epoch. It seems to be the function of the Mars period to break down the previous hegemony, and thus it may be not until we enter, or at least approach, the subsequent Venus period (which begins around 2040) that we can expect clear victors and a new hegemony to really take hold.

And yet, while we have seen extreme events such as the Black Death during previous Mars periods, there is nothing inherent within the Venus-Mars epoch itself to suggest that we are nearing a complete collapse, or the end of civilization itself. Rather than the "aberration" which Blaschke described, the erratic activity of the Mars period is actually an inherent part of a larger cycle. Like the autumnal and winter quarters of the solar year, it seems perhaps the function of the Mars period is to break down and re-cycle the meme-stuff of a culture. And yet, as Rudhyar so poignantly reminds us, the break-down of the leaf detritus serves as an incubator for the seed of a new cycle.

Civilization is, at first, both leaf-decay and seed-rebirth. It is for human beings to choose the currents to which they are inwardly, yet most often unconsciously, drawn…At such times, whether or not they are aware of this compulsive fact, the people of the culture-whole are forced to make a symbolic choice: to disintegrate with the leaves, or to participate in the formation of seeds, foundations of future cycles of vegetation—a cycle that will begin with their ritual death, germination.[28]

It is always within the darkness of breakdown that the seed of a new cycle germinates. I am reminded here of how the words of Rudhyar above echo those of Empedocles, with which we opened. This begs the question, where is our Mars era's Dutch Miracle, or seed of Venus? For progressives, it would seem that perhaps the Social Democracy model of Northern Europe might represent the seed of the future—with their high GDP per capita, low unemployment, and high scores on measures of wellbeing.[29] But rather than simply look outward for the seeds of the next Venus period in governmental structures, perhaps it is the responsibility of each of us to look inward and find our own personal "Dutch Miracle." After all, anyone younger than 68 years old was born within the current Mars period. Perhaps it is ultimately our personal responsibilities to dig down into the detritus of our disintegrating cultural meme-stuff and find the shining seeds of a new way of living—the coming renaissance of the next Venus era.

Since we are technically past the culminating point of the Mars era, where the triple conjunctions disappear and the cycle extends to 940 days, we could see the current situation as similar to what the Chinese philosophers refer to as "declining from Yang." The Mars force is still dominant, but it is waning; meanwhile, the small seed of the new Venus era is slowly waxing toward visibility. Perhaps then on an individual level, it is the task of the "Mars types" to "decline from yang," that is, to complete their separation from consensus and individuation process and then seek to join with others that share their new values. Conversely, the task of "Venus types" is to be, or understand how they have already been, penetrated by a seed-vision of the Venus era to come—and then protect the tender seed/shoot of growth from being overwhelmed by the still dominant Mars forces. Together, perhaps the Mars/leaves and Venus/seeds of the astrology community can dream a new philosophy which heals or transcends the "nothingness" resulting from the Ptolemaic/Copernican split and whereby astrology and metaphysics will be welcomed back to the mainstream. May we make Empedocles proud with our ingenuity!

Endnotes

1 Richard Parry, "Empedocles," in *The Stanford Encyclopedia of Philosophy,* edited by Edward N. Zalta, Online: https://plato.stanford.edu/entries/empedocles/

2 G.W. Trompf, *The Idea of Historical Recurrence in Western Thought* (Los Angeles: UC Press, 1979).

3 Some basic web references on Parmenides include: http://plato.stanford.edu/entries/parmenides/

http://www.historyofphilosophy.net/parmenides

http://www.iep.utm.edu/parmenid/

4 For examples of French and British usage of *translatio imperii*, see; http://cla.calpoly.edu/~dschwart/engl513/courtly/translat.htm; For American usage of *translatio imperii*, see Mark Bradley, *Classics and Imperialism in the British Empire* (Oxford: Oxford UP, 2010), Ch. 11.

5 Though the details of the stories vary, it's not difficult to see a common thread: Sargon: http://www.sacred-texts.com/neu/mbh/mbh02.htm ; Romulus: http://www.sacred-texts.com/neu/mbh/mbh12.htm ; Moses: http://www.sacred-texts.com/neu/mbh/mbh03.htm

6 Some basic web references on Heraclitus are: http://plato.stanford.edu/entries/heraclitus/

http://www.historyofphilosophy.net/heraclitus

http://www.iep.utm.edu/heraclit/

7 Nietzsche was explicit in his philosophical relationship to Heraclitus. Christoph Cox, *Nietzsche: Naturalism and Interpretation* (Berkeley, CA: UC Press, 1999), 184–93.

8 See, for instance, http://www.mapsofwar.com/ind/imperial-history.html

9 Some basic web references on Empedocles include: http://plato.stanford.edu/entries/empedocles/

http://www.historyofphilosophy.net/empedocles

http://www.iep.utm.edu/empedocl/

http://www.mycrandall.ca/courses/grphil/empedocles.htm

10 William Ellery Leonard, *The Fragments of Empedocles* (Chicago: Open Court, 1908).

11 In a telephone conversation on 2/16/14 classics scholar Demetra George confirmed that Empedocles' Love and Strife can definitively be seen as Aphrodite/Ares and also suggested that, since by the time of the Pythagoreans the associations between planets/gods had already been worked out (transferred from Egyptians) then I should also consider assigning the children of Venus and Mars that are most like each parent to the two periods which correspond to each planet within the larger Venus/Mars epoch.

12 Stephen M. Trzaskoma, R. Scott Smith, Stephen Brunet, Thomas G. Palaima, *Anthology of Classical Myth: Primary Sources in Translation* (Indianapolis: Hacket, 2004).

13 We can only wonder if George W. Bush's statement characterizing the current "war on terror" as a "crusade" was simply a Freudian slip—or in fact a kind of "dog whistle" politics, wherein those trained to hear such keywords would understand that he was declaring, or renewing, a holy war against Islam. In either case it represents a diachronic pattern, as the First Crusade also happened during a Mars era: http://web.archive.org/web/20100505200651/http://www.nydailynews.com/archives/news/2001/09/17/2001-09-17_a_fight_vs__evil__bush_and_c.html

14 For Regiomontanus as an astrologer, see, http://www.hps.cam.ac.uk/starry/regioastrol.html ; for Regiomontanous' other activities, see http://www.britannica.com/EBchecked/topic/496038/Regiomontanus#ref710409

15 Clayton J. Drees, ed., *The Late Medieval Age of Crisis and Renewal, 1300-1500: A Biographical Dictionary* (Westport, CT: Greenwood Press, 2001), 462ff.

16 Ibid.

17 http://copernicus.torun.pl/en/biography/1503-1543/9/

18 Noel M. Swerdlow, "Regiomontanus on the Critical Problems in Astronomy," 188, in *Nature, Experiment, and the Sciences: Essays on Galileo and the History of Science*, edited by Trevor H. Levere and William R. Shea, (Dordrecht: Kluwer, 1990).

19 Kepler's first two laws were published in *Astronomia Nova* (*New Astronomy*) in 1609; Kepler discovered his "third law" a decade after the publication of the *Astronomia Nova* as a result of his investigations in the 1619 *Harmonices Mundi* (*Harmonies of the World*).

20 Eric Voegelin, "The Origins of Scientism" *Social Research* 15.4 (Dec. 1948): 462–94; Eric Voegelin, *The Collected Works of Eric Voegelin, Vol 10, Published Essays 1940–1952* (Columbia, MO: University of Missouri Press, 2000), esp. Ch. 7.

21 For the divergent views on the various causes of the General Crisis, see Philip Benedict and Myron P. Gutmann, eds., *Early Modern Europe: From Crisis to Stability* (Newark: University of Delaware Press, 2005); Geoffrey Parker, *Global Crisis: War, Climate Change, and Catastrophe in the Seventeenth Century* (New Haven, CT: Yale UP, 2013) http://www.foreignaffairs.com/articles/140759/deborah-r-coen/the-first-cold-war

22 Jonathan Israel, *Radical Enlightenment*: Philosophy and the Making of Modernity 1650–1750 (Oxford: Oxford UP, 2001); Wiep van Bunge, *Spinoza Past and Present: Essays on Spinoza, Spinozism, and Spinoza Scholarship* (Leiden: Brill, 2012), 195; for general info on Spinoza, see http://plato.stanford.edu/entries/spinoza/

23 Dane Rudhyar, *Culture, Crisis and Creativity* (Wheaton, IL: Theosophical Publishing House, 1977).

24 http://galileo.rice.edu/sci/observations/comets.html

http://galileo.rice.edu/sci/brahe.html

25 Nietzsche proclaimed that "Heraclitus will remain eternally right with his assertion that being is an empty fiction." Cox, *Nietzsche: Naturalism and Interpretation*, 169.

26 Cox, *Nietzsche: Naturalism and Interpretation*, 170–76.

27 For a detailed explanation of Bismarck's success with this simple formula, see this excellent lecture by Kathleen Burk on the balance of powers in nineteenth- and twentieth-century Europe. http://www.gresham.ac.uk/lectures-and-events/britain-and-germany-from-ally-to-enemy

28 Rudhyar, *Culture, Crisis and Creativity*, 20, 65.

29 http://www.commondreams.org/further/2009/05/11/worlds-happiest-countries-social-democracies

---

GARY P. CATON is a transdisciplinary astrologer who embraces an organic process-oriented approach to spiritual transformation via engagement with the living sky. Initiated an astrologer by a magnificent dream in 1993, Gary has since become an accomplished stargazer and astro-photographer, combining the experiential power and dynamic images of the living sky with classic horoscopy and metaphysics, and delivering this alchemical blend through the matrix of bleeding edge modern research and pioneering technique. Gary is the author of a new book, *Hermetica Triptycha: The Mercury Elemental Year*. You can also catch Gary online via the popular Hermetic Astrology Podcast, or live, on one of his frequent lecture tours, across the US and abroad, including the upcoming Sky Astrology Conference II, in Moffat, CO August 9–12, 2018. www.DreamAstrologer.com E-mail: gary@dreamastrologer.com

---

ELODIE ST-ONGE-AUBUT is a French Canadian Astrologer, photographer and writer living on the island of Newfoundland. For the last fifteen years, Elodie has immersed herself in the Northern landscape of the Boreal forest, learning the ways of the land and prioritizing a self-sustaining lifestyle. Much of her time is dedicated to being in direct relation with nature and its many languages. Observation and contemplation plays an important role in her practice of astrology. Elodie is a certified astrologer with the Nightlight Astrology School. She is also an active member of APAA and AYA. You can find her writing at www.9thhouseastrology.com.

Brian Demeter, Medusa (2018)

BRIAN DEMETER is an artist/illustrator from Central Florida. His works are typically acrylic on wood-burned wood. His inspiration is derived from mythology, fiction, elemental, nature, wildlife, and abstract. You can find more of his work at: www.briandemeter.com

A Critical Review of the Babylonian

Berossos' Contribution *to the* History of Astrology

by Estebon S.R. Duarte

THE TRANSMISSION OF A SINGLE and pure historical astrological tradition is not something that can be presented textually with absolute certainty, though familiar echoes of ancient cosmogonies are present with astrology in all its various incarnations.[1] What can be attested to is the persistence of astrological traditions and cosmologically based world-views that have connections, whether conscious or not, to the more ancient astral-theism traditions that are recorded in one of humanities' oldest mediums, the clay tablet, and provide anchors to a often fragmented historiographical picture of astrology and the path of practice and participation.[2] A single instance in the progression of the history of astrology can sometimes provide an excellent cross-section of transmission and syncretism in the abstract and often misunderstood study of astrology.

During the third century BCE a figure emerged from within a historical textual tradition that was then undergoing a culturally relevant transition period that has since marked a decisive intellectual shift in power and presentation from Ancient Near-East to Greek authority. The Babylonian *Bel-re'usu*, transcribed in one of various ways by Greek authors as Berossos (Berosos, Berossus), was an active writer, astronomer, and later leader of a school promoting the astrological arts.[3] This assessment of Berossos does not come easily, as his own writings are lost and only survive today as fragments taken from later authors, some contemporary and others distanced by time. What is certain though is the astrological and cosmological importance Berossos maintained as a source and a symbol for the universal nature of astrology, and the syncretic tendency of the "science" or "art" of astrology, where Babylonian ideas about the heavens met Greek culture and the reflection this had on the historical progression of astrology.

A symbol of the shift was the mode of communication used for information, both political and religious, that Greek conquerors had imposed upon culture and language from ancient Mesopotamia. When the Greek language took over the literary record, effectively absorbing the intensity and imagery of the Egyptian temple traditions and Mesopotamian astral-theism, it shed some remnants of the past.[4] From 3500 BCE cuneiform was the preferred mode of recording events and communications. Developed in southern Mesopotamia, the use of cuneiform was spread among different cultures for official use until the Greek takeover. However, this did not dissuade the continued use of cuneiform, given the evidence of clay tablet use into the first century CE.[5] The slow erosion of the transmission of history and language for Mesopotamian and even Egyptian culture, initiated by the dependence on the Greek language, and the parallel introduction of Aramaic "alphabetic" style letters both perpetuated by a naturally syncretic Greek culture made the intellectual allegiances of this period's characters hard to determine by modern standards and labels.[6] The Hellenistic Era created an environment that made it even more difficult to distinguish a cultural source, as Nicholas Campion relays, "The problem is simple: as Greek became the educated language of Asia Minor, Syria, Mesopotamia, and Egypt, the distinction between who was or was not Greek becomes a distinctly difficult one to answer."[7]

Berossos' thoughts survive, albeit circuitously, in twenty-two quotations and paraphrases of his work by a variety of authors spanning different time periods, and eleven statements concerning his name made by classical Jewish and Christian writers. These are representations of what was known in his own time as an encompassing history of Babylonian culture, monarchy, and astronomy written some time around 290–278 BCE, and dedicated to a Greek king Antiochus I, the *Babyloniaca*,[8] or "History of Babylon." This was a "priest" of Belrus/Marduk's attempt at preserving and presenting the collection of his astral-rich heritage to new and receptive Greek rulers. The term priest in this instance must be approached with caution as Joachim Oelsner warns, because while Berossos was well versed in Akkadian and most likely could write in cuneiform, being trained in the traditions of Babylon as representing priesthood may be overusing the term.[9]

Born between 330–323 BCE, Berossos' *History of Babylon*, known to "ancient authors as the *Chaldaica*, the *Chaldaen History* or *History of the Chaldaeans*,"[10] was an incorporation of creation myth, cosmogony, and royal record of the dynasties that reputedly ruled over Babylon. And while some of the various feats are reflections of recognized ancient Mesopotamian myths,[11] there are many intriguing elements in the *Babyloniaca* that have cross-cultural relevance and reveal the continued transmission of a unique ontological presentation. Most participants in Babylonian culture still wrote in Akkadian-Summerian, using cuneiform tablets in the time of Berossos, and Campion has shown that horoscopic birth-charts were being produced for Greek aristocrats on clay tablets during the first century CE.[12] Despite this the *Babyloniaca* was written in Greek. This can be understood in light of its dedication to a Greek king, though it did little to draw major attention during the period as Lambert reports, the works of Berossos were not known to be widely distributed.[13] Berossos' decision to compose in Greek should not be taken as a reflection of the Greek impression upon Berossos, but perhaps the opposite. As Oelsner states, "he intended to bring near the traditions of his country to the new overlords."[14] The composition of Berossos' history includes pieces of the vast myth-based historiographical tradition established in Mesopotamia for millennia, which included the Enuma Elish and the various astronomical-event tablets that are indicative of that era.[15] And while both Drews and Lambert have differing views on how the Babylonian scribal tradition viewed or implied its motivations for record keeping, research suggests that historical chronicles were complementary to astronomical diaries.[16] Some claim that Berossos is responsible for the transmission of astrology into Greek culture during that period; van der Suijs references Campion's and van der Warden's versions of the historical roots of astrological practice as a syncretic sign of the integration of Greek astronomical models and the detailed and immense set of eclipse records of Mesopotamian and Babylonian origin.[17] There are currently eight quotations of Berossos concerning astrological and astronomical matters recorded by later authors: Pliny the Elder (23/25–79 CE) transmitted Berossos' achievements via his *Natural History* (VI 121); Flavius Josephus (37–c.100 CE) discussed Berossos' account of the flood myth for comparison with Christian motifs; and Marcus Vitruvius Pollio (c.80–70, died c.15 BCE), who transmitted astrological fragments regarding the exploits on Cos.

Yet-to-be translated cuneiform tablets may surface, which could shed more light on Berossos and his contributions, though his historical position is not in question. Here we are concerned with the importance of what his contribution meant to astrology, used by later authors such as Seneca concerning events such as the "Great Year" and other theoretical-practical transmissions of an astrological tradition. The following passage is supposedly read from Berossos, presented by Seneca:

> Water and Fire dominate earthly things. From them is the origin, from them the death. Therefore whenever a renewal for the universe is decided, the sea is sent against us from above, like raging fire, when another form of destruction is decided upon. Berossus, who interpreted Belus, says that these catastrophes occur with the movements of the planets. Indeed, he is so certain that he assigns a date for the conflagration and the deluge. For earthly things will burn, he contends, when all the planets which now maintain different orbits come together in the sign of Cancer, and are so arranged in the same path that a straight line can pass through the spheres of all of them. The deluge will occur when the same group of planets meets in the sign of Capricorn. They are signs of great power since they are the turning-points in the very change of the year.[18]

Campion lists the Roman writer Vitrivius (c. 50 BCE–26 CE) as a prominent reporter on Berossos; "we must give way to the calculations of the Chaldean astrologers, because the casting of nativities is special to them so that they can explain the past and the future from astronomical calculations. Those who have sprung from the Chaldean nation have approved themselves of great skill and subtlety. And first, Berossus settled in the island of Cos as a citizen and opened a school there."[19] Campion labeled Berossos' move to the island "either particularly shrewd or a happy coincidence" as this was a historic center of learning that was once the site of Hippocreates' medical school as well as the Asclepion healing sanctuary part of an "Islander's League" connected to an emerging intellectual hub in Egypt that would come to be under Ptolemaic control by the time Berossos' school was established.[20] With such large pieces of the *Babyloniaca* fragmented among different authors who did not have direct access to his works themselves, scholars maintain a certain amount of skepticism at taking such statements like Vitruvius' at face value. Evans has suggested that with little evidence in the fragments pointing to a cohesive astronomical tradition there is little reason to assume Berossos was a crucial link in the transmission of astrology from Babylon to Greece, however, "if it was not Berosus, we can imagine another priest or scribe of Babylon writing some sort of astronomical compendium in Greek for some other Greek patron. Other writers have pointed out that it is sufficient to assume that Babylonian scribes emigrated and took their skills with them or that Greeks who talked to the priests in Babylon picked up the essentials of Babylonian astronomy."[21]

The underlying Babylonian contribution to Hellenistic astrology—and thus horoscopic astrology as well—has been investigated by various scholars to sometimes opposing outcomes.[22] The nature of syncretic representations imported from ancient tradition and applied in a Greek setting makes it difficult to interpret one as the inspiration of the other or as purposeful blending of recognized universal elements. Van der Suijs analyzes previous scholarship by Jacoby and Neugeberger, which demoted Berossos' place in the transmission of celestial ideas as either uninformed or out of place.[23] Both Drews and Burnstein have effectively agreed that there should be no reason to doubt a singular Berossos, cultural emissary and astrological prognosticator par excellence. Pliny reported that the Athenians had erected a statute of Berossos dedicated to his fame as a predictive astrologer and his reputation grew so far as to put in him the realm of heroes as legendary father of Sibyl.[24]

Oelsner has investigated the effect of Babylon history being transmitted in Greek by Berossos, if such is a literary example of the "Hellenization of Babylonian culture," with an in-depth analysis of how syncretism of Greek and Babylonian cultures should be measured when discussing the Hellenistic Era. The mixing of cultures under Macedonian rule was not one of necessarily subjugation or subversion, even though the Platonic dialogues speak of foreign influence on tradition with expected Greek skepticism. Oelsner cites Robertus van der Spek in agreement with the conclusion that Babylonian cities and systems under Greek rule were "superficially hellenized" and for the most part respective communities were kept separate. As Oelsner personally summed up the situation, "Berossos lived in a world in which Babylonian religion, literature, and traditions were alive."[25]

Though the connection between the publication of Berossos' *History* and the various astrological fragments that have been reproduced under his name by different authors has yet to be firmly established, this is mostly due to previous scholarship's perception that Babylonian astronomical and astrological knowledge was not sophisticated enough to produce cyclic theories about celestial events. This perception produced a "Psuedo-Berossos," who was considered a later Latin author of the astrological related material transmitted by Seneca, *et al.* As stated above scholars have mainly dismissed that idea, it has been since shown that the Babylonian framework established in the Neo-Babylonian period or earlier that is considered a feature of Ancient Near-Eastern astronomy and cosmology[26] does not necessarily represent the whole of Berossos' astrological knowledge or practices. He was a Babylonian applying his knowledge to a Greek world. Though there is some agitation at the idea of a Babylonian astronomer presenting descriptions of lunar operations in spherical terms, which according to Pingree and Reiner in Lambert's investigation, has been seen as a strictly Greek invention.[27] Van de Sluijs notes that sources used by Berossos could be contemporary products of the Hellenistic era, when planetary periods were widely introduced. When tracing the Babylonian roots of the cosmic cycles relating to the "Great Year," van der Sluijs mentions that in writings attributed to Berossos "it may often be impractical to distinguish between strictly Greek and 'foreign' concepts." Berossos is also known for transmitting a theory on lunar astronomy that has been preserved by Burnstein:

> The Moon is a ball, one half luminous and the rest of a blue color. When in the course of her orbit she has passed below the disc of the sun, she is attracted by his rays and great heat, and turns thither her luminous side, on account of the sympathy between light and light. Thus being summoned by the Sun's disc and facing upward, her lower half, as it is not luminous, is invisible on account of its likeness with the air.[28]

From an astronomical point of view, historian of astronomy James Evans does not take this to be descriptive of particular Babylonian lunar theory: "One can know that the bright side of the Moon always faces the Sun without realizing that the Moon shines by reflected sunlight. This is abundantly clear in the 'explanation' of the Moon's phases attributed by Vitruvius to Berosus."[29] If the astrological fragments attributed to Berossos are designed to fit into the *Babyloniaca*, then these astronomical presentations could be designed to cater to a Greek audience, who would expect a theory based on spherical geometry of some kind. Evans admits it is clear that Berossos had a part in the dissemination of Babylonian astronomical knowledge among the Greeks but cautions against taking the above description of lunar phases as indicative of early Babylonian astronomy: "From the point of view of Babylonian astronomy, Berosus is rather late. Living among the Greeks, he may well have been influenced by the Greek desire for a physical explanation."[30]

Some scholars have presented the idea that the astrological fragments have their place within the pages of what would be a complete version of the *Babyloniaca*. As important as celestial matters were to the Babylonian culture, there should be no doubt that any real synopsis of its cosmogony would include a thorough assessment of the heavens and theories on planetary motions and prognostications. Drews points out that much of Book 3 has plenty of room and relevance for a section on Babylonian astrology: "I suggest that here [Book 3], constituting about a quarter of the whole work, was to be found the 'astronomy and philosophical doctrines of the Chaldaeans,' the presentation of which secured for Berossus whatever reputation he did enjoy in the classical world."[31] Coupled with Vitruvius' statements regarding the astrological school on the island of Cos these ideas present Berossos as cultural emissary and active historical astrologer, trained in the temple traditions but attracted to a natural Greek system that was contemporary with Aristotle. Astrology was a multicultural endeavor in the Ancient-Near East, even more so when the Greek impetus was added. As Franz Cumont states, "the Chaldeans entered into close relations with the learned men who came to Asia in the train of their conquerors, and proceeded to carry their precepts throughout the land of Greece."[32] Proclus had mentioned the quality of Babylonian astrology in his commentary on Plato's *Timaeus*, quoting Theophrastus' *Book on Signs*, on the Chaldeans of his time, whom "could predict every event, and the life and death of every person."[33]

Where eventual textual evidence may add more to the story of Berossos and his place among the Greeks as a Babylonian representative, the implicit version of his contribution should be seen in light of the vast cultural ground that astrology has covered since its roots in ancient Mesopotamia. From astral-theism in a religious context within the ancient divination tradition, Berossos can be viewed as a literary example of the universal nature of astrology as it crossed into the Hellenistic era, a representation of the shift of astrological use from Babylonian priesthood to technical theorizing and dissemination of practices.

☿

Apkallu, a protective spirit of the type reported by Berossos ~850 BCE. Image adapted from Osama Shukir Muhammed Amin FRCP(Glasg) CC BY-SA 4.0.

Endnotes

1 Nicholas Campion, "Introduction," *Astrology and Cosmology in the World's Religions* (New York: New York University Press, 2012), ii.

2 Gerald P. Verbrugghe and John M. Wickersham, *Berossos and Manetho, Introduced and Translated: Native Traditions in Ancient Mesopotamia and Egypt* (Ann Arbor: University of Michigan Press, 1996), 2–3.

3 Nicholas Campion, *A History of Western Astrology Volume I: The Ancient World* (London: Continuum, 2008), 85.

4 Campion, *History*, 131.

5 Verbrugghe and Wickersham, *Berossos and Manetho*, 5.

6 Joachim Oelsner, "Hellenization of the Babylonian Culture?", 'Melammu Symposia 3: Ideologies as Intercultural Phenomena', *Proceedings of the Third Annual Symposium of the Assyrian and Babylonian Intellectual Heritage Project, Chicago US October 27–31 2000* (Milan: University di Bologna & Islao 2002), 183–96, here 184.

7 Campion, *History*, 84.

8 Stanley M. Burnstein, *The Babyloniaca of Berossus: Sources for the Ancient Near East, Vol.1* (Malibu, CA: Undena Publications, 1978).

9 See Oelsner, "Hellenization of the Babylonian Culture?"

10 Robert Drews, "The Babylonian Chronicles and Berossus," *Iraq* 37 (1975): 53.

11 Verbrugghe and Wickersham, *Berossos and Manetho*, 2–5.

12 Campion, *History*, 175.

13 W. G. Lambert, "Berossus and Babylonian Eschatology," *Iraq* 38, no. 2 (1976): 171–73.

14 Oelsner, "Hellenization of the Babylonian Culture?," 185.

15 Francesca Rochberg, "Empiricism in Babylonian Omen Texts and the Classification of Mesopotamian Divination as Science," *Journal of the American Oriental Society* 119, no. 4 (1999): 559–61; Paul-Alain Beaulieu, "The Social and Intellectual Setting of Babylonian Wisdom Literature," in Richard J. Clifford (ed.), *Wisdom Literature in Mesopotamia and Israel* (Atlanta: Society of Biblical Literature, 2007), 3–19.

16 Drews, "The Babylonian Chronicles and Berossus," 54.

17 Marinus Anthony van der Sluijs, "A Possible Babylonian Precursor to the Theory of *ecpyrosis*," *Culture and Cosmos* 9, no.2 (Autumn/Winter 2005): 5.

18 Thomas Corcoran, *Seneca, 10 Vols.*, Loeb Classical Library (Cambridge, MA: Harvard UP, 1971), 284–87.

19 Frank Granger, *Vitruvius on Architecture*, edited from the Harleian manuscript 2767. Loeb Classical Library (Cambridge MA: Harvard UP; London: Heinemann 1962), 444–47.

20 Campion, *History*, 176.

21 James Evans, *The History and Practice of Ancient Astronomy* (New York: Oxford UP, 1998), 176.

22 Chris Mitchell, "Did the Division of the Year by the Babylonians into Twelve Months Lead to the Adoption of an Equal Twelve-Sign Zodiac in Hellenistic Astrology?" (MA Dissertation, Bath Spa University College, 2008).

23 Van der Suijs, "A Possible Babylonian Precursor to the Theory of *ecpyrosis*," 3–5.

24 Lambert, "Berossus and Babylonian Eschatology," 172.

25 Oelsner, "Hellenization of the Babylonian Culture?," 191.

26 Beaulieu, "The Social and Intellectual Setting of Babylonian Wisdom Literature," 5–9.

27 Van der Sluijs, "A Possible Babylonian Precursor to the Theory of *ecpyrosis*," 172.

28 Burnstein, *Babyloniaca*, 16.

29 Evans, *The History and Practice of Ancient Astronomy*, 44–45.

30 Ibid., 45.

31 Drews, "The Babylonian Chronicles and Berossus," 53.

32 Franz Cumont, *Astrology and Religion among the Greeks and Romans*, American Lectures on the History of Religions 8 (New York and London: G.P. Putnam's Sons, 1912), 56–57.

33 Peter Kingsley, "Meetings with Magi. Iranian Themes among the Greeks, from Xanthus of Lydia to Plato's Academy," *Journal of the Royal Asiatic Society* 5 (1995): 206.

ESTEBON S.R. DUARTE AMA, MACAA. Received Certificate in Medieval Astrology from the Academy of Predictive Astrology, London 2003, studied under Robert Zoller in 2004–2006 for the title of AMA. Graduated July 2013 with a Master's Degree from the University of Wales under the auspices of the Sophia Centre for the Study of Cosmology in Culture directed by Dr. Nicholas Campion. With a focus on traditional astrology from the medieval Arabic period, Duarte has a foundation in nativity delineation and prediction, though in recent years has centered studies on mundane techniques involving eclipses and ingresses. Follow on social media channels for musings and check www.organic-astrology.com for research and related materials. Twitter: @S__R__D Google+: google.com/+organicastrology

aum namo nārāyaṇāya
aum namo bhagavate vāsudevāya
aum viṣṇave namaḥ

Hindutva and Indian Astrology's Modernization
by Freedom Cole

ASTROLOGY IS an integral aspect of Hinduism and therefore to understand the development of Hindu astrology into the modern age it is important to understand the political and cultural history of the Hindu people and what we know as "India" to provide a proper context. The Indian subcontinent had advanced empires while Europe was living as what the Greeks called barbarians. Then India suffered eight hundred years of genocide and three hundred years of colonial oppression and is presently rebuilding its polytheistic self in a world of rationalistic scientism.

History

What we presently call "India" as a country was established in 1947. Previous to that, the Indian subcontinent was composed of many kingdoms as different as the countries of Europe, each with their own individual languages and culture. To talk about "India" in ancient times is similar to talking about the European Union before the Common Era: you are talking about the lands occupied by the modern political power.

Kingdoms in north-western India had the primary land routes through the Middle East. What we now call Afghanistan, in the third century BCE, was one of the main centers of Vedic culture and eventually Buddhist culture. The present state of modern day Afghanistan, which has been devastated by Islamic infighting, hides the sophistication of ancient Hindu and Buddhist empires.

The Indus Valley civilization (from the area of present day Afghanistan, Pakistan, Rajasthan, and Gujarat) had trade with Sumer in southern Mesopotamia from about 3000 BCE,. Harrapan seals, cubical weight measures, lapis, and statues have been unearthed in Mesopotamian urban sites.[1] Carnelian beads made in the Indus Valley decorate the dead found in the royal tombs of Mesopotamia.[2] From the earliest records, the north-western kingdoms were filled with trade, arts, and universities. There was a high level of education in mathematics, linguistics, and other social sciences.[3] This area was a place where ideas and merchandise from South East Asia, China, and the Middle East mixed. It took a messenger about two weeks and merchants about a month to get to what is now Baghdad (previously ancient Babylon), which we understand as the heart of astrological observation in the ancient world, since the civilization wrote in clay, and their records have survived. After Alexander the Great, the Northwest culture was a mix of Hinduism and Hellenism for four hundred years.

The South Indian subcontinent is composed of Dravidian ethnic groups that have a different linguistic foundation than the north. The kingdoms in the south had maritime trade routes with the Egyptians, Greeks, Romans, and other Mediterranean kingdoms.[4] The Eastern kingdoms and the Vijayanagar Empire of South India were less devastated by the Islamic invasions, and have kept more of their traditional culture.

Each of these regions had their own culture and subcultures which also had their own schools of astrology that can be seen reflected in regional chart formats. Eastern India had maritime routes with the rest of South East Asia, which it colonized in various ways. The Chola Empire in East and South India was one of the longest standing dynasties in India. It endured from 300 BCE, to 1279 CE,. Their culture (and astrology) spread to Myanmar, Thailand, Laos, Cambodia, Vietnam, the Philippines, Malaysia, and Java during the prosperous times of the sixth to eleventh centuries. The architecture and religious overlay of places like Angkor Wat provide an image of Ancient East and South India before the Muslim invasions.

Kingdoms rose and fell over the centuries. In the North, the Mauryan empire (322–187 BCE,) stretched across North India to present day Myanmar, including Nepal and Bhutan. In the northwest, the Greco-Bactrian kingdom (250–12 BCE,) was overrun by the Indo-Scythians and then they were subsumed into the Kushan Empire in the first century, which is now the area of Afghanistan, Pakistan, Gujarat, and Madya Pradesh. In the fourth century, the Hephalite Empire took the area of Afghanistan and the Gupta Empire took the rest of the Kushan Empire and expanded east to include most parts of the northern Indian subcontinent. This then fell into three different kingdoms in the sixth century. While I bring up a few of the major kingdoms of the ancient Hindu world, the goal is not geography, but to share how the land we call India is a composite of many ancient kingdoms.[5] The name Hindusthan (land of the Hindus) is often use to delineate the geography of these ancient cultures. The terrain continued to change, and there was no "India" but a mix of cultures that all participated in developing astrology to a very high level. Muslim attacks in the north-eastern regions

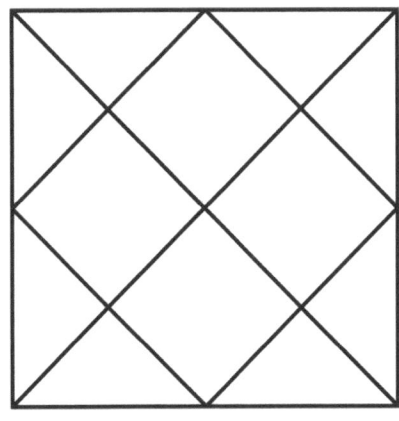

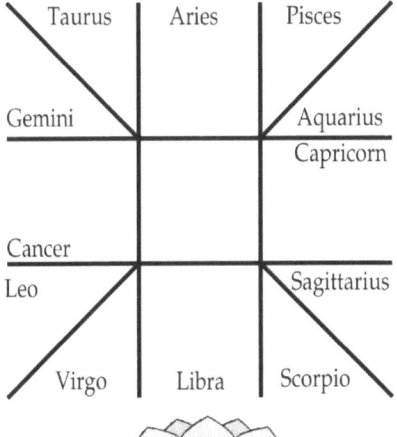

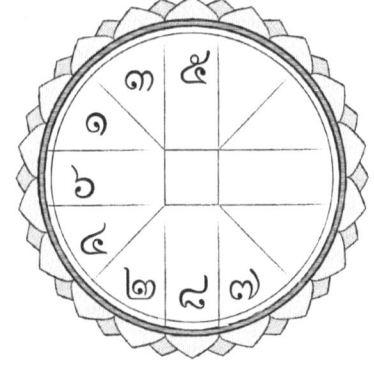

The North Indian chart is called the diamond chart, and has the ascendant at the top with static houses and sign placements that move through the house positions similar to a western circle chart. The South Indian chart is a square and the signs remain static while the ascendant and houses are moveable and placed in different sign positions. The East Indian chart is said to represent the Sun and it has static sign placements, similar to the southern chart format.

started in the eighth century and in 725 CE the Somanath Temple was sacked and destroyed the first time. This temple, in what is now Gujarat, has become a symbol for the persistent Hindu struggle and resilience of Vedic culture. The temple was rebuilt in 815 CE.

During the early eleventh century, Mahmud of Ghazni conquered the Kabul Valley and Gandhara (now called Khandar) and then conquered parts of northern India. He forced conversions to Islam, beheaded and enslaved thousands of Hindus,[6] and looted and destroyed temples. Women were mass raped, libraries were burned and universities destroyed. This was the beginning of a bloody and genocidal period of which Buddhism did not survive in the Indian subcontinent, and a huge amount of history was lost. In 1026, Mahmud of Ghazni sacked and destroyed the temple of Somanath again.

Somanath Temple

Soma means Moon and *nath* means lord. This temple was a place to worship Śiva as the Moon-lord and is said to represent the Moon in its exaltation sign of Taurus. The location of the temple is called Prabhās Kṣetra. Sanskrit has many words for light: hot light, burning light, blinding light, inner light, and Prabhās is gentle illuminating light, similar to the Moon or stars. The land around the Somanath (Moon-lord) temple is that place shining with the light of the Moon and the stars. The original temple is said to have been established by Kṛṣṇa, who is understood to be the lunar Viṣṇu avatar.[7] Pilgrimage to this site removes afflictions to the Moon in one's birth chart. Similarly, the Rameśwar Śiva temple in South India was said to be established by Rāma, who is the solar Viṣṇu avatar, and its pilgrimage removes afflictions to the Sun and paternal curses in one's birth chart.

My teacher's lineage of astrology traces its roots back to the Atri Brahmins who were priests of the Somanath temple. After the destruction in 1026, the family migrated to the university area of Mithila in central-north India, famous for its libraries. The most famous was the library at Nalanda University, spread over fourteen hectares and said to have more than a hundred thousand texts on grammar, logic, astronomy, astrology, and other ancient literature. This library was destroyed by Turkish Muslim invaders in 1193 CE under Bakhtiyar Khiliji, and it took weeks to burn. At this time, the Gajapati king invited my teacher's family to the kingdom of Kalinga (modern day Odisha). The Sun worship in this eastern part of India was influenced by the Maga Brahmins (Iranian priests), who had migrated during the previous centuries, and knowledge of astrology was highly valued. This is how the family lineage of my teacher traces its roots from the Somanath temple in the northwest to Odisha in the East.

Back in Gujarat, the Somanath temple was rebuilt, but in 1296 the temple was destroyed a third time after the local king was defeated by Islamic forces that bragged of killing fifty thousand Hindus and making twenty thousand slaves. The Mughal Empire began in 1526, and brought with it more tolerant views which supported the arts and literature. The last astrology classics were written at this time.[8] The Mughal Empire conquered farther south into the Indian Subcontinent than any previous Islamic empire; it covered the area from present-day Afghanistan to the South Indian Empire of Vijayanagar.

Traditionally a family lineage had its text, which was memorized and passed down orally. Occasionally the text was written for others, but within the tradition, it was memorized and passed down orally. My teacher's lineage, carries a text called the *Jaimini Upadeśa Sūtras*. My teacher memorized the text at the age of eight and not till he was older did he learn the astrological import of what he had memorized, along with all the contrasting opinions over the centuries. He also read and learned other texts, but the lineage revolved around the family transmission which persisted like the Somanath temple. My teacher does astrology differently than his uncle who practiced differently than his father, but the thread of the lineage runs through the text which lives inside of them.

Colonization and Modernity

In the 1500s, the Portuguese, Spanish, Dutch, Danish, and French had set up trading posts. The last Mughal Emperor, Aurangzeb, famous for his cruelty, devastated the Somanath Temple again in 1665. Mughal power waned and rich British investors began controlling parts of India. In 1757, the British East India Company took control of India. Religious persecution stopped, and in 1783 the Somanath temple was rebuilt next to its ruins, symbolic of the perseverance of the Hindu spirit. In 1857, the British government assumed complete control over "India" through military power. While they were unable to control the Afghan region, they did take South India, which the Mughals could not.

Western superiority and white supremacy was used to justify British colonialism and the Indian people were treated as servants. Thomas Babington Macaulay designed the Indian education system to degrade Indian culture and promote European ideology. Indian history and literature was degraded as "barbaric," and ancient Greek and European history were taught in their place as superior. Materialistic scientism taught that Hindu spirituality and astrology were primitive. The British did not physically persecute the Indian people, but they did so intellectually.

Traditional teacher student schools (gurukula) survived in the rural villages, but there was little mainstream expression. Sanskrit, rituals, and astrology continued to be practiced as part of the Indian culture. My teacher's grandfather, Jaganath Rath, was able to use an ephemeris and do all chart and daśā calculations in his head. He passed the lineage teachings on to his eldest son, Kaśinath Rath, who had a government job during the day and taught astrology in the evenings and weekends. My teacher, Sanjay Rath, was the nephew who took the lineage teachings. The other children chose IT or doctor professions and followed the pursuit of the British/American dream that the 1947 Independence now made available. Many traditions have died or are dying because teenagers are choosing modern jobs, and there are too few taking the time to learn the ancient ways.

The Power of Nomenclature

Astrology was seen as an inherent part of Hindu culture, though *Hindu* or *Indian* are not words that the people traditionally called themselves. The word Hindu was originally the Persian name for those living in the area of the Sindhu River, which is now Pakistan and the Punjab. Islamic invaders conquering that area began using it to refer to all non-Muslims of the Indian subcontinent (and even the Chinese for a time). The British continued using *Hindu* to refer to the ethnic Indian as well as all the *Hindu's* non-Abrahamic religions.

In the late nineteenth century, Indian leaders began to use the term Hindu to link the people of the various Indian kingdoms and diverse cultural and linguistic heritages under a single "Hindu" ethnicity. In origination, it was debated whether "Hindu" was a cultural/ethnic/racial term or a religious term, and various opinions still exist.[9] But this term allowed the Indian subcontinent to unite against the British colonial power.

Religious organizations such as the Brahmo Samaj (1861) and Arya Samaj (1875) worked on systematizing (and Christianizing) the Vedic teachings to focus on the monotheist aspects of Vedic thought to counter the missionaries working on "converting the heathens." Swami Vivekananda gave modernized interpretations of Vedic teachings that made them intelligible to the Western mind. He spoke of an eternal universal religion (Sanātana Dharma) that included all the religions of India. Śrī Aurobindo defined the eternal religion as including all of the pagan open-minded religious practices that India had saved. These two figures influenced Gandhi and many future freedom fighters to promote a single Indian cultural identity. What was once a simplistic grouping of a subcontinent's ethnicities and religions became a way to unite the "Hindu" people.

Resistance to British colonialism required fostering a patriotic movement. Indian kings that had risen up against the Mughals were made heroes for the youth, along with ancient scholars, astronomers, and astrologers. Today, the astrologer Varāhamihira and the astronomer Āryabhaṭa hang on the walls of Indian schools alongside other political and religious heroes.

Hindutva was a term popularized by the atheist V.D. Sarvarkar in 1924. Sarvarkar used it to mean ethnic Indian and gave it no religious connotation. To him, Hindutva was Hindu/cultural nationalism as a resistance to Colonial oppression. Hindutva promoted Indian culture over westernization. Indians were being modernized and industrialized, but the Hindutva movement worked to keep Indian culture from being westernized.

Astrologers

Astrology had been kept alive among Brahmins who often kept the knowledge exclusive amongst themselves for career purposes. They cast the chart of new born children and would make life predictions. They chose marriage dates, beneficial times of action and would print ephemerides with holiday schedules. Religious Hindus had a family astrologer whom they would see like a doctor when life had problems. There were no major astrological personalities or classic works, at least that were able to be recognized, during the British rule during the seventeenth to the nineteen century, as astrology was degraded with everything else "heathen" in India. In the twentieth century, the religious tide began to change. Hindu literature from the Brahmo Samaj, Swami Vivekananda, and the occult works of Sir John Woodroffe were influencing English culture. The dynamics of oppression changed in India, and the Hindutva culture grew.

In 1895, Professor B. Suryanarayan Rao, the grandfather of Dr. B. V. Raman, started the *Astrological Magazine* in the English language for the modernized Indian. It had the intention to support the cultivation of traditional Indian culture in the younger generation. Dr. Raman became the editor of this magazine from 1932 till his death in 1998 and was one of India's most important Astrologers in the twentieth century. He rose to fame during World War II by making successful predictions about the war. Dr. Raman wrote fifteen books on Hindu Astrology, translated three classic texts, and wrote numerous articles—all in English.

After World War II, India gained independence. Previously, British India had about 500 provinces that were then merged into states along the lines of the major 22 languages, though there are 122 major languages spoken (with a few hundred dialects).[10] English remains the primary language in India since the southern states will not accept Hindi, which has a large Persian and Arabic influence which they never had imposed upon them. Printing in English allowed astrology to be communicated both nationally and internationally.

When we say "Western astrology," it includes many different systems and approaches. Similarly, when we say "Hindu astrology" there is not just one. There are many traditions and variations from different regions and lineages. Iranian historians even call this ancient astrology as "South East Asian astrology" to indicate the complete geography of its practice. In Vedic culture it is called *Jyotiṣa* and is a branch of the Vedas (*vedāṅga*) composed of astronomy (*gaṇita*), its interpretations (*horā*), and omenology (*saṁhitā*). B. V. Raman used the term Hindu astrology in the mid twentieth century because he was promoting cultural nationalism and inspiring the younger generation to study. "Vedic Astrology" is another translation that came into use in the 1980s in America. These names are for Westerners, since in India it is called Jyotiṣ or just astrology.[11]

In 1984, B. V. Raman founded the Indian Council of Astrological Science (ICAS) to create certifications and regulations for astrologers outside of traditional lineages. He is called the father of modern Hindu astrology. His writing inspired astrologers around the globe and reinvigorated astrology in India itself. Dr. Raman was an inspiration for a generation of practicing astrologers, astrology teachers, and translators of astrological texts. Many texts have been translated since and made available, nonetheless, there are hundreds more in Sanskrit and colloquial languages still untranslated. Many texts are still on bamboo leaf manuscripts.

C. S. Patel (1915–2007) was another star in the astrology world who opened the doorway for Western scholarship. He was especially loved for his teachings on the Nāḍī texts, which is an advanced school of astrology in India. Narendra Desai (1924–2001) had a technique of determining the rising sign based on the thumb print. He was also said to allow ancient sages to speak through him. He is appreciated by many Western astrologers who start to practice Hindu astrology as he interpreted a statement in the Vasiṣṭa Nāḍī as predicting the discovery of the outer planets. Uranus, Neptune, and Pluto are called Prajāpati, Varuṇa, and Yama. Desai developed the use of the outer planets within Hindu astrology.

There are other respected teachers for various traditional lineages and modernizations of astrology after independence, but to name them would be to name some and not others, and there are many schools. Within schools there are different opinions. For example, my teacher from Odisha gives a Jaimini timing method called Dṛg daśā which is used to calculate spiritual growth and experiences in a person's life. Śrī Iranganti Rangacharya in Andra Pradesh teaches the same technique but uses a slightly different calculation. Both are official lineages carrying the *Jaimini Upadeśa Sūtras*, but interpretation has subtle differences. There are also modern interpretations of the same text that have no lineage associations.

India has many astrology masters who would never share their teachings outside of a small group of Brahmin disciples. And then there are great astrologers who only know their colloquial language and could not share their knowledge, even if they wanted. B. V. Raman is a grandfather of modern astrology in that he opened the doorway with English and translated a general form of Hindu astrology for the entire world.

Temple

After Independence, the ruins of the old Somanath temple were pulled down and it was properly rebuilt. A temple is a place to journey to the deity, outside of us and metaphorically inside. The deity in a temple is empowered by constant worship which infuses it with prāṇa and the power to impact our lives. The Western mind differentiates planets from deities, but in Hindu astrology planets are the deities; Venus *is* the goddess Aphrodite who manifests our self-love and the love we share with others. When the ancients said that the gods were not happy, they were not talking about the ones in the temples, they were talking about the planets in the sky. Temple architecture was a reflection of the macrocosm and the microcosm. The deity that lives in the temple is the empowered doorway between the deity in the heavens and the deity within the human being.

In Hindu astrology (see *Praśna Mārga*), planets in the ninth house require a journey to their temple as part of their propitiation. The journey to visit the deity awakens something in us related to that deity. If the lord of the ascendant is in the ninth house, a journey to that deity will bring clarity and good decision making, as well as good health. If the second lord is in the ninth house, then the journey to the deity will help family and financial issues. If the fourth lord is in the ninth house, then a journey to its temple will clean the heart, bring cures for diseases, and can manifest a home for one who is seeking.

The ninth house represents our world views. For a community, the ninth house represents the community temple and the collective view. A church or temple radiates and impacts the psyche of the whole vicinity. The rebuilding of the temple which exalts the Moon; does more than just provide a place to worship. It rejuvenates a nation, and all those who live in the boundaries of its king/governance.

Culture

The Hindutva movement that united the country for independence continues to work on restoring the Hindu identity in a post-colonial era. At the time of Independence, the schools and universities were teaching a British standard with Eurocentric ideas. The Hindutva movement is rewriting history books to promote Indian achievements and culture. A problem arises between the Islamic community (15%) and the Hindutva movement, as India is officially a secular government, and small actions or poor wording can lead to riots and deaths.

In the process of Independence, the Muslims partitioned India and created Pakistan and Bangladesh which displaced fourteen million people and created religious tension not present when all Indians were united against the British. Hindu-Muslim tension goes through phases but is constantly present in modern day India. Violence and bombing on the border with Pakistan and murder, pillaging, and burning of Hindu homes, temples, and Āshrams in Kashmir is regular. Mosques stand on top of ancient Hindu temples of which the previous gods have small temples nearby where they are still worshipped. Fundamental Islamic terrorism is common, and major Hindu temples have sandbags and machine guns guarding them from attacks.

The weaving of politics and culture has an impact on concepts in science and astrology. Between 1998 and 2004, a Hindutva national party held political power. Astrology was promoted and expanded in the universities as a *science*. Westernized scientists fought this before the Indian Supreme Court and lost. Hindutva ideology considers astrology (*jyotir vijñāna*) one of the main subjects of traditional and classical Indian knowledge. There are criticisms about the quality of a university program compared to the traditional system where astrology was passed down in families and took a decade or more to fully transmit, but I believe it is a cause for celebration that astrology is living in a place of respect.

Hindutva

The Hindutva movement comes with advantages and disadvantages. It is protecting Indian cultural values against materialistic scientism. Western theories that invalidate traditional teachings, give simplistic dating, or fail to honour South East Asian ingenuity are seen as degrading Eurocentric propaganda. The negative side of this happens when taken to the extreme, where good reasoning and logic are cast out and all Western research is seen as propaganda. India has become adverse to Western theories that try to link monotheistic Europeans/Americans to the philosophy of Greek pagans who were more similar to Indians than the present culture of scientism.[12]

The difference in perspective shows itself in how we look at the history of astrology. Many religious and astrological texts lack an author's name and are attributed to the gods the authors worshipped. Putting an author's name in some traditions was considered egotistical. It was proper to offer authorship to the divine origination of all knowledge (one's deity) or to the sage of the lineage one followed, as the knowledge was handed down, not owned. Many teachings are said to come from Brahmā, the creator, who represents the root of all ancestors going back tens of thousands of years. Some Hindutva take this to the religious extreme, treating some texts as if a deity or a 10,000 year old sage actually wrote them, and calling any other view propaganda. Western researchers call that literal approach primitive and argue against the ancient mythological timeline with Eurocentric theories of dating. For example, David Pingree theorizes that the astrology that forms the cornerstone of South East Asian religions was imported into India through a single Greek text. The over-simplistic, over-rational theory not just conflicts with mythological thinking but, from an archaeological view, ignores centuries of shared culture and science. The attempt at Eurocentric sourcing of astrological science is seen in India as British white supremacist indoctrination. The Hindutva are actively fighting that viewpoint and fighting for an equal honouring of traditions, which is sometimes taken to the opposite extreme. The last few decades have seen an increase in this extremism.

Myth

The traditional Hindu mind allows itself to fully believe its myth and understands that it is myth. The Western analytic mind has killed its myths. The gods are dead stories and to believe in Zeus or Aphrodite as real entities is considered the fringe of insanity. In India, people who graduate first in their class from MIT with high-level technical jobs allow themselves to approach the gods as archetypal frequencies of the universe in a personal form that they can interact with. They have the ability to hold multiple points of view and to utilize archetypal images to work on deep levels of their psyche. Science does not disprove the causal realm of gods, who live both outside and inside the human being. Ritual is seen as a traditional science that works with a realm that physical science does not yet understand. From this perspective, astrology is *the science* that allows vision and analysis of this causal realm.

Myth and ritual are passed within family traditions, and rituals vary from family to family. Sometimes the myths are completely opposite from one part of India to another. In Northern India, Gaṇeśa has two wives and his brother, the war god, is celibate. In South India, Gaṇeśa is celibate and his brother, the war god, has two wives. There are no wars over the different myths, though, as there is space for variation.

Myth is real and imagined. Because it is imagined does not mean it is not real. Gandhi once said, "Whether Rāma of my imagination ever lived or not on this earth, the ancient ideal of Rāmarājya [righteous rulership] is undoubtedly one of true democracy in which the meanest citizen could be sure of swift justice without an elaborate and costly procedure." Gandhi fully believed in his deity—whether real in the sense of rationalism or real in the sense of paganism. There are some extremist Hindus that have more limited perspectives, but they are rare. In my lineage of astrology, the texts are very clear that the image/form of god is created by the mind for the need of the human being. The Supreme is far beyond anything the mind can perceive, but the image/form is important for guiding the mind. The imaginal realm has a real impact on our reality. In an astrological text that comes through as the voice of the ancient sage Parāśara, it is taught that divinity can be approached through a visualized personal form. How our individual psyche approaches divinity will vary according to the planetary positions that give access to that divinity.

Western culture lives in rationality; myth and magic are suspect, and astrology is pseudo-science. Even the Western practitioner of astrology and magic is plagued by their ingrained rationality. The classic Hindu mind works with rationality yet lives in myth; ritual/magic and astrology are a science. This gives space for both the science of the material realm, and the science of the mental and causal realms. The causal language of archetypes that manifests in the symbolic language of myth and astrology is part of everyday life in Hindu culture. This difference in perspective is important for the future of astrology. The cultural perspective on reality shapes the definition of science and determines what is taught in our universities.

Western scientism describes a world of matter that evolves and eventually attains a consciousness (often limited to the brain). From this materialistic perspective, the gravitational pull of planetary bodies having an impact on human behavior will never be validated; it is like describing atomic energy with Newtonian physics. Hindu philosophies describe how the universe manifests as a densification of consciousness into mind and then into matter. In a world manifest from the seeds of karma through the subtle worlds of thought, the planets are gods who weave consciousness and manifest the life we perceive.

I believe in a few more decades India will find more balance between myth and a rational research-oriented perspective, but will Western culture be able to find that balance? For Westerners, raised on cartoon characters and materialist science, it is important for us to learn the gift of living in ancient myth and allowing for more than one realm of perspective. I believe that learning to live in myth opens the doorway to enlivening an archetypal language in which the stars speak. Not just as an analogy, but as an imaginal consciousness that has the potential to affect reality.

Endnotes

1 Steffen Laursen and Piotr Steinkeller, *Babylonia, the Gulf Region, and the Indus: Archaeological and Textual Evidence for Contact in the Third and Early Second Millenia BCE* (Indiana: Eisenbrauns, 2017).

2 Many of these beads are on display at the British Museum in London. An article on them can be seen at https://www.harappa.com/blog/carnelian-feast-british-museum

3 In the fifth century BCE, Pāṇini, the philologist and formalizer of modern Sanskrit grammar lived in Gandhāra, the present day border of Afghanistan and Pakistan.

4 Ancient trade routes discussed by S. Chandra and A.K. Jain, *Foundations of Ethnobotonay: 21st Century Perspective* (Delhi: Scientific Publisher, 2017), 30.

5 For a historical overview, see Kulke, Hermann, and Dietmar Rothermund, *A History of India* (London: Routledge, 2004).

6 Buddhists and Jains were also called Hindus as the term Hindu referred to the ethnic people of the Indian subcontinent and did not have religious affiliations other than non-Muslim. There was no religion called Hinduism; there were Vaiṣṇavas, Śaivas, Śāktas, Tāntrics, Sauras (Sun worshippers), Buddhists, Jains, Christians, Cārvākas and more, each of which had many sects within themselves.

7 According to Bṛhat Parāśara Horā Śāstra, Incarnation Chapter

8 Praśna Mārga from Kerala in South India and Jataka Tattva from the Rajasthan area both written in the sixteenth or seventeenth century.

9 The Indian Supreme Court voted in 1995 to use the word in a secular way to emphasize the way of life of the Indian people and the Indian culture or ethos, though scholars and religious studies still use the word to refer to the various religions found in India.

10 Europe has 23 officially recognized languages and sixty indigenous regional minority languages.

11 The ṣ in Jyotiṣ is pronounced as a cerebral sha, like the seashore not palatal sha (ś) in a word like share. Jyotiṣa is Sanskrit and Jyotiṣ is Hindi.

12 Rajiv Malhotra, *Being Different: An Indian Challenge to Western Universalism* (Delhi: Harpercollins, 2013).

Freedom Cole is a practitioner of Jyotiṣa, Āyurveda and Yoga therapy. He is initiated into a traditional Jyotiṣa lineage which traces back to the royal astrologers of Odisha, India. Freedom is the author of two books and numerous articles. With his training in Sanskrit, Vedic philosophy, modern psychology, and two decades of practice, he is able to translate the ancient principles into practical clinical application. Freedom is presently working on a PhD focused on applying the framework of Yoga and Āyurveda to modern clinical psychology.

Pluto's *Weird* History:
Dumb Luck? Dumb Note? *Dumbbell?*
An Exploration of the History of Pluto in Astrology
by Kenneth D. Miller

In 1897, thirty-three years before the discovery of Pluto, the French astrologer Formalhalt published his belief that

> *"The Planet beyond Neptune exists. It is called Pluto. Pluto (nature of Mars) would rule Aries."*[1]

Dumb Luck?

¶ Before Pluto, Neptune

Due to an irregularity of Uranus' orbit, a mathematical prediction was made by an astronomer, and on the night of September 23rd 1846 the planet we would all soon call Neptune was discovered.[2] Ironically Neptune—whose keywords include nebulousness[3] and delusion[4]—was found within only a few minutes of searching. In the chart of its discovery, Neptune is partile conjunct Saturn and in the whole-sign eighth house—perhaps contributing to its mystical associations.

In time, astronomers noticed that Neptune was not behaving as expected. There were what appeared to be perturbations in its orbit. Perhaps there was yet another planet, beyond Neptune, that would account for the irregularities. The search for this "Planet X" was on!

Astronomer Percival Lowell began to search for "Planet X" in 1905 and continued until his death in 1916 at the observatory named after him in Arizona. His nephew picked up the search in 1920 and for nine unsuccessful years used the calculations based on his uncle's thinking to search for the giant mysterious planet that must surely exist. In 1929 young Clyde Tombaugh was hired by Lowell Observatory to continue the work. He quickly realized that the calculations alone and direct telescopic observations would not work and began searching using another approach. This included flashing between slides taken of the night sky some time apart, to see if any object appeared to move between slides. Since the stars would remain fixed, any object moving would be the mystery planet. It worked! On February 18, 1930 at 4 pm the planet "Lowell" was discovered.[5]

However, Lowell was not the only astronomer who had worked out a hypothetical orbit for Planet X. Venkatesh

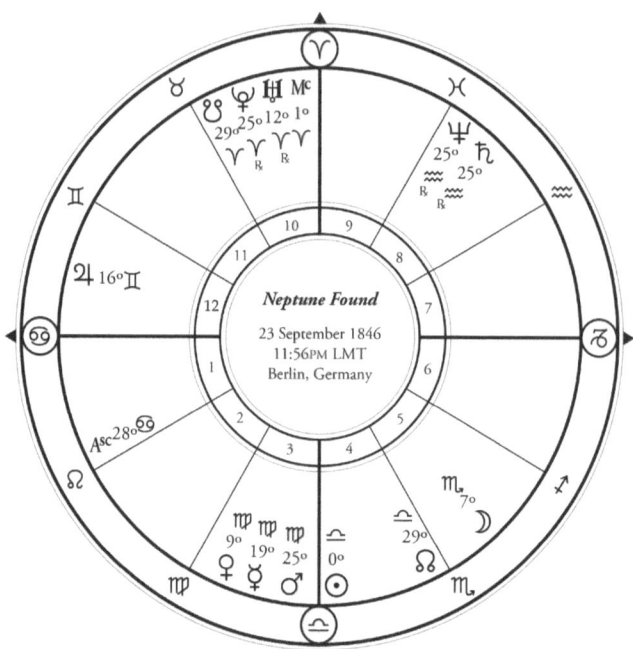

Percival Lowell (WikiCommons).

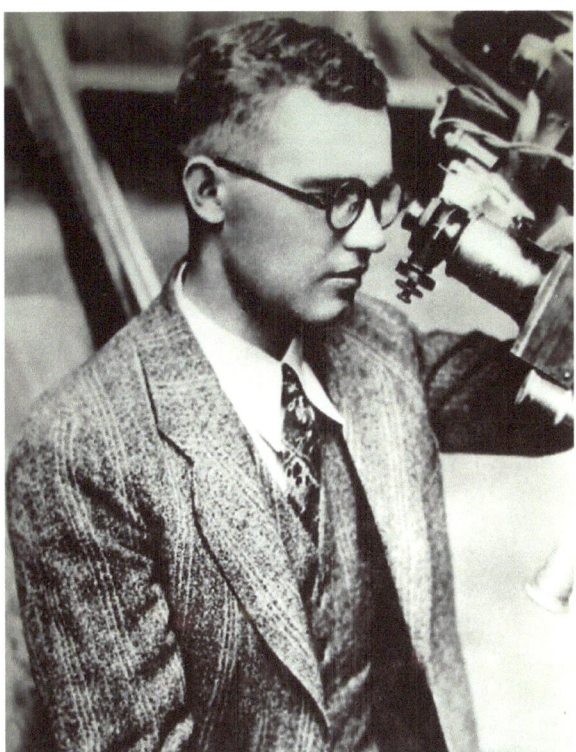

Clyde Tombaugh (WikiCommons).

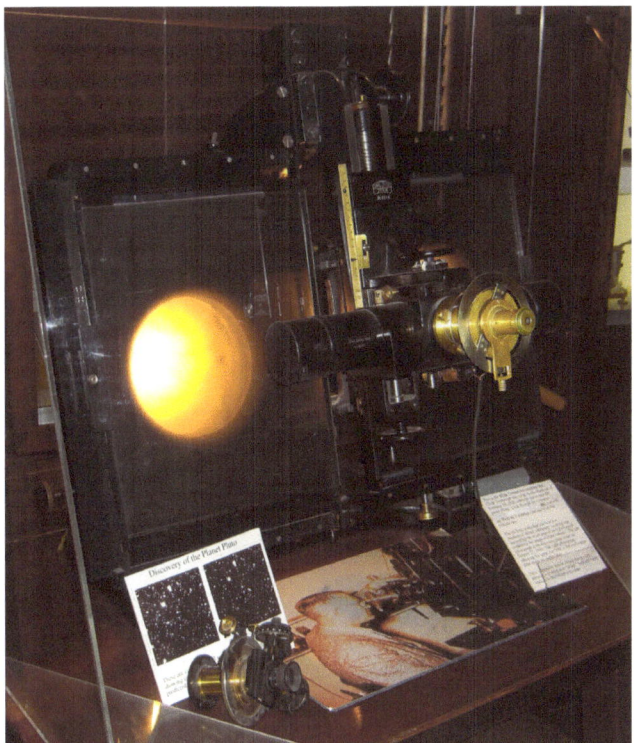

The machine Tombaugh used to find Pluto (WikiCommons).

Ketakar had published in 1911 that a trans-Neptunian planet he called Brahma would have an orbital period 242.28 years, bringing it close to Pluto's actual 248-year orbit. The less accurate Lowell had estimated it at 282 years.[6]

In the years following 1930, astronomers realized they had a problem. The newly named Pluto was much smaller than anticipated. It should be the size of Neptune if it was going to explain the orbital irregularities. In addition, the observed position of Pluto at the time of discovery only coincidently corresponded well with Lowell's calculations, which were in fact quite off the mark.[7] To add insult to injury, advances in celestial science would soon demonstrate that Neptune's orbit is in fact quite normal...there was no need to postulate another planet to account for it! Was the discovery of Pluto the result of false pretenses and *dumb luck*?

Dumb Note?

In addition to scientists, astrologers began speculating on planet(s) beyond Neptune. In an amazing bit of foresight "the French astrologer Fomalhalt stated definitely in 1897 that there was (a planet beyond Neptune) and that its name would be Pluto."[8] And he was not the only one.

In the March 1906 issue of *Modern Astrology*, G. E. Sutcliffe published position tables for a planet he called Isis with an orbital period of 360 years. As late as 1931 some British astrologers still actively monitored Isis in charts, even though discussion of Pluto was viewed as a kind of replacement.[9]

Maurice Wemyss, a Scottish archaeologist and medical astrologer, (and likely influenced by Alfred Witte, the founder of what eventually became known as Uranian astrology) postulated several hypothetical planets in the 1920s, including one "Pluto" whose orbit was estimated at 1,366 years. When the "real" Pluto was discovered he assigned it co-rulership of Virgo, and said it should be called Lowell-Pluto, to distinguish it from his own hypothetical Pluto.[10]

But how did Planet X become Pluto in the first place? Was it named after Mickey Mouse's dog? Nope![11]

More than a thousand names were submitted to the Lowell Observatory including Constance, Atlas, Artemis, Zymal, Zeus. And let's not forget Ketakar's Brahma, creator god of Hinduism. But none of these were selected.

Instead, on March 14, 1930, the day after the discovery was announced to the world (as it was both the anniversary of Uranus' discovery and Lowell's birthday), eleven year old Venetia Burney suggested the name "Pluto" because it was so far and distant and invisible to the eye, just like the Roman god Pluto had the power to make himself invisible. Her grandfather was friends with the astronomer at Oxford observatory, and he cabled Lowell Observatory with the suggestion. Astronomers there immediately liked the name because the first two letters of PLuto also stand for Percival Lowell. On May 1, 1930, the name Pluto was officially announced.[12]

Astrologers wasted no time in considering the meanings of the new planet.

Venetia Burney (WikiCommons).

¶ THE EARLY YEARS

As we have seen, astrological predictions pre-dating 1930 speculated that the new planet would be called Pluto and have the nature of Mars. Sepharial published this in 1918 and was remembered by the astrologers of 1930.[13] However, from the beginning views were diverse.

Writing in the December 1930 issue of *Astrology* (a UK publication), J. P. Gross, after mentioning the obvious association of Neptune with Cancer(?)[14] makes a case for Leo being the proper home for Pluto. Pluto wears a crown like Apollo, is King of the Underworld, autocrats and dictators have arisen since its discovery. The connection between Pluto and wealth, and wealth and gold, and the removal of the gold standard, makes him think Leo is the natural choice. He concludes with "I further believe that Pluto, ruling from his own original sign, will prove a benefic, if a stern one."[15]

Writing in 1931, Charles E. O. Carter[16] considers Pluto to be related to Cancer, reasoning that mythologically, Jupiter, Neptune, and Pluto are brothers and with Neptune associated with Pisces, perhaps it makes sense that Pluto would be associated with Jupiter's exaltation point in Cancer. However, he adds "as we have not yet agreed on the rulerships of Uranus and Neptune, we ought, I think, to be in no great haste to 'fix' Pluto. In any case I am one who stands by the ancient and traditional rulerships and I regard the new planets as being at best not true rulers, but merely, as it were, *interested parties*."[17]

At this point he had not been able to find many natal charts which feature a prominent Pluto, but based on keen observation from his own life, his preliminary analysis shows four main themes:

1. Upheaval, beginnings, and endings.
2. Discoverer and revealer of the hidden
3. Acute disease and death
4. Relief, "as when a swelling is lanced."[18]

Meanwhile, some astrologers, such as Mabel Baudot, were writing extensively on the Persephone and Pluto myth, at a time when many others were concerned more with Pluto himself.[19] Believing that Mars is incapable of bestowing "the deep, occult tendencies of this marvelous sign," she firmly gives Scorpio's lordship to Pluto. She writes, "Pluto possesses enormous potentialities...not only on our subconscious mind, but on our intuitive faculties, according to our state of evolution... here we have an opportunity of drawing to ourselves the vibrations of a trans-Neptunian planet perhaps wonderful beyond the farthest flight of our dreams!"[20]

By 1934 many opinions had been published. Charles Carter reports that "when we ask (astrologers) to give their votes in respect of its nature, we are met with considerable difference of opinion. Its name has probably been responsible for the widely accepted view that it rules Scorpio but others suggest Taurus, Aries, and Aquarius." Carter recommends empirical data be collected to suss out the true delineations and rulership. At this time he relates Pluto to "health and death... that its nature is to bring to the surface, like a volcano...what has accumulated unperceived over long periods. Thus is seems the planet of the *healing crisis*."[21]

The first to publish a book on the new planet, German astrologer Fritz Brunhuber's *PLUTO* appears in 1934 and would go on to be translated into English throughout 1943 in the American Federation of Scientific Astrologers' monthly journal.[22] He tells us that "while mythology can give us a few useful points and facts for the astrological praxis, such material should be used cautiously."[23] He is an early adopter of Pluto's rulership of Scorpio "on account of its watery nature."[24]

Brunhubner notes that Pluto's influence appears irregular and thinks its "rays" haven't connected fully to the Earth yet. Ruling the pineal gland, he encourages us to study the birth charts of mediums and seers to help delineate Pluto's meanings, which he feels will be psychic in orientation.[25] He writes that the planet can be "confusing and chaotic" indicating transitions, turning points, and self-discovery. Pluto has a kind of kinship with Jupiter, we are told, in that he "gives abundance with extreme goals." Giving both fore-

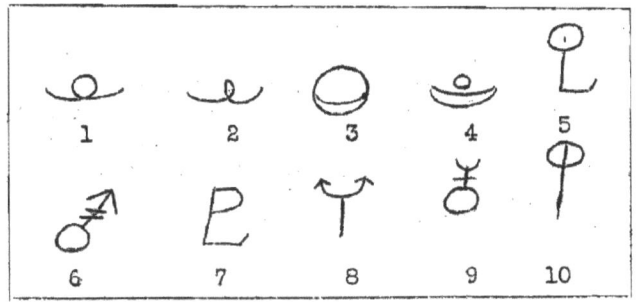

Glyphs for Pluto by Brunhubner (scan by K. Miller)

sight and hindsight, he suggests that Pluto may be better described by Janus, the two-faced god.[26]

He gives some natal delineation principles: Pluto aspects are felt with Neptune, Uranus, Sun, and Moon. Aspects to the other planets are weaker unless Pluto is very strong. If applying the aspects have a driving power, while separating aspects will have spiritual effects. With Pluto and Moon aspects there is an "eagerness to accomplish great seats bravery fanaticism violent outbreak of temper." When Pluto and Venus combine it is "love at first sight and they stay together for a lifetime."[27]

With regard to transits he writes that "Pluto is a malicious ache in the greatest form" and "is the planet bringing death."[28] And while he cautions us that it is difficult to time events by Pluto, they will have a lifelong lasting effect. Squares and conjuctions bring out the worst, but the opposition is "much weaker."[29]

Back in the US, C.C. Zain (aka Elbert Benjamine) claimed in 1939 to have examined several thousands of charts and "investigated what had happened in the many hundreds of people's lives when a progressed aspect had formed *to* Pluto." His conclusion: "Pluto is never wishy-washy. Cunning and daring to attain its own ends, permits nothing to stand in its way." He considers the planet to, on the one hand, instigate horrendous crimes, and on the other to manifest forcefully "but works invariably for the benefit of all."[30]

He gives several keywords including: Co-operation, inversion, spirituality. A special ruler over groups as diverse as criminal and charitable. Its house placement "represents a department of life readily affected by co-operation and the activity of groups."[31]

In the 1940s, Elman Bacher an astrologer writing for The Rosicrucian Fellowship described Pluto as "Frozen Fire" based on his association of the new planet to Scorpio and says "Pluto...is abstracted essence of the fixed, congealed, and compressing nature of Scorpio—the most rigid of all the signs."[32] He describes the planet as a kind of dark Mars, but frankly most of his article on Pluto talks about Scorpio and the 8th house, and he offers no specific delineation information beyond the above abstractions.

Grant Lewi (1902–1951) was known for using transits exclusively for predictions. And he ignored Pluto. As he never published on the subject, we can speculate that he was unable to discern any clear meaning for the planet.[33]

Writing in the 1950s, Margarete Hone gives the keywords "elimination, renewal, regeneration" to Pluto and tells us that "astrologers had to work by trial and error to find out which signs seem to be the ones most likely to be ruled by the new planets." She is inclined to give Pluto co-rulership of Aries and Scorpio. "Pluto seems to have relation to the working of the life force itself in its stages as the sexual act and birth, and death. When considering a personal chart, the judgment of the ability for quick eliminative getting-rid-of action will depend largely on Plutonian characteristics. This planet, less understood than any other at the time of writing (1950), has been known to astrologers for only twenty years. Also, it is so far from the earth and can have such wide latitude that it may be that its meaning cannot be taken too personally (unless prominent in a chart), but has more a mass effect."[34] Associating Pluto with beginnings and endings, Hone further makes reference to the secrecy with which the atom bomb was developed, and the timing of Pluto and the beginning of World War II. Gangster activity is also associated with Pluto since it is an underground activity. Again the keywords for Scorpio and the 8th house continue their migration to Pluto's camp.

In fact, organized crime in America actually pre-dates the discovery of Pluto by decades and atomic research, depending on where you want to draw the line, either begins way before 1930 or eight years after.[35] However, Hone was not alone in linking nuclear power with Pluto. Many astrologers of the time also speculated on this connection. Although it is important to note that during the 1950s and 1960s, nuclear power was billed as a boon to society, soon to provide electricity "so cheap that it wouldn't even be metered."[36]

By 1970 Reinhold Ebertin writes that he has investigated thousands of example charts and that Pluto's effect was stronger the closer its orbit brought to earth. What was that effect? He tells us "Pluto equals power and mass when combined with another body." And "an extraordinary increase of character and intensity must be attributed to that body," for example Venus and Pluto will increase intensity of love, Pluto when angular to the Sun will promote an "extraordinary rise in vitality." Pluto with Venus and you have charm or licentiousness. Pluto with Moon/Mars for a woman "has extraordinary powers to succeed." But for men it is "one-sided fanaticism."[37]

Also at this time, Edward Whitman complains that as yet no definitive planetary principle has been determined. Pluto "seems to conform to a blending of Mars and Neptune."[38] He observes two modes of operation: transformation in a constructive sense, versus annihilation. He calls Pluto a "higher octave of earth." It shows "the capacity to release into action unrealized powers for good or for ill, which resides within the human form and brain."[39] Its house position and bad aspects to other planets indicate banishment or a halt in one's affairs.

After more than thirty years of professional astrological work, Isabel Hickey in 1970 devotes a separate chapter to Pluto in her textbook. It is less than two pages. She tells us that "its effects are so subtle and so hidden that what it has done when it transits a natal planet will not be apparent until much later."[40] And "to many of the earth children Pluto is a dumb note and it is better so. The invoking of this energy through too much concentration on it will bring trouble in its wake."[41] I think many modern Western astrologers would agree with her, considering the amount of attention Pluto receives *and* the frequent lamenting of the trouble associated with it.[42] Still, she tells us that it "has more to do with civilizations than it does with personal matters." And "know that in the house Pluto is placed there must be transformation and redemption, but do not delineate it in a personal way."[43]

In the end she advises us to simply "study its effects in the world conditions since 1930 but do not attempt to interpret it in the personal chart for it will remain a *dumb note* (and luckily so) until the person has developed enough power to be a force in the world."[44]

Three years later in her booklet titled *Minerva* she adds "For some people Pluto remains apparently a *non-functioning* influence because they are sleeping souls neither their heights nor their depths have been stirred…. If you consider Pluto as important in the horoscope of those who are young souls you will not interpret the natal chart correctly." Pluto by house location appears to be where a purging takes place.[45]

In 1974 Virginia Elenbaas writes, "Some forty odd years after its discovery in 1930, Pluto remains elusive and mysterious in the minds of many students of astrology. It seems to be the big question mark… A blank spot in the horoscope, vaguely related to 'group involvement,' 'regeneration,' etc. Such terminology, while perhaps accurate, fosters interpretations which are long on confusion and short on usefulness."[46]

Almost benignly she adds "Pluto is of itself neutral; it simply lends to any person or situation the unique ability to carry-on further than the usual limits. This is sometimes easier to comprehend in terms of extremes, since Pluto is certainly the arch-extremist."[47]

Dumbbells. WikiCommons.

Dumbbell?

If the period from 1930 to early 1970s saw astrologers being reserved about Pluto's role in the nativity, the period after that saw an explosion of information that continues to this day. Suddenly Pluto is the new darling of astrologers, and its importance in the life of humanity grows like a kombucha until for many it is the de facto most important point in the chart.[48]

In 1976 Ted George considered Pluto "in many ways like Gemini" and is neutral in nature "like Mercury."[49] Pluto "is the planet of the unseen, but all-powerful knowledge of the psychic mind. To learn where the person's psychic ability is, check the nature of this planet in the natal chart."[50] His book then becomes a little surreal as he goes on to say that "if Pluto is needed in Aquarius by the year 2000, it will be there," and he believes that it stays in each sign as long as it is needed. This would put a new twist on the whole World War II connection, as perhaps Pluto "came" to help defeat evil. George's sign and house delineations are almost all positive; Pluto reads like a benefic! While not giving it rulership, he does claim that the three best signs for Pluto are Leo, Capricorn, and Pisces.[51]

1976 also saw the publication of Robert Hand's seminal and still in-print *Planets in Transit*. Pluto is delineated quite extensively. He says that the nature of Pluto is similar to that of the Hindu god Shiva, the creator and destroyer.[52] "Pluto usually begins by breaking down a structure; then it creates a new one in its place. The entire cycle of death, destruction, and renovation is accompanied by tremendous powers, for Pluto is not a mild or even very subtle planetary influence. You can always see its effects very clearly, ranging from machines breaking down and needing repair to full-scale construction or death. Decay at one level or another, followed by new life from the old is the typical Plutonian process."[53] In six short years we have gone from "dumb note" to "tremendous power"!

Hand continues, "the energies of the planet that Pluto is transiting become a source of change and transformation in your life. You may get involved in serious power struggles with others about changes in the areas of your life associated with that planet. Often a Pluto transit will signify the arrival of a person who transforms your life, either for good or evil. Or it can symbolize an event or circumstance that has the same effect."[54]

He also believes that the house transited undergoes radical transformation, which means at any time of your life something is undergoing a "radical transformation." There is hope, however, and by accepting the inevitability of change, the process can be somewhat easier. "For reasons that are not entirely understood, Pluto also has to do with secretive and subversive elements of society—revolutionary groups, organized crime, and the like. A Pluto transit may bring such elements into your life, although it is often quite dangerous to allow this during a Pluto transit." Hand's detailed analysis of Pluto's contacts with each planet makes this text one of the clearest and unambiguous expositions of Pluto's influence.[55]

In the same year (1976), Don Jacobs had an article published in *Astrology Now*[56] about transits. He teaches that when you are looking at transits you are to give more weight to the slower moving outer planets. He recommends starting with Pluto, and working your way back down through each planet in reverse order (i.e., Pluto, Neptune, Uranus, Saturn, etc.) to identify significant events by transit. This answers the question as to what to do when the Moon conjuncts Pluto. You know, every month, nothing.

Jacobs elevates Pluto to essentially the most important planet in the chart: "The natal and solar houses through which Pluto is moving—the related areas of life—assume such importance *that everything else* must be understood within that context. *Pluto brings transformation, deep basic change, and obsessive interest to that activity.*"[57]

In 1978 we find Alexander Ruperti in his book *Cycles of Becoming* beginning his section on Pluto with a discussion that it may be bigger than earth due to some new theory (which time and science eventually proved wrong).[58] He takes a more cautious approach than Hand, writing that Pluto is tied up with the collective approach to life, i.e., society's activities. "Pluto will significantly 'work' in a person's natal chart from the moment he begins to question the collective approach to life, or tries to find an individual solution to the problems generated by the collective mentality of his generation. As long as one remains identified with the collective mentality, there is no problem and therefore his natal Pluto will not 'work.'"[59] That said, he then makes a point that the *transit* of Pluto will always work as it is measuring the changing pressures of life, which is felt by the collective itself.

Also in 1978, astrologer Donna Cunningham writes that Pluto is the planet of female sexuality. "Pluto represents a female type of reproductive process in which you allow something new to grow within yourself out of the substance of yourself. Like the female sexual organs this process is internal and hidden and, like pregnancy, it develops over a long period."[60] Blurring the distinction between Pluto, Scorpio, and the 8th house she says, "Plutonians include people with planets in Scorpio, a number of planets in the 8th house, and those whose Pluto is near the Ascendant or Midheaven or aspecting the Sun or Moon."[61] She posits the negative expression of Pluto to include: possessiveness, manipulative control freaks, vindictiveness, rigid control over anger "and a deep fear that any expression of anger will be violent." Both isolating and smothering, Pluto is also linked to the disease cancer, because the person "is being eaten up with resentment." The positive expressions are the transformation which happens when one can "let go" of problems. One must accept change and transformation that Pluto brings and psychotherapy is one (Plutonian) way to do that.[62]

In delineating Pluto transits she says "A major issue that can come up…is that of control and the use of power." And "almost any problem area in your chart and your life can be healed by a Pluto transit to that area. You often go through a purging process." The problem at first intensifies, forcing you to look within and deal with the inner issues involved. This begins the actual healing/transformative process indicated by Pluto.[63]

We are really starting to see how Pluto seems to take on more and more keywords associated with Scorpio and/or the 8th house, at a time when the use of signs and houses is fading into the background of late twentieth–century astrology as aspects become the dominant interpretive tool. Even today at astrology clubs you hear people talking about planets in aspect first and foremost.

Alan Epstein in 1983 tells us that "Pluto represents the function of elimination" and "serves to cleanse us by ejecting material before it begins to decay and rot." In order to align ourselves with this process we need to let go "of old feelings, old ideas, old practices, etc." Otherwise Pluto may manifest bodily through "constipation and diarrhea."[64] We will soon learn the startling mundane source of this concept.

Arlene Robertson and Margaret Wilson (1979) believe that Pluto's discovery in Cancer is linked with the development of psychotherapies and that people are now, post-Pluto, more in touch with their feelings. They call Pluto's influence subtle on page 7 but on page 6 say power, control, domination, destruction, and renewal from a deathlike experience are part of the Pluto portfolio.

Pluto as a receiver of transits has significant influence. For example, when the Sun is transiting by soft aspects to Pluto, those three days "can be used beneficially by encouraging possibilities previously overlooked. The Sun beams positive rays and aligns itself with the depth of Pluto to penetrate and strength willpower, purging the self of accumulated and unnecessary residue."[65]

Pluto transiting other natal planets "can be compared to the impact of a gentleman who arrives for a lengthy stay, leaves his signature in the guest book, rearranges the furniture, cleans out the attic and the basement and, when he departs has altered forever the values lifestyle and commitments of the hosts." A sextile "is similar to a next-door neighbor who was unobtrusive, friendly, and cooperative. The trine represents the neighbor who actively participates in our life, and when she borrows a cup of sugar, returns with the whole cake. A square describes a neighbor whose property abuts ours and who causes tension in ceaseless complaints about Pluto's rubbish blowing over in their yard or our weed straddling under the fence. The opposition is the fellow across the street who keeps us awake with loud parties and barking dogs, but he cheerfully lands the lawnmower or gives us a lift to work when it rains."[66]

Tracy Marks (1980) writes that Pluto leads us to experience and intense release of either physical, emotional, intellectual, sexual, or spiritual energy. A big playing field for Pluto, to be sure. Pluto "teaches us how to live in the state of extreme intensity" and more often than not indicates a kind of psychological death, rather than physical. "If we've not been living in harmony with the universe, if we are overly attached to parts of ourselves or our lives which hinder rather than promised our own development we may feel as if we are falling into a black endless pit."[67]

In Debbie Kempton Smith's 1982 best-seller, she says of Pluto "you will strive against all odds and logic to achieve rare depth and understanding. It takes some willpower but you have it. If you want it badly enough. Pluto shows you where you will find your treasure, for it is the ultimate jackpot. You must aim very high and act with noble intentions in the will of steel. Make a mistake and Pluto will french fry you."[68]

Liz Green (1983) says that Pluto is concerned with the urges the types of which are uncivilized and primordial. She points to the wild raging passionate instinctual creature that is the core of one's animal self. "Pluto represents power, the power of the unconscious and the instincts. There's always the problem with Pluto that the person who is meant to learn to work with power must first be the victim of power for a time. Otherwise he cannot use it responsibly."[69]

The following year she writes, "with Pluto placed in a given house of the horoscope, some sphere of life becomes the place where one meets the retributive justice connected with ancestral sin, the limitations of nature visited congenitally upon the individual through what appear to be 'my problem,' 'my incurable wound.'" The implication is we are all damaged goods. "The confrontations with power and powerlessness, loss and frustrated desire, and the potential healing that arises from the acceptance of Necessity are characteristic of Pluto in every house."[70] A sad fate to any house Pluto tenants.

Howard Sasportas (1989) identifies Pluto with the unconscious, linking it to the symbology of the underworld. Clearly influenced by C.G. Jung he says "beyond the ego level of awareness lies the unconscious, all those attributes and elements of our being which we've not yet contacted or integrated… In the name of wholeness Pluto forces us to confront anything that is buried in us—he is our untapped potential or a repressed Demons and complexes."[71]

Rejecting the notion that the outer planets are good only for understanding the Collective (or Collective Unconscious), Joan Negas (1989) tells us that "once a planet is placed in your horoscope, it becomes as personally yours as your Sun or Moon."[72] She is among the first of our post-1970 astrologers to say "enormous wealth falls under Pluto, but so does abject poverty." Pluto also "mercilessly brings to the surface and eliminates anything that stands in the way of positive development." Elimination, even going so far as cleaning closets and drawers out, can provide a positive expression to the Pluto influence. And let's not forget power and power trips, whether surrendering that power to another or claiming it as your own is a key feature of the Pluto experience.[73]

It is at this point that the associations seem pretty fixed for Pluto. It seems that the post mid 70s were the defining moment. Perhaps the popularity of Hand's *Planets in Transit* indelibly stamped the morphic field of Pluto.

Elizabeth Greenwood's curious book on Freudian astrology (1990) says that after twenty years of research she's identified Pluto as the representative of "the function of the individual superego…in the horoscope," and that it functions as a conscience. Imagine Pluto as the moral principle of right and wrong.[74] This is in stark contrast to the Jungian approach; in fact it is an inversion of that approach!

Stephen Forest (1988) writes that, "Pluto represents a special wisdom in each of us, a precious gift it must be found and cultivated… We may find ourselves expressing insights we did not know we had. The nature of the wisdom depends on the position of Pluto in the birth chart. But whatever its form, when we speak from our Pluto consciousness, people listen as if it were the voice in the burning bush."[75]

In 1994's *Book on Pluto* Stephen notes that "Since its discovery in 1930, astrologers have noted a tendency for the planet Pluto to loom large in one's birthchart during life's darker moments;" and "our potential readiness to integrate wounded aspects of ourselves—is signaled by Plutonian triggers… where Pluto lies in the chart we are particularly vulnerable to distortions and navigational errors based on unprocessed wounding experience."[76] He also believes that since Pluto's discovery humanity has become "vastly more psychological" in their thinking.[77] Maybe you can make a case for that among middle class Westerners, but I am not sure that would apply to other cultures. I am not sure how you would measure it.[78]

In the Aug/Sept 2004 issue of *The Mountain Astrologer* Donna Cunningham gives us a list of Pluto keywords: "Seeking control, amassing power, subjective, intensely emotional, psychological, focused on inner life, private, covert, mistrustful, fusing, healing, regenerating, slow-deep transformation."[79] Essentially the same themes that have been elucidated by our various authors from the mid-70s to the present.

PLUTO: GOD OF CONSUMERISM?

Steven Weis published a book in 2005 that became a bestseller in its field. *The Consistent Consumer* made no mention of Pluto or astrology. It was some time later he revealed that the birthdate-based marketing categories that his authors created actually corresponded to Pluto's occupation of tropical signs. Reviewing the statistical data they accumulated, they found distinctive buying patterns and marketing methods that corresponded to the various Pluto generations. The lasting values associated with specific generations broke down into distinct Pluto periods. Appeal to someone's core values, and they'll be more likely to buy. When I asked him if he thought this would apply to other cultures, say Japan as an example, he thought no, it worked on the US market. Which begs the question, could Pluto be the planet of consumerism? And since we are the preeminent consumer culture in the world, could Pluto have a special influence/relationship on Americans?[80] Remember the advice President Bush in the years following 9/11? He told us to go shopping more.[81]

¶ PLUTO AND INDIAN (VEDIC) ASTROLOGY

Traditional Indian astrology uses only the seven visible planets and the nodes.[82] However Pluto's influence is incorporated by "Neo-Vedic Astrologers" (viz., Western astrologers who have converted to Indian astrology but still hold on to some Western concepts like the outer planets) in their work. Edith Hathaway describes Pluto simply as "a bully who doesn't operate in a straightforward, civilized manner."[83] However she cautions against bringing it over wholesale, and prefers to look at it in the context of mundane astrology. She also sees a relationship between Pluto and the deities Yama and Kali.[84]

Joni Patri, another Neo-Vedic astrologer, says that "Pluto resembles Rahu"[85] and gives the keywords "power, control, manipulation, transformation, underworld, sex, obsessions, compulsions, birth and death, and healing." Taking a page from her Western astrological siblings, she states unequivocally that "Pluto relates to the energies of Scorpio and the 8th house."[86]

Most Indian astrologers reject the use of the outer planets, as do many traditional astrologers in the West. For instance, John Frawley (traditional astrologer from England) is very critical of the outer planets explaining that "the workings of the traditional system are based on light and the providential appearance of the Heavens to the naked eye: a planet with no light has no power, hence the weakness of whichever of the luminaries is darkened during an eclipse. The new planets…have no appreciable light. They cannot be seen from Earth without artificial aid. Light is the visible manifestation of truth, the substance of creation."[87] Further he says "thus the main role of the outer planets and their asteroid cohorts is to fuel the contemporary obsession with titillation." On Pluto specifically he adds, "Pluto is much beloved by our eccentric, idealistic modern astrologer: dark, mysterious, and passionate (just like him/her), the repository of all manner of anti-social but rather thrilling vices, it is the astrological equivalent of curling up with a vampire novel."[88]

¶ UNPUBLISHED PLUTO

During 2006–2009 I interviewed some contemporary professional astrologers to get a feel for how Pluto was being handled in the here and now. Andrea felt Pluto brought "intense energy" to any aspect and that it had an intensifying quality. She also mentioned power struggles, tearing down and rebuilding, purging, and recycling as keywords. She distinguished different qualities based on the specific aspectual relationship—e.g., trine can be cathartic, square can be power struggles. She was influenced by Hand's *Planets in Transit*.[89]

In 2006 Wonder made extensive use of the mythology around Hades and the Underworld; and associated Pluto with compulsions, secrets, and a lack of choice often resulting in a need for domination. She was influenced by Stephen Arroyo, Jeffrey Wolf Green, and Amanda Owen. In 2009 she added issues around controlling or being controlled to Pluto's portfolio. And the solution to these problems is to experience personal power. Also she observed that when Sun is conjunct or opposite transiting Pluto, it was not uncommon to experience the death of a father figure.

Tamira called Pluto the planet of transformation and said "…very painful, deep dark stuff. If you resist it, it goes away." Nick thought of Pluto as a planet of change. If things are good you will lose something, if things are bad they will improve. A time of consequences that are brought on by ourselves. Alan said it "takes small things and makes them big, takes big things and makes them small."

Sarah told me that "Pluto is a good planet, but it sucks while it happens." Her keyword was "re-do" like a phoenix arising from the ashes; the phoenix is beautiful, the burning process unpleasant. At its worst it can mean violent tendencies, vindictiveness, even betrayal. But whatever it touches in your chart it wants to "re-do." She learned about Pluto by reading books and through her own experience.

In fact, all of my interviewees drew from personal experience in understanding Pluto, and gave me concrete examples of how their keywords specifically showed up in their life and the lives of the people around them.

Voting on the Status of Pluto at the IAU, 24 August 2006. (WikiCommons)

¶ The Astronomy of Pluto, 2006–2015

On August 24, 2006 the few remaining astronomers (about 17%) still attending the last afternoon of the last day of the General Assembly of the International Astronomical Union voted to demote Pluto from Planetary to Dwarf status. At Pluto's discovery, astrologers were quick to mythologize the discovery into its meaning. There was something important about that moment, and the world of 1930 that indicated what Pluto would mean. However, in 2006 quite the opposite was happening. Rather than re-evaluate Pluto's role, perhaps there was some mythic meaning to the demotion that would now involve the astrological meaning. Perhaps those born after August 2006 would see a Pluto whose influence has been "dwarfed." But no, our community seems to have doubled-down on malefic keywords.[90]

In 2015 NASA's New Horizon spacecraft collected astonishing data as it flew close to and then past Pluto. We learned several things:[91]

1. It has (the appearance of) a giant heart on the surface! (*photo below, ©NASA*)
2. It was larger than we thought.
3. It has a mysterious internal heat, as yet unexplained.
4. There appears to be plenty of water ice.
5. It has a blue atmosphere!

Far from being the lifeless, cold dark ugly planet, it turned out to be astonishingly beautiful, with sufficient internal heat to keep the surface smooth. So smooth it is like a giant mirror. Has Pluto simply been reflecting our own fears back at us? As astrologers, if we are going to attach significance to its initial scientific discovery, it behooves us to consider these latest discoveries as they unfold. Perhaps, as Edward Whitman speculated in 1971, Pluto is a kind of "higher octave" of Earth.

Conclusion

Pat Geisler, an Ohio astrologer with 44 years' experience, wrote in 2013 "Perhaps in 100 years we will realize more about Pluto's actions. Pluto's discovery was only some 70 to 80 years ago, so we are hardly in a position to judge completely."[92]

Her take on the planet is more benign than most, she sees Pluto "prominent in the natal charts of people who like to refurbish old furniture, resellers of auto hubcaps, antique store owners, used car lots and second hand clothing stores. It is also strong in those who manage money and who manipulate money well to their own benefit. Anytime transiting Pluto makes an aspect to your Moon you may get the urge to clean closets, for the basement, or the attic." She adds that sometimes it cleans out your pocket book by triggering your more extravagant tendencies.[93]

"I've always thought of Pluto as the Ex-Lax planet, in a way—it purges our lives

of so many things."[94]

I have lost count of how many astrologers associate Pluto with "purging" or "eliminating." He is not the god of pooping or barfing, so what is up with this attribute? Did he steal these keywords from medical astrology's Scorpio or the eighth house? He might have, but he in fact didn't. And here is why:

In 1930, if you said the word "Pluto" to anyone, the first thought that would come to mind is America's best-selling constipation remedy PLUTO WATER.[95]

Introduced in the early twentieth century, by 1919 it was a best-selling brand. No doubt by 1930 astrologers had this very same remedy in their medicine cabinets, and it would not take long for the connection to be made to the planet. Advertised as "America's Laxative," Pluto Water used the slogan "When Nature Won't, PLUTO Will." The bottle featured a devil image and since the water came from underground, Pluto (the god) was a good fit.

So what are we to make of the journey little Pluto has made over these 88 years? The basis for the associations seem to be born out of the world of World War II. Once Pluto and Scorpio got linked, the keywords started migrating over from both the 8th sign and house. At the same time modern psychological astrology downplayed somewhat the role of signs and houses in planetary dignity, allowing Pluto to take up the slack. And there is the tradition of looking at the world to see what was going on at the time of discovery. The war was still nine years away and the depression had already started. I find it puzzling that the associations to Pluto are historical events that were temporary. World War II ended, the depression ended. The era of dictators ended (kind of—at least in the first world). There are plenty of things that are still with us from the 30s that no one has associated with Pluto.

In addition to imbibing America's favorite laxative, what was going on in 1930 anyway? Well, you had the invention of photo flashbulbs, Nancy Drew Mysteries, and the Golden Age of Radio began. Also "Lowell Thomas begins first regular US network newscast."[96] Also in 1930 the first Mickey Mouse comic strip is published in the *New York Mirror*, and "Gandhi and small group of followers begin the Salt March, a march to the sea where he intends to manufacture salt in defiance of the British government monopoly on salt production."[97] This kicked off the civil disobedience movement that ultimately resulted in India's independence from Britain, creating what is now the world's largest democracy.

As far as I can tell none of these themes were incorporated into Pluto's meaning although they have all had a lasting impact on our world.

Admittedly this is only a beginning foray into the complex world of Pluto and more work needs to be done. A more thorough examination of the literature would be a good place to start, as I was limited to whatever books and journals happened to be in my library. The thing that strikes me as weird, and the questions we must wrestle with as astrologers are…. how is it, why is it, and what is it that drives Pluto from being this nebulous influence, debated by the top astrologers of the day, to being a metaphorical *dumbbell* that almost all contemporary astrologers believe falls on people's heads with such intensity as to have usurped Saturn as the most feared planet in the sky.

☿

Works cited, courtesy of Kenneth D. Miller.

Endnotes

1 James H. Holden, *A History of Horoscopic Astrology* (Tempe, AZ: AFA, 1996), 229.

2 Neptune had been observed earlier than this, but not recognized. Galileo is believed to have been the first to see it.

3 Margaret E. Hone, *Modern Text-Book of Astrology* (Romford, UK: L.N. Fowler, 1978), 34.

4 Isabel Hickey, *Astrology: A Cosmic Science* (Watertown, MA: Fellowship House Bookshop, 1970), 44.

5 "Clyde Tombaugh" - Wikipedia. Accessed 9 March 2018. https://en.wikipedia.org/wiki/Clyde_Tombaugh.

6 J.G. Chhabra, S.D. Sharma, and Manju Khanna, "Prediction of Pluto by V.B. Ketakar," *Indian Journal of History of Science* 19, no. 1 (1984): 18–26.

7 Ibid.

8 Holden, *History of Horoscopic Astrology*, 229.

9 Harold Harvey, "Pluto and Isis," *Astrology* 5, no. 1 (May 1931): 34–38.

10 Holden, *History of Horoscopic Astrology*, 199.

11 Pluto the Dog was actually named after Pluto the planet, and premiered about six months after Pluto was discovered. See: https://en.wikipedia.org/wiki/Pluto_(Disney)

12 https://en.wikipedia.org/wiki/Venetia_Burney

13 Sepharial, *Science of Foreknowledge* (London: n.p., 1918), 29. Quoted in the pages of *Astrology* magazine in the early 30s.

14 Yes, there was debate about Neptune, with others like Sepharial making a case of a Capricorn rulership for Neptune. Based on my reading of the literature, these questions seem to disappear as the new planet dominates the imagination.

15 *Astrology* (Dec. 1930), 222–23.

16 Considered the dean of British Astrologers in the first half of the twentieth century. See Holden, *History of Horoscopic Astrology*, 196.

17 Charles E.O. Carter, "Observations on Pluto," *Astrology* 5, no. 2 (Aug. 1931): 92–95, here 95.

18 Ibid., 92–94.

19 This begins a long tradition of astrologers who give pride of place to Persephone when telling the Pluto myth. We do not do this for any other planet. For example, we do not discus Zeus' wife Hera when talking about Jupiter, nor do we discuss Mercury's mom Maia. An interesting topic to explore in a future article.

20 Mabel Baudot, "Observations on Pluto," *Astrology* 5, no. 2 (Aug. 1931): 123–24.

21 Charles E.O. Carter, *Some Principles of Horoscopic Delineation* (Seattle, WA: Dorothy B. Hughes, 1934), 30.

22 Known today as American Federation of Astrologers or AFA.

23 Fritz Brunhubner, *PLUTO* (Washington, DC: AFA, 1971), 4.

24 Ibid., 11.

25 Ibid., 13, 34.

26 Ibid., 13, 16.

27 Ibid., 41–42.

28 Ibid., 71.

29 Ibid.

30 Elbert Benjamine, *The Influence of the Planet Pluto* (Chicago: Aries Press, 1939), 4.

31 Ibid., 4–5.

32 Elman Bacher, *Studies in Astrology* (Oceaside, CA: Rosicrucian Fellowship, 1962), II:100.

33 Holden, *History of Horoscopic Astrology*, 219.

34 Hone, *Modern Text-Book of Astrology*, 35–36.

35 See: http://www.u-s-history.com/pages/h1596.html and http://www.atomcentral.com/atom-bomb-history.aspx

36 J. Lee Lehman, "Human Use of Radioactive Isotopes," *The Ascendant* 1 (2014): 55.

37 Reinhold Ebertin, *The Influence of Pluto on Human Love Life* (Aalen: Ebertin Verlag, 1970).

38 Edward W. Whitman, *Astro-Kinetics, Volume 2: Influence of the Planets* (Norwich, UK: L.N. Fowler, 1971), 195.

39 Ibid., 200.

40 Hickey, *Astrology*, 273.

41 Ibid., 274.

42 At astrology conferences and local society meetings, I have noticed over the years it is quite common to hear people lamenting about some horrible Pluto transit.

43 Hickey, *Astrology*, 273, 275.

44 Ibid., 274, emphasis mine.

45 Hickey and Bruce Altieri, *Pluto or Minerva, the Choice is Yours* (Watertown, MA: Fellowship House Bookshop, 1977).

46 Virginia Elenbaas, *Focus on Pluto* (Washington, DC: AFA, 1974), intro.

47 Ibid., 51.

48 Although it does seem like Chiron is giving Pluto a run for his money these days.

49 He was a prominent Florida astrologer and founded the North Florida Astrological Association.

50 Ted George, *Lives You Live as Revealed in the Heavens: A History of Karmic Astrology and Pertinent Delineations* (Jacksonville, FL: Arthur, 1976), 113.

51 Ibid., 113–17.

52 In Indian Astrology Shiva is associated with the Sun and Saturn, and plays a special role in remedial measures involving these two *grahas* (planets).

53 Robert Hand, *Planets in Transit: Life Cycles for Living* (Gloucester, MA: Para Research, 1976), 477.

54 Ibid.

55 Ibid., 477ff.

56 This was *The Mountain Astrologer* of its day, published by Llewellyn.

57 Don (Moby Dick) Jacobs, "Getting Specifics Out of Transits," *Astrology Now* (May 1979), 22ff. Emphasis mine.

58 Alexander Ruperti, *Cycles of Becoming: The Planetary Pattern of Growth* (Davis, CA: CRCS Publications, 1978), 247.

59 Ibid., 248.

60 Donna Cunningham, *An Astrological Guide to Self-Awareness* (Vancouver, WA: CRCS Publications, 1978), 119

61 Ibid., 119.

62 Ibid., 120–25.

63 Ibid., 128.

64 Alan Epstein, *Psychodynamics of Inconjunctions: The Semi-Sextile and Quincunx* (York Beach, ME: Red Wheel/Weiser, 1983), 54–55.

65 Arlene Robertson and Margaret Wilson. *Power of Pluto: The Complete Book*. Birmingham, MI: Seek It, 1979), 184.

66 Ibid., 195–96.

67 Tracy Marks, *Pluto: From Darkness Into Light* (n.p.: Sagittarius Rising, 1980), 2–7.

68 Debbi Kempton Smith, *Secrets from a Stargazer's Notebook* (New York: Bantam, 1982), 288–89.

69 Liz Greene, *The Outer Planets and Their Cycles: The Astrology of the Collective* (Reno, NV: CRCS, 1983), 139.

70 Liz Greene, *The Astrology of Fate* (1984; York Beach, ME: Weiser Books, 1995), 54–56.

71 Howard Sasportas, *The Gods of Change: Pain, Crisis, and the Transits of Uranus, Neptune, and Pluto* (London: Penguin, 1989), 226.

72 Joan McEvers, *Planets: The Astrological Tools* (St. Paul, MN: Llewellyn, 1989), 331.

73 Ibid., 332–36.

74 Elizabeth Greenwood, *Freudian Astrology: Pluto, the Superego* (Tempe, AZ: AFA, 1990), 3, 81.

75 Steven Forrest, *The Inner Sky: The Dynamic New Astrology for Everyone* (New York: Bantam, 1988), 134.

76 Steven Forrest, *The Book of Pluto: Turning Darkness to Wisdom with Astrology* (San Diego, CA: ACS, 1995), viii, 7, 13.

77 Ibid, 313.

78 The notion of "are we more evolved" or "are we more psychologically sophisticated" than we were in the past is a kind of glorification of the present, and I am not sure would really hold up to scrutiny. It is a complex topic that will be explored in a future paper.

79 Donna Cunningham, "Uranus and Pluto at Midlife" *The Mountain Astrologer* (Aug./Sept. 2004): 30ff.

80 See: http://www.businessinsider.com/birth-of-consumer-culture-2013-2

81 See: http://www.washingtonpost..com/wp-dyn/content/article/2008/10/03/AR2008100301977.html

82 This isn't strictly true as there are a variety of extra mathematical points that can be calculated called Upagrahas. [Editor's note: see also Lars Panaro's article in this issue, which introduces this briefly.]

83 Edith Hathaway, "Pluto Gandanta and Kali's Zone of Influence," *CVA Journal* 1, no. 2 (2005): 12–17, here 13.

84 Traditional Indian astrology has these two associated with Saturn.

85 The north node of the Moon.

86 Joni Patry, *Eastern Astrology for Western Minds: A Compilation of NewVedic Astrology*, 2nd ed. (CreateSpace, 2004), 46.

87 John Frawley, *The Real Astrology* (London: Apprentice, 2001), 64.

88 Ibid., 67, 70.

89 My thanks to the as here presented semi-anonymous astrologers for their time and patience in answering my Pluto questions.

90 To be fair, there were some astrologers who thought this may herald a change, but their numbers are few and their influence negligible as of this writing.

91 https://www.theguardian.com/science/across-the-universe/2015/jul/28/pluto-ten-things-we-now-know-about-the-dwarf-planet

92 Pat Geisler, *The Plain Vanilla Astrologer* (Epping, NH: ACS, 2013), 92.

93 Ibid., 90. 94 Ibid., 272.

95 https://en.wikipedia.org/wiki/Pluto_Water

96 http://www.mediahistory.umn.edu/time/1930s.html

97 http://xroads.virginia.edu/%7E1930s2/Time/1930/1930fr.html

---

KENNETH D. MILLER has an MA in Eastern and Western Traditions: History and Transmission of Astrology from Kepler College. He is on the Boards of the current incarnations of Kepler College and ISAR, and teaches astrology online and in-person. Awarded Jyotish Medha Shree from ICAS, Jyotish Kovid from CVA, and Level II Certification from ACVA. Based in San Diego, he maintains a practice as a consulting astrologer. He is the author of *Mars: Passion or Strife—The Confounding Influence of Culture on Astrology*, and the forthcoming new translation/commentary of *On the Bright Fixed Stars* by Anon of 379 (with Andrea Gehrz). E-mail him at kenneth@celestialintelligencer.net

An *Astrological View* of the Nuclear Age in Light of TNO Borasisi

by David Leskowitz

From Orbits to Orbitals

LOOKING DOWN FROM Alpha Centauri, our solar system resembles an atom, and a very heavy one at that. Our solar atom model is complete with a wildly abundant electron/Oort cloud forming a sparkling aura, covering over rings of oddly inclined Kuiper belt objects, alongside the outer gas giants. Within lies a minuscule nucleus made up of inner planets and Sun. In the same way that the modern physicist had to grapple with atomic structures of such greater complexity than did the earlier student of the Bohr model, it might be the work of the twenty first–century astrologer to come to terms with this complex new model of our solar system and its effects on human consciousness.

On January 25, 2018 the Bulletin of Atomic Scientists moved the minute hand of its Doomsday clock to two minutes before midnight. From the final minutes of Scorpio, anaretic Mars lurched equally close to a cusp. Pushing ahead into a tight square aspect to the past summer's Great American Eclipse (conjunct the President's Mars), the red planet of war did its darnedest to make eclipses greatly relevant again. Closing out its sojourn through Scorpio, Mars traced a path through degrees we will see retraced over and over as we look into the astrology of the Nuclear Age.

Broadly speaking, the discovery of Pluto in 1930 presaged the Atomic Age, which began in the decade following the sighting of our neighborhood Hades. Early pangs of the nuclear age began with the first successful nuclear fission in 1939, and the development of Plutonium in 1940. The transiting outer planets did their part to inscribe the outlines for this picture also, with the Neptune-Pluto synod in the late nineteenth century preceding both planets finding their opposition to Uranus through the first years of the twentieth century. In that decade many ideas and ideologues were born who bear directly on this story: Einstein's theories of relativity, Max Planck's quantum theories, and thermonuclear energy, along with major shifts in mystical perception by seers including Rudolf Steiner, Sri Aurobindo, and Edgar Cayce.

In "Human Use of Radioactive Isotopes" published in *Ascendant* Vol. 1, Dr. Lehman cites sound reasons to let Pluto signify nuclear energy, and yet remains "not so convinced that Pluto is the only ruler for radioactivity." As a process of decay (and destruction), the association of nuclear radiation with Pluto makes sense. As a release of energy, though, radiation seems Uranian, too. Lehman notes how Uranus was at the MC of Hiroshima, and rising during both the first nuclear chain reaction and the Chernobyl disaster. I have found that one way to hone in on the genesis of nuclear science through the symbols of astrology is to include the trans-Neptunian object Borasisi, in concert with two asteroids named for the founding scientists of modern physics—Albert Einstein and Max Planck.

Introducing *Borasisi*

Eric Francis Coppolino mentions how one "proving" moment of Borasisi occurred prior to the earthquake which distressed the Fukushima Daichi Nuclear plant.[1] A New Moon happened to conjoin Borasisi the week before the nuclear disaster at Fukushima in 2011; and on the date of the earthquake-tsunami, Mars hit Borasisi, showing us how an activated Borasisian lunation behaves, and proving the new planet's nuclear significance. In the present work we will review many of the steps along the path of nuclear theory, development and deployment, and notice Borasisi's heavy footprint throughout the astrological moments involved.

The Goddess Asteroids are in, Centaurs are on the up and up, and the many "more Plutos" recently discovered are making their homes in all twelve astrological houses. Certain Kuiper belt objects are already trending with intrepid students of the sky, with Sedna and Eris gaining some slow ground in the mainstream. Some astrologers (such as Coppolino, Philip Sedgwick, and Sue Kientz) have been tracking TNOs Haumea, MakeMake, Orcus, Quaoar, and Varuna ever since they hit the most *avant garde* of electronic ephemerides in the early 00's.

Out there, in the Kuiper-belt field beyond ideas of right and wrong, there is a little body proud to serve its cosmic duty as the patron planet of the mad scientist. There we meet the trans-Neptunian object Borasisi (66652). Astrologers may have to delineate this new guy with a dose of irony, seeing as he is named after neither Greco-Roman god, nor Aboriginal, nor Viking deity, but a fictional one out of a Kurt Vonnegut novel.[2] Personally, working with Borasisi stretches my mythopoetic imagination into that field[3] where nothing makes sense, but things clearly happen. In these examples we see just how very real Borasisi's effect on Earth-life can be, and how appropriate is the mythic basis of its astrological qualities. I hope this case

Denitsa Toneva, "66652 Borasisi" ~ "Borasisi, the Sun, held Pabu, the Moon, in his arms and hoped that Pabu would bear him a fiery child", Kurt Vonnegut. Oil pastel, paper. 44×46 cm (2009).

Denitsa Toneva practices design and visual communication occasionally at yesyes.studio and kodplod.bg, although she is mostly obsessed with projects that are still cooking at denitsatoneva.net. She is also a fencing coach at plovdivfencing.com.

---

study will contribute to the debate over whether and how a new body's naming can effect and express its function.

Co-discoverer Chad Trujillo named the real-life planet in fanciful reference to a favorite dark comedy. Gods of the fictitious *Bokononist* religion in Vonnegut's *Cat's Cradle* name the far-off denizens of our solar system, Borasisi and its binary twin, Pabu, which orbit our Sun every 288 years.[4] The story's internal myth tells of the ill-fated love of Borasisi, the Sun, for Pabu, the Moon, a wife who begat the fiery father only frozen worlds, to his dismay. The sheer fictitiousness of any entity known as "Borasisi" is triply so, for the island characters of *Cat's Cradle* are only haphazard believers in a cargo-cult spun of spontaneous Calypso verses penned by an eponymously pseudonymous Mr. Bokonon writing in his *Book* from various hideouts and alleyways as he copes with his own war trauma. Thus, the deity Borasisi only exists in an imaginary imagination.

Planets met myth in September 2007, when the astronomer gave Borasisi and Pabu their names. This event happened to coincide with the binary planet's conjunction to Earth's lunar North Node. Maybe this lends its silly name some cosmic weight. Even such a name, for an object which, according to astronomical standards, requires the mantle of a tribal creator god, is terribly *Borasisian*: the rational mind taken too far along the path to absurdity.

An essential tenet of Bokononism is *foma*: the lies upon which one may base a happy life. Such sardonic genius drips from the pen of Kurt Vonnegut, Jr. His nativity is a fine place to begin our discovery of Borasisi.[5] The writer's natal humor is apparent in a close Mercury-Jupiter conjunction, iconic in charts of wit. Yet squeezed in between that partile conjunction in Scorpio? Borasisi, 8 arc minutes from his Mercury. For theologians of Bokonon, this is a trove of exegetical wisdom. Such true lies as only astrology can generate: the guy who made up a deity has his own mental astrology configured in alignment with a planet arbitrarily designated as our solar system's very own center of *foma*-gravity. The gods could not be more transparent in hoping we play with this rigged tarot deck. Well there it is, but how do we know what it signifies? Coppolino suggests at the personal level Borasisi tells us about "the lies that we believe even when we know better."[6]

Requisite synastry check for Mr. Trujillo, born November 22, 1973 (I am not yet aware of a birth time or place for this astronomer): if born on the east coast of the US in the morning, then indeed his Sun in the first minutes of Sagittarius would be "on the cusp" of Scorpio. Also notable is a mid-Capricorn stellium of Planckia conjunct Borasisi and Venus! The planet of love is one arc minute from the planet of lies, at 16° 50' and 16° 51' Capricorn: the man just loves his Borasisi.

Spoiler alert: the frigid destiny of Vonnegut's world could not be escaped. The Earth of *Cat's Cradle* ends frozen over by an engineered derivative of water called Ice-Nine. The fatal liquid was created by Dr. Hoenikker, a character who claims to have played a leading role in the invention of the atomic bomb. With the story taking place just following the Allied bombing of Hiroshima and Nagasaki, this apocalypse serves as a nuclear allegory. Its anti-hero Bokonon is a voice of conscience who bears tragic witness to Vonnegut's own war experience.

Borasisi's discovery on September 8, 1999 as it meandered through Aquarius 26°, links the trans-Neptunian object with Neptune itself: these two faraway planets share the degree at which they were discovered.[7] The gas giant of illumination and deception was spotted during its exact conjunction with limit-defining Saturn at 26 Aquarius in 1846. Such a major synodic event as this conjunction between outer planets creates a significant landmark in zodiacal space—a sensitive degree. According to Mike Harding's research, Neptune was discovered during the first time in a millennium that a major planetary conjunction fell within that degree area.[8] Since Neptune marked the boundary between the old and new solar system, its discovery marks a watershed, especially since this took place at a peak moment in its *coincidentia oppositorum* of a synodic cycle with Saturn. Formerly, the outer-most known planet and thus symbolic of limitation, Saturn structures time, while Neptune gives us the oceanic space for dreams and timeless experiences. Transits to the degree of this synod, such as the discovery of Borasisi, suggest harbingers of the conceptual "beyond."

Astrologically, Borasisi appears to act like a meta-Neptune, along with that planet's dual character of insight and confusion. His myth tells us of the destructive potential of science undertaken within a moral vacuum. Its discovery degree of Aquarius 26 is symbolized in the series of degree symbols I rely on as, "A scientist measuring the mineral levels in a sample of water."[9] This is an apt symbol, both for Neptune—the union of Saturn and Neptune reflected in the image of a *container* of *water*—and Borasisi, in light of its origin story derived from Vonnegut's world, iced over by a single lab scientist run amok.

That scientist (of the symbol's very-short-short-story) sounds like one engaged in an innocent enough pursuit of experimental research. But as this is Borasisi's degree of discovery, we can see how the symbol can allude to darker details drawn from the lore of mythical Ice-Nine. Since it relates to the signifier of science gone mad, Borasisi's discovery degree as symbolized in that Pleiadian degree series does appear to provide insight into its astrological meaning. Borasisi, here depicted as a chemist on the brink, measures out the deadly efficacy of his most threatening invention. Coppolino notes how it portends that "technology without conscience is very dangerous."[10] It is historically clear that the development of nuclear science inspired Vonnegut to write his cautionary novel.

Enter *Einstein* and *Planckia*

With Borasisi at our side, let's turn toward a brief history of nuclear energy and the development of the atomic bomb. For an early example of Borasisi's nuclear power, we may look to Marie (and Pierre) Curie's discovery of the highly radioactive element Radium in late 1898, when Borasisi lay in square to that week's lunar eclipse. If we include Borasisi in the chart of the Nobel winning Curie's birth, a dense square between Jupiter and Saturn-Venus-Mars broadens out to a full T-square of scientific discovery.[11]

Guiding us on this expedition will be the distant, dim light of a nerdy minor-planet squadron led by our fictional solar deity, followed by professorial asteroids *Einstein* (2001) and *Planckia*

(1069). The asteroids named for these thinkers each orbit different bands of the main belt in a phase of 1:2 (*Einstein: Planckia*).[12] *Planckia* commemorates the rare colleague with whom Einstein could bounce around his new theories.

Max Planck's own *Planckia* conjoined Neptune, in synastry with Einstein's Sun, at 24° Pisces.[13] The biggest ideas of these asteroids' namesakes, Einstein's Relativity and Planck's Quantum Theory, form the two antagonistic paradigms of modern physics; though the theorists collaborated on an equation that mediates the gulf between waves and discrete photons of light.

The then-futuristic-sounding planetary designation "Asteroid 2001" was given especially in honor of Albert Einstein in the late 1970s to an asteroid that had been discovered in 1973 in Bern, the same city which hosted the legendary patent office where he had labored while having the deep thoughts that would give rise to his Nobel-winning equations.

At his birth, Albert Einstein's namesake asteroid also lurked out in space prior to its discovery. Inhabiting Virgo 29°, natal asteroid Einstein spoke: "A long sought after formula is finally found in a rare old book." This makes a portentous placement for an asteroid named after a man we remember for conceiving a formula, in the birth chart of that same man. (Incidentally the natal North Node of our demiurge Vonnegut is at the same degree).

Bringing the story back to the more dangerous mythos of Borasisi, it might seem unfair to attribute its traits to the biography of a man of peace such as Albert Einstein. Although his theoretical wonder was wrestled along the path to nuclear invention by historical forces beyond his control, it was his insight into the vast quantities of energy contained within matter ($E=MC^2$) that laid the foundations of nuclear theory. If, through the theory of Special Relativity, he hadn't learned that the greatest source of energy existed within the nucleus of an atom, Enrico Fermi might not have pioneered nuclear energy.

Einstein thus shares responsibility for the mighty knowledge upon which nuclear experimentation depends. At first he spoke out against developing this insight into a nuclear weapon. Yet with the growing fear that the Third Reich might come to realize one first, he found himself lobbying in support of such a fearsome invention, even hand-delivering a letter to the American President that would initiate the Manhattan Project. So while we have Einstein's theories to thank for technologies of great social benefit, he is connected to the Promethean invention of atomic weaponry, too.

From late Aquarius, Einstein's natal Jupiter[14] links him to the discovery degree of both Neptune and Borasisi; he is appropriately remembered as the giant (Jupiter) of twentieth-century physics (Borasisi-Neptune). Drilling deeper into the discovery moment of Borasisi, asteroid *Planckia* was conjunct the Moon, and these were at the place of Einstein's own natal Borasisi. If *Planckia* brings genius, then planet Borasisi here wears it well; and Albert Einstein, as an exponent of genius itself, was attuned to its revelation over time. Further down the synchronistic rabbit hole, there is another synastric linkage between nerd-asteroids in the history of Einsteinian astrology. Einstein's own Planckia is exactly conjunct asteroid *Einstein's* "natal" Borasisi. Also, weirdly, another shared degree hosts both Albert Einstein's natal Planckia, and asteroid *Einstein's* "natal" Borasisi (Capricorn 19). [Recap: Borasisi's *Planckia*=Einstein's Borasisi (9 Virgo) & Einstein's *Planckia*=Einstein's Borasisi (19 Cap)]. And Pholus—the Centaur which brings the "small cause with big effect"[15]—marched on through that zodiacal sweet spot of Capricorn 19 when Enrico Fermi blew the lid off of nuclear physics.[16] What smaller cause with greater effect can we imagine than atomic weaponry?

Nuclear Daydreams

Physics lore relates a famous thought experiment, when at age sixteen Einstein imagined himself riding a beam of light.[17] It was this daydream, at least in the popular imagination, that precipitated his eventual theory of Special Relativity and its memorable $E=MC^2$. At Albert's sixteenth birthday, solar return Borasisi was at 29 Virgo, symbolized in that degree series as "A long sought after formula is finally found in a rare old book." That year would augur well for a budding theorist. Recall that this return-chart planet conjoins his natal eponymous asteroid. Such a connection shows this asteroid at work in the life of its namesake. Secondly, it shows the two minor planets' (Borasisi and *Einstein*) affinity as astrological timers of scientific innovation.

In 1923, Enrico Fermi wrote an addendum to a work about the theory of Relativity in which he memorably described how it might look if the energy promised in that equation were to be tapped: "The first effect of an explosion of such a dreadful amount of energy would be to smash into smithereens the physicist who had the misfortune to find a way to do it."[18] Fermi, who would become that same physicist, proves also to be an astrological avatar of Borasisi: our TNO is *cazimi* his natal Sun.[19]

These nuclear planets are activated in charts of the elements involved, too. Glenn Seaborg co-created Plutonium at the Berkeley cyclotron in 1940. According to his diary, Seaborg first bombarded a sample of Uranium with deuterium nuclei at 8:00 PM on December 14.[20] When through this elemental alchemy the spirit of Uranium transmigrated into the new body called Plutonium, the neo-element's namesake Pluto was rising.

Nick Kollerstrom notes how the outer planets which lent their names to elements 92 (Neptunium), 93 (Uranium), and 94 (Plutonium) made inter-aspects across a configuration of midpoints throughout nuclear energy's formative period of 1939–1941, (Neptune at the Uranus-Pluto midpoint). At Plutonium's birth, Pluto at 4° 00' Leo squared the Jupiter-Saturn conjunction in Taurus. If we involve our fledgling nuclear mascots in this equation, we see that Planckia (5° 34' Aquarius) joined the midpoint picture: opposing Pluto across the chart's horizon, making a clear T-square with Jupiter-Saturn. The midpoint picture for Planckia-Pluto=Jupiter/Saturn might read: A spark of genius innovating Hades' domain through the powerful dynamics of expansion and contraction available during Grand Conjunctions such as these.

Then, Borasisi was in the final minutes of a move from the Scorpion into the realm of the Sage, (which now appears to be familiar territory). Borasisi reached for Ceres, as she separated from their conjunction across signs. This minor planet named for the Goddess of grain mediates between Earth and the Underworld. Seasons are a mythic compromise between Earth-Goddess Ceres/Demeter and King of Underworld Hades; nuclear winter, the marriage of Earth and Hell, is a season no-one wishes to experience. Nuclear concepts were grounded onto our planet with Borasisi conjunct Ceres as Hades' own element took birth.

Nuclear outer planets Uranus and Pluto formed a quintile, while from the other side of the zodiac, *Einstein* made another quintile to Pluto. Plutonium took birth right after a Full Moon; when the cyclotron switched on, the Moon precisely aspected Uranus, Pluto, *Einstein*, and *Planckia* by aspects within the quintile family. This is an aspect that John Addey linked with the drive to power and its potential abuse—a creative impulse that can end in violence.[21] The symbol for *Einstein's* journey to the Cyclotron, 15 Libra: "A spiral path that never seems to come to an end."

When, on December 7, 1941, events prompted America's involvement in World War II, *Planckia* ticked through the 22nd degree of Pisces. Near to Einstein's Sun, the so-very-Einsteinian symbol for Pisces 22 reads "A scientist discovering new equations that more completely explain the nature of the universe," darkly echoing the path his knowledge travelled. One of the initiating moments for the eventual use

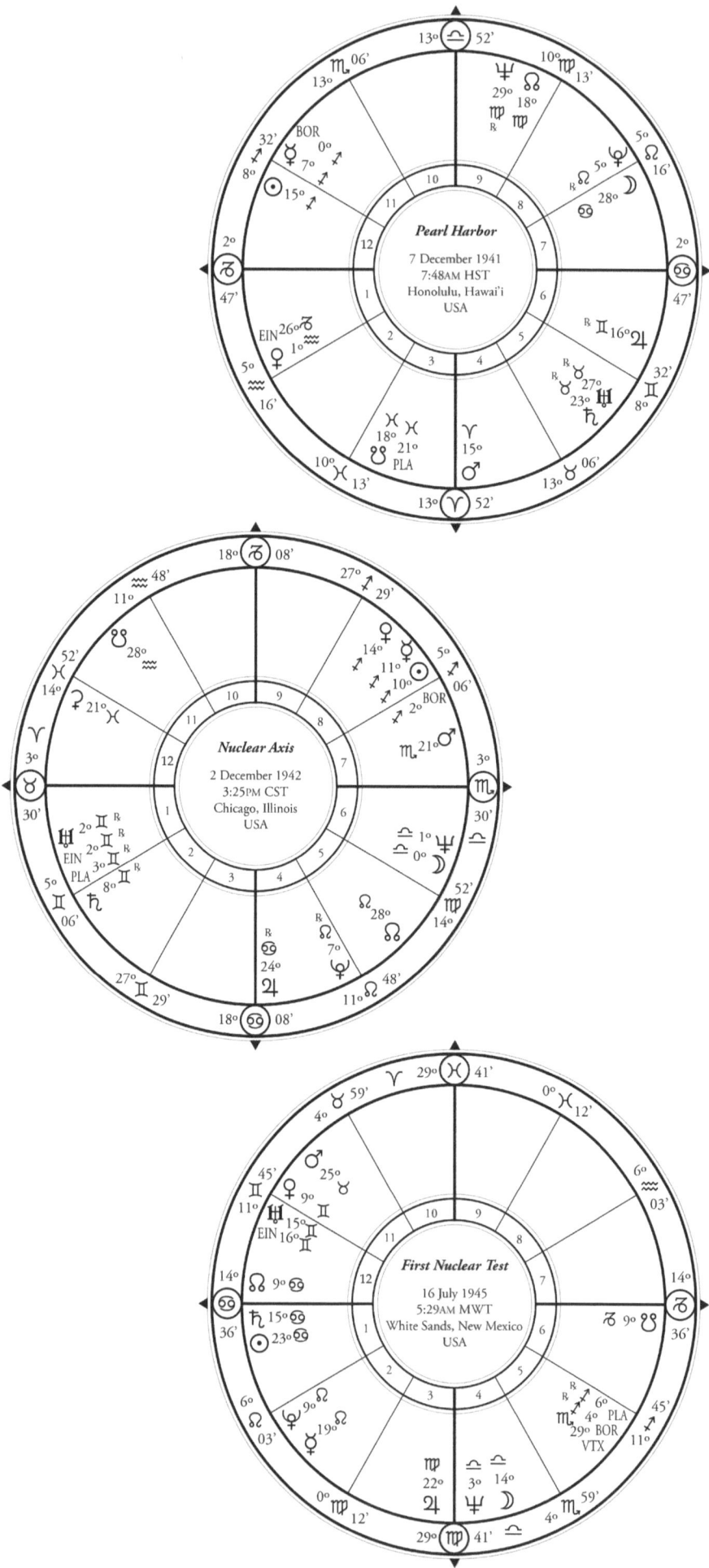

of history's first nuclear weapons, the bombing of Pearl Harbor presaged the holocausts of Hiroshima and Nagasaki. Action and reaction, if not simple cause and effect: Pearl Harbor <—> Hiroshima.

In the chart of Pearl Harbor,[2] Borasisi opposed Uranus within three degrees. More banal notes of war in this chart include an angular Mars at the 4th cusp, and Pluto at the 8th cusp of death. Capricorn rises, with ruling Saturn nearly conjunct Uranus. The opposition of these outer planets to Borasisi brings the astrological eye back to the devious scientist, here in 11th house Sagittarius: the high-minded experiment gone awry. Planckia at that key degree conjoins the South Node of the Moon, a point which always carries with it the shadow of the chart's dark past. What genius (Planckia) would be misused as a result of this event?

The theoretical science (Planckia) behind the nuclear blasts of uranium and plutonium was already under development, and in astrological alignment, when Japanese planes bombed the American base. In that chart, Ceres made an exact sextile to Planckia at its key degree of scientific discovery. Planckia's supportive aspect to Ceres is a minor piece of the chart, yet, as we will see, more ominous than it looks.

Less than one year after Pearl Harbor ignited World War II, Fermi mastered nuclear fission. This moment of genius is linked by a fateful synastry to Pearl Harbor, which instigated a sequence that would end in the fallout of that same nuclear invention. When Fermi's ground-breaking chain reaction occurred, it was then Ceres (formerly in aspect to Planckia at that degree) occupying that crucial degree of Pisces 22. As signifier of earthy substance, Ceres planted the science into a tangible form. Ever in dialogue with the king of the underworld, Ceres grounded the degree of "new equations" as she mid-wifed Relativity's more unexpected manifestation into life.

The astrological charts for the world's first nuclear reactions reveals a strong basis for delineating these new planets. The first successful fission occurred back on January 25, 1939, when German chemists Otto Hahn and Fritz Strassmann managed to split Uranium into lighter isotopes. Significantly, Uranus was partile conjunct the South Node. Mars conjoined Borasisi in late Scorpio, astrologically depicting an invisible dimension under bombardment by a scientist.

Enrico Fermi initiated the nuclear age on December 2, 1942, in what has been called "the Nuclear Axis Chart."[23] This marks the day when the Italian ex-pat in Chicago commandeered a university squash court, loaded it up with graphite and Uranium-235, and manufactured the first self-sustaining nuclear reaction. Procuring a nuclear weapon's "dreadful amount of energy," as he had once mused, was thereby proven to be possible. (The Nuclear Axis date—October 11, 1939—marked the lunar return of Albert Einstein's delivery to the President of his letter in support of the Manhattan Project.) This nuclear birth chart contains a stellium of Uranus conjunct asteroids *Planckia* and *Einstein*. The merger of these scientific minds, conjunct the radioactive element itself, delivers the nuclear goods. This trio is precisely in opposition to Borasisi, forming a real "nuclear axis" in early Sagittarius, as if to intone: "Beware, O Nuclear Scientist! Especially one with Borasisi in the heart of your natal Sun! You are playing with Fire. Prometheus' fate awaits if you dare!"

Testing Death

Trinity was the name given by Robert Oppenheimer to America's first nuclear bomb, a prelude explosion tested just weeks before Hiroshima. On that date Planckia was near to Borasisi, both in trine to Pluto.[24] At the precise time of this test explosion, the Vertex at the end of Scorpio conjoined Plutonium's invention Borasisi. The insane "science" symbolized by Borasisi found its portal to the event level (Vertex). Symbolically, this degree of 30 Scorpio is "a man in a death's head mask."

When the awful fruit of the Manhattan Project fell to Earth in war, on August 6, 1945, Planckia had recently stationed direct, and on this date the asteroid of genius clicked into the next degree from its station. On Hiroshima Day, Mercury itself stationed retrograde, precisely in square to Borasisi, (and now notably, in a sextile aspect to Ceres). Historians still debate whether the damned bombs were even necessary to end a war against an opponent already prepared to surrender. Mercury retrograde problems, indeed. Those days in 1945 mark two of Earth's darkest, at least since humanity has been around to intervene. Cue Penderecki's *Threnody* on the loudest sound system, on repeat, for as many thousand years as the half-life of Plutonium persists.

With the exception of a few miraculous diplomatic near-misses in the ensuing decades, these two bombs are the only nuclear devices overtly used in combat (besides a hideous number of tests), yet. For comparative reference, the Cuban Missile Crisis, a standoff between nuclear armed powers, unfolded during Borasisi's final minutes in Sagittarius in October 1962. Days after the TNO entered sober Capricorn, the crisis was averted. Well aware that this correlation does not imply causation in this instance, it is worth noting that Borasisi's previous entry into the sign of the Archer correlates with the Nuclear Axis Chart, while its exit from that sign correlates with the resolution of an episode that could have exploded into an armageddon of mutually assured destruction.

Never Again?

Sadly, the bombs dropped on Japan were fractions of the strength of our worst invention: the thermonuclear (hydrogen) bomb. Based on the theories of William Teller, such bombs were catastrophically tested by the Americans at Bikini Atoll, and again with Russia's even larger "Tsar Bomba,"—and hopefully, never again. Teller himself was born amid the epochal Uranus-Neptune opposition of paradigm shifts and shifters (Jan. 15, 1908). Moreover, these natal outer planets were aligned with the Nodes of the Moon, thrusting that tumultuous energy into his path. His predicament was furthered by a conjunction of Ceres-Borasisi at odds with the Nodes and Uranus-Neptune, priming a natal T-square of nuclear planets. A nodal dilemma, one "the father of the hydrogen bomb" did not appreciate living.

The Teller-Ulam design for thermonuclear weaponry was published (in classified form) on March 9, 1951, during a grand fire trine of Venus, Borasisi, and Pluto. The ensuing testing of such a device at Bikini Atoll displaced an entire population and yielded a destructive power far beyond the government's intention. Eight years into the systematic radiation poisoning of the island, the United States tested its first thermonuclear (hydrogen) bomb: Castle Bravo. At dawn on March 1, 1954, Borasisi was culminating opposite Jupiter in Gemini.[25] Years later, the Soviet bomb nicknamed Tsar Bomba exploded 50 megatons of "test" energy.[26] Borasisi at 29 Sagittarius trined Uranus in the last degree of Leo (fit for a Tsar). At the end of Sagittarius, Borasisi was exactly one sign beyond its placement at Plutonium's birth.

Borasisian Diplomacy

Today we find ourselves in a new era of nuclear agitation. World leaders ill-equipped to handle diplomatic crises have taken center stage among the nuclear powers. The 45th President of the United States was born with Borasisi in Sagittarius, quincunx his sensitive Cancerian Mercury. But that personality, and its potential compensatory mechanisms, is a chart for another day.

The North Koreans allege that their People's Republic is armed with nuclear-powered ballistic missiles. Their dynastic leader Kim Jong Un's birth date happens to be contentious as well. The boy-king brags about a maturity-enhancing 1983 birthdate, one that is at odds with a reports by an aunt now living in the US, who claims Kim was born in 1984.[27] If we use this latter date—January 8, 1984—it gives a Jupiter-Neptune-Mercury conjunction across the Sagittarius-Capricorn cusp. Throughout 2017's nuclear tensions, Saturn (with Pholus) crossed the North Korean leader's path at these degrees. I worried how such a transit might trouble this idealistic stellium in the chart of a saber-wielding dictator. That natal chart shows a forebodingly close Borasisi-Pluto square; Pluto transited his Capricorn Sun exactly throughout calendar year 2017. Maybe we can take solace in the amenable sextile between the two Premier's synastric Borasisis, with the Elder Statesman's also conjunct the Younger's Venus.

Another contemporary test of nuclear mettle sprang out of nowhere on January 18, 2018, to startle the cellphones of Hawaii's chillest citizens. At 8:18 AM, an Emergency Alert displayed in all-caps: "Ballistic Missile Threat Inbound to Hawaii. Seek Immediate Shelter. This is not a drill." Yikes. It was an apparent mistake, however. That morning's Sagittarian Moon was void of course if we consider only traditional planets.[28] We can feel further details of the prevailing mood that morning by including the Moon's applying trine to nuclear Uranus, mixed with an applying square to Borasisi. The public was given the excuse that an employee pressed "the wrong button" during a changing of the guard, a very void-of-course kind of situation. Nuclear shenanigans on the Sag-Cap cusp once again, with disaster averted, *à la* the Cuban Missile Crisis.

Conclusions?

In some indeterminate timeframe, the elements were not just discovered, but *created*. Having a chart for the literal birth of Uranium is no more tangible than a natal chart for the Earth. Recently, though, physicists made a discovery that for the first time allowed them to theorize where and how Uranium would have been created. In the summer of 2017, the LIGO team (inspired by Einstein's theory of General Relativity) received the wobble of a gravitational wave from a distant *kilonova*, the explosion caused when two neutron stars collide. LIGO's measurements determined that this enormous, ancient collision was responsible for generating gold and other heavy elements, including Uranium. This is a moment relating to the creation of *some* quantity of Uranium—mere epiphenomena, not an actual birth chart—but a thing along those lines.

This discovery (LIGO: 8/17/17, 8:41AM EDT, Livingston, LA) provides a fitting coda to the nuclear tale, with Borasisi having stationed retrograde at the 22nd degree of Pisces over the summer of 2017. Retrograde stations act as standing waves in time, marking out sensitive degrees on the zodiac. Borasisi was in that degree when the kilonova's gravitation waved on past LIGO's laser—this symbolic degree of new equations that continually refine our understanding of the universe. Planet Borasisi's happy place. Exaltation even?

How Borasisi—an idea created by a novelist and then plastered over a tiny and distant rock—can meaningfully correspond to the unfolding of the historical events for which that novel is an allegory, is the mystery of astrology, thriving in our discovery of plentiful worlds beyond Neptune.

☿

Endnotes

1 Eric Francis Coppolino, "Beyond the Veil: The Minor Planets in Astrology," *The Mountain Astrologer* 165 (Oct. 2012): 28..

2 Kurt Vonnegut, *Cat's Cradle* (New York: Delacorte Press, 1963).

3 Rumi by way of Coleman Barks, *Open Secret* "There is a Field."

4 Perihelion of ~40 AU and Aphelion 47.3 AU make Borasisi a Pluto-hugging-and-transcending Kuiper belt TNO.

5 Kurt Vonnegut: Nov 11, 1922, 8 AM, Indianapolis, IN. (Note that birth times are not relevant to citing TNO longitudes throughout)

6 Coppolino, "Beyond the Veil," 28.

7 Here referring to degrees as "whole numbers" in the style of degree symbolism; mostly throughout.

8 Michael Harding, *Hymns to the Ancient Gods* (New York: Arkana, 1992), "A Degree of Meaning," p. 221.

9 John Sandbach's reworking of the Sabian symbols called the Pleiadian Symbols, published in *The Circular Temple,* Kindle edition (ADS, 2012).

10 Coppolino, "With Love from Borasisi" Planetwaves Member letter, March 4, 2011 http://planetwaves.net/astrologynews/with-love-from-borasisi.html

11 Marie Curie, Nov 7, 1867; Radium, December 26, 1898.

12 Though not obviously by design, since according to Wikipedia: Einstein 2001 was named in 1978 due to the connection between its discovery city and his life; while Planckia was named on the occasion of Planck's eightieth birthday. Phase: E-2001 982 days, Planckia 2020 days.

13 Max Planck: April 23, 1858, Kiel, Germany, (no time) (X: AstroDataBank).

14 Albert Einstein: March 14, 1879 at 11:30, Ulm Germany. Rodden Rating: AA: Birth record in hand (AstroDatabank); Jupiter at 27° 29' Aquarius.

15 Robert van Heeren, www.kentauren.info, "Pholus."

16 December 2, 1942, first chain reaction.

17 *Autobiographische Skizze*, Schweizerische Hochschulzeitung Festnummer 1855–1955, found; in Carl Seeling, ed., *Helle Zeit—Dunkle Zeit:, In Memoriam Albert Einstein*, ed. Carl Seeling, (Zurich: Europa Verlag, 1956), 9–17.

18 Luisa Bonolis, "Enrico Fermi's Scientific Work," in Carlo Bernardini and Luisa Bonolis, eds., *Enrico Fermi: His Work and Legacy*, 314–94, (Berlin: Springer, 2001).

19 Enrico Fermi, September 29, 1901 at 19:00, Rome, Italy. Rodden Rating AA: Birth Record (AstroDatabank); cazimi refers to being in the heart of the Sun, and is most commonly defined as a celestial object being conjunct the Sun's exact degree within 17 arc minutes. Fermi Sun: 5° 53' Libra, Borasisi 6° 06' Libra. Source of this insight is Linda Lee Berry, http://www.astrologicaldepth.com/TNOInfo/Borasisi.htm

20 Obtained by Nick Kollerstrom, in "Pluto and Plutonium: Any Connection?" *The Astrological Journal* 26, no. 4 (1984): pp. 249–53.

21 Bil Tierney, *Dynamics of Aspect Analysis* (Petaluma, CA: CRCS, 1992), 46.

22 Pearl Harbor: December 7, 1941, 7:48 AM, Honolulu, HI. Time cited in First Bomb Drop, *Smithsonian Magazine*, https://www.smithsonianmag.com/history/children-pearl-harbor-180961290/

23 Eric Francis Coppolino, http://members.planetwaves.net/of-nuclear-bombs-and-reasoning/

24 July 16, 1945 5:29 AM, Socorro, New Mexico.

25 MC for Bikini Atoll at dawn that date was 14°45' Sag; Jupiter at 16°58' Gemini, Borasisi 19°41' Sag.

26 October 30, 1961.

27 https://www.telegraph.co.uk/news/2016/05/27/aunt-of-north-korea-dictator-kim-jong-un-runs-dry-cleaners-in-ne/

28 See Chris Brennan's Astrology School discussion of three varieties of void-moon phenomena, "When is the Moon Really Void of Course": https://www.youtube.com/watch?v=7qMV_JcrsQ0

Grant Hanna, Venus in Pisces, 2017

David Leskowitz first met astrology when Chiron and Neptune approached his Pisces Ascendant. After seeing how a cycle in the sky aligned with this new knowledge, he never looked back. Now an evolutionary astrologer, he practices astrological healing with help from Chiron and friends. A graduate of Vassar College, David was invited to his alma mater to lecture in an astrology course in religion. He is writing a book about how the history of spiritual experience makes better sense when timed by planetary cycles, especially those of Chiron, Chariklo, Pholus, and Okyrhoe. Please follow his work at www.centaurs.space

Telling the Story of our Future
What Will Astrology Be Like in 2025?

by Kent Bye

IN THE LAST ISSUE OF *The Ascendant*, I speculated on how virtual reality (VR) could create immersive experiences with astrology. Over the last four years, augmented reality (AR) and artificial intelligence (AI) have emerged as key technological drivers, and so I will be exploring how these technological trends could help shape what astrology looks like in 2025.

Moving into the Experiential Age

Archetypal cosmology provides a good framework for looking into the past in order to more clearly see patterns of the future. We are 130 years into a 500-year Neptune-Pluto cycle, which was followed by a Uranus-Pluto conjunction in the 1960s. The last time these two outer planet cycles followed each other like this was in 1454 when the Gutenberg press became the dominant mass communications modality for the next 500 years. Computers are the printing press of this era. Just as books proliferated access to information and knowledge, computing technologies proliferate access to experiences.

I see that we are moving from the Information Age into the Experiential Age. Rather than consuming products, there's more of an emphasis on having experiences. Services like Netflix and Spotify provide ubiquitous, on-demand access to a vast library of entertainment, which is worth a lot more than owning physical copies of the media.

Another quality of the Experiential Age is that it is cultivating a deeper sense of presence into the quality of the moment of the time. Snapchat snaps and Twitch livestreams provide ephemeral experiences that are meant to be fully experienced in the moment, and then they disappear. Immersive technologies like VR have an explicit design goal of cultivating presence. The Experience Age is leading people towards experiences that are interactive, embodied, social, and immersive.

So where does astrology come in to this equation? The common thread between VR, AI, and astrology is that they are all *experiential* technologies. Each of them has a foundation of storytelling that use symbolic patterns of reality to reflect upon the human experience. VR creates an archetypal representation of reality to convince your sensory perception that you are in another world and your mind believes it is real. AI is trained by providing it an experience of data where it discovers the underlying patterns of intelligence. And astrology uses a mathematical and symbolic system, developed collectively over millennia, to describe the non-linear dynamics of the individual and collective human psyche, which we use as a narrative technology to help people discover the story of their lives and to make meaning of larger cultural trends.

Astrology and the Power of Storytelling

Storytelling expresses the complexity and paradox of the human experience, which is not based upon a set of logic or reason that can be reduced down to a mathematical equation. Author Steve Almond says, "I've placed my faith in stories because I believe them to be the basic unit of human consciousness. The stories we tell, and the ones we absorb, are what allow us to pluck meaning from the rush of experience. Only through the patient interrogation of these stories can we begin to understand where we are and how we got here."[1] Astrologer Jenn Zahrt argues that astrology itself is a narrative technology helps us tell the stories of our lives.[2] In some ways astrology is the most comprehensive symbolic system we have for describing the complexity of the human experience: Who we are, why we are here, and how we change over time.

As we move from the Information Age to the Experiential Age, the next step is going to be personalized stories and transformational stories. We are going to want to have an immersive and interactive experiences that lead us deeper down our favorite rabbit holes, and tell us stories that are deeply meaningful to our lives.

The future of storytelling will be immersive and interactive, which reflects the balance between the passive yin of receiving a story and active yang of participating in the story. This balance between authorial control and open-ended possibility spaces is biggest open challenge for immersive storytelling. I have found the four elements provide profoundly powerful experiential design framework.

Immersive storytelling combines the Air and Fire of video games, the

Water of Film, and the Earth of VR to create a direct experience. Video games are about an outward yang expression of agency where you make choices (Mental and Social Presence/Air) and take action (Active Presence/Fire). Film is primarily about the emotional engagement that happens when receiving a story (Emotional Presence/Water). VR adds full embodiment into computing, and it is about stimulating your sensory experience (Embodied Presence/Earth) to create a sense of presence.

Astrology will have a huge role to play in experiential design, creating interactive stories, as well as developing compelling, complex, and nuanced characters. AI is going to be on the front lines of implementing the technology that makes interacting with computers more like interacting with humans, but it is *astrological thinking* that will inform how AI gets to the point of being able to understand and tell stories by itself. AI telling a compelling story is one of the next generation's Turing Tests—a classic benchmark for evaluating the intelligence of an AI system. Can astrology provide a model to describe the aspects of character development through signs and aspects, the quality of experiences through the signs, and the domain of human experience with the houses? It not only can, but it will.

Storytellers of the future will be creating worlds and possibility spaces, which means that they are going to be designing the personalities, temperaments, and character arcs of AI characters. Imagine a story that changes every day that reflects that world's current transits. Imagine that the characters are growing and evolving through a number of multidimensional layers of character development. What would a storytelling system look like that balances authorial control of a human storyteller with the generative possibilities of a world filled with characters that feel alive? What if you could use the astrological chart of the audience member to look at difficult natal aspects or outer planet transits? Is it possible to customize an archetypal experience that serves as a form of astrological remediation? What if you came out of an immersive story experience with deeper insight and understanding more about yourself and the dynamics of the world?

Astrology provides a robust experiential design framework that can be used to create balanced immersive experiences, architect realistic AI characters who change over time, and design personalized narratives that have transformative potential.

Uranus in Taurus and Unlocking Embodied Wisdom

As we head toward 2025, Uranus will move into Taurus. From what I am learning from the technology pioneers I interview on my *Voices of VR* podcast, this appears to correspond with innovations in consciousness hacking and biofeedback technologies that help people reach a deeper state of embodiment, and ultimately help them become more focused, present, and achieve profound flow states in their lives. Over the next seven years, as Uranus goes through Taurus, I expect there will be a lot of insights gained by watching the development of immersive haptic (touch-based) technologies, the spread of immersive theater that focuses on sensory experiences, the modeling of neural network architectures for artificial intelligence, the advancements of robotics as the embodiment of technology, and spatial computing technologies with AR and VR technologies.

Consider this: We now have the capability of curing deafness through technology and touch. David Eagleman's NeoSensory haptic vest can translate speech into sensory input through an array of 32 buzzers. As long as the signals reach the brain in a structured format that can be correlated with other sensory input, then the brain can eventually figure out how to make sense of the input. So Eagleman has been able to cure deafness by turning the torso into an ear—by rewiring sound input to the brain through the body rather than the cochlea. Not only is sensory substitution possible, but the cultivation of entirely new senses with sensory addition is also possible.

So if we carry this over to astrology, what types of intuitions could be cultivated by translating the spatial geometry of astrology into haptic input that could be subconsciously processed by our bodies in massive quantities? How will the mass distribution of embodied practices change not only culture, but how we practice astrology? How can astrological temperamental analysis help match people up with embodied immersive experiences?

Embodied cognition is a significant advancement in neuroscience where our thinking is not happening within our brains, but rather throughout our entire bodies. The way we move changes the way we think. Augmenting our identity through facial filters, like on Snapchat, taps us into undiscovered aspects of our personality and changes the way that we interface with the world. Changing avatars in virtual reality with limb tracking can invoke the virtual body ownership illusion, where you believe that you have become that character. Not only do you believe it, but other people believe it as well. It takes what you are wearing to new levels that can change how other people respond to you to a degree that transcends what you can do with just clothes, makeup, and a hairdo. How about trying on a new natal chart?

Will we be able to make huge advances within the cultivation of intuition and body awareness? How will adding new sensory input expand the palette of what is possible within the human experience? Can astrocartography give us insights into how our relative position in space and time changes what types of experiences and qualities of consciousness are possible? Will we discover new latent human potentials?

I expect that there will be a lot of interest in technologically mediated, embodied sensory experiences over the next seven years as Uranus traverses through Taurus up to 2025, and I expect that this increased focus on embodiment will cultivate new forms of intuition that will refine astrological delineation.

What Applications Will Astrology have in 2025?

So, what will astrology look like in 2025? I expect to see a continuation of growth in popularity of astrology from esoteric niches into larger mainstream audiences, and it will likely start to cross the chasm into the mainstream in larger ways as we move more into the Experiential Age. Computing technologies have already democratized access to astrological information through software programs, and I expect there will be a number of popular interactive and immersive experiences that provide people with their own embodied experiences of astrology. So be on the look out for a number of popular immersive apps that proliferate access to astrological knowledge. Here are some of my suggestions for some of the popular applications and new possibilities:

- Astrology as a map of your unconscious behaviors
- Astrology as a model of character development over the course of a lifetime
- Astrology as a conversational portal to the enchanted universe through embodied omens
- Astrology as a roadmap for the cultivation of flow states and creativity
- Astrology as an experiential design framework and drama manager for interactive storytelling
- Astrology as a system to embed deeper symbolic and geometric meaning to the spatial placement of objects
- Astrology as an augmented reality annotation layer for stories of space and time
- Astrology as a mathematical structure of consciousness
- Astrology as an organizing principle for the deeper story of historical cycles
- Astrology as the decentralization of time zones to planetary hours and solar time for a deeper connection to your local time and space
- Astrology as a form of integrative medicine for healing the body, mind, and spirit
- Astrology as a recipe for transformational experiences
- Astrology as a model for electing virtual worlds and birthing AI consciousness
- Astrology as a transfer learning language for interdisciplinary collaborations
- Astrology as the ultimate empathy machine

Astrology as a Mathematical Structure

As astrology continues to grow in popularity, questions will continue to be asked about the nature of astrological knowledge. An open question for the astrology community is: "Is it worth specifying how and why astrology works?" Saying "I don't know. It just works," is not a satisfying answer to the Western mind, and it is also a weak philosophical foundation. Updating astrological metaphysics to be current with current cosmological discussions would not only make astrology stronger as it continues to grow, but it could also have profound implications on the philosophy of math and helping us understand the nature of consciousness.

Consider astrology as a mathematical object for a moment. Mathematical objects describe underlying patterns of reality, and some argue they are indispensable to science. And yet the exact nature of mathematical objects is an open question in the philosophy of math. Are mathematical objects invented or discovered? Do we discover mathematical objects through some sort of mathematical intuition of a non-local, Platonic realm of eternal ideal forms? Or are mathematical objects a semantic invention of the human mind that provides useful descriptions, but do not require non-spatiotemporal realms to exist outside of the empirically observable and natural world?

The next time someone asks you to prove astrology with science, then ask them to describe the exact nature of a mathematical object. It is possible that astrology is more similar to math than science. Mathematical objects are used to describe patterns of empirical reality just as astrological configurations are used to describe patterns of behavior. Math and astrology both use an axiomatic method rather than the scientific method that relies upon falsification or repeatability. It is a mystery why mathematical objects derived from an axiomatic set of rules would describe patterns of reality, just as it is a mystery why astrological rules could describe patterns of reality. The phenomenology of astrological delineation is more similar to mathematical intuition than it is to the scientific method. If astrology is a math object, then the relationship between astrology and reality could be the same as the relationship between mathematical objects and reality.

Perhaps reality itself a math object. Max Tegmark's Mathematical Universe Hypothesis says that objective reality could be isomorphic to a mathematical structure. So perhaps the Pythagoreans were right all along that "All is number." But the exact relationship between mathematical objects/astrology and reality is an open metaphysical question. If mathematical objects exist in a Platonic realm beyond space and time, then perhaps they exert some type of Aristotelian formal cause upon material reality. Then it would not be to much of a stretch to believe that the movement of the planets could have a corresponding

Mariana Palova, Astronomy, (2011)

Platonic realm of astrological patterning that is either correlated to or directly influences the underlying patterns of the objective cosmos and subjective psyche.

We live in a world where science and physics form the foundations of our dominant models of reality, yet these scientists have made metaphysical assumptions about the nature of mathematical objects. It is not surprising that reductive materialist scientists have a vastly different idea about the nature of math objects from how most practicing mathematicians think about them.

I interviewed three dozen professional mathematicians for my *Voices of Math* podcast and asked them whether they believe math is discovered or invented. Most of them felt like they are discovering these patterns rather than inventing them. It was surprising to hear so many mathematicians readily accept the possibility of a metaphysical Platonic realm that cannot be falsified, but their beliefs are grounded in their direct experiences of mathematical research. Their experiences feel more like discovering something that is already there, more than exerting their will to put something there that was not there before. They express awe and wonder about something larger than themselves in these mysterious patterns of reality, and they cite the importance of elegance, beauty, and mathematical intuition in the process of discovering mathematical truths.

There were some mathematicians who reject mathematical Platonism because there is not a clear mechanism for how humans can interface with a non-spatiotemporal realm of eternal forms. Could it be intuition, imagination, visualization, or an embodied gut feeling? Or perhaps consciousness itself is a universal or fundamental field that extends beyond the structures of space and time. Naturalists view supernatural Platonic realms to be an extraordinary claim that requires extraordinary evidence, and any experience of this realm of eternal forms is purely subjective or phenomenological. But the counterargument is how is it that mathematical objects that humans created are able to describe quantum electrodynamics to twelve decimal points of precision? Quine and Putnam argue that we should have an ontological commitment to all entities that are indispensable to our best scientific theories, and therefore we should believe in the reality of mathematical entities because they are indispensable to science.[3]

Some mathematicians think math objects could come from some combination of discovered Platonic forms and invented tools through social construction. Perhaps it is more of a cultivation process akin to a community garden where eternal form seeds are planted, but they have to be cultivated by the community into functional mathematical tools. Perhaps astrology provides some evidence that math objects are some combination of invention and discovery where our lives are the nexus point between the fate of our Platonic astrological patternings that are interfacing with our free will, subjective experiences, consciousness, and intentions. Perhaps astrology will lead to the fusion of the philosophy of mind and the philosophy of math in order to reveal underlying patterns of human consciousness.

So if astrology does turn out to be a mathematical object, then what are its axioms? Discerning a formal set of astrological axioms can be problematic as it is similar to reducing the multivalent nature of an archetype down to a single word. Astrology rejects being reduced down to a set of fixed rules or simple equations, and has inherent inconsistencies and paradoxes that are difficult for the Western mind to tolerate. It might prove to be really

Astrology could be thought of as form of paraconsistent logic that is able to deal with internal contradictions and paradoxes of human behavior, but it is often through the discretion of the astrologer rather than through a formalized set of axioms.

difficult to replace astrologers with AI or a computer algorithm because there might be something about astrological delineation that requires the subjective participation of a human astrologer to navigate contradictions, make subjective judgments, and tell the story of quality of a moment with imperfect and incomplete information.

In 1931, Kurt Gödel proposed two incompleteness theorems, which showed that completeness and consistency are mutually exclusive in mathematical systems. Most mathematical systems choose consistency, which means that most math systems are consistent but incomplete. This means that new math in consistent systems will always be discovered until the heat death of the universe. Yet, if we want to use math to describe humans, consistency becomes problematic because people and language are paradoxical; in an odd way, our human inconsistency is our one consistency.

Inconsistencies within a logical system can destroy the entire system of logic because it means something could be both true and false, which leads to the principle of explosion where anything can mean everything, and then nothing means anything. In the past half-century, a branch of logic called paraconsistent logic has emerged in order to handle such paradoxes and inconsistencies as long as they do not explode. There has been a resurgence in interest in paraconsistent logic in 2016 during the Saturn square Neptune, and it has been finding many fruitful applications in AI, knowledge representation, and natural language processing.

Astrology could be thought of as form of paraconsistent logic that is able to deal with internal contradictions and paradoxes of human behavior, but it is often through the discretion of the astrologer rather than through a formalized set of axioms. Therefore the Western mind would resist describing astrology as a mathematical system of logic because astrologers make subjective deductions independent of axioms that feel too unconstrained. Each symbol and archetype is like a multi-faceted diamond that has a multi-valent possibility space of interpretation. In addition, human behavior has many factors and variables. An astrological delineation can feel like a violation of the explosion principle because you can make any truth statement you want without any supporting evidence in an axiomatic system without well-defined axioms. It is no wonder that the Western mind views astrology as being susceptible to the worst aspects of unconstrained New Age thinking, especially when astrologers themselves cannot clearly articulate all of the axiomatic rules or previous experiences they are referencing.

As the astrological community continues to grow, then astrological significations could be become unmoored from their roots, and claims may be made that are not based in inductive experience, but in flights of fancy. As a community, what do we do if a dubious advocate of astrology starts to become famous and popular? What is our tolerance for inconsistent symbolic correlations that deviate too far from the accepted cannon of the collective wisdom of the astrological community? Is there a way to capture and model a representation of esoteric knowledge? Will AI and natural language processing help us collect astrological delineations so that we can reflect upon them or aggregate them? Is it worth trying to more clearly define the axioms of astrology as a mathematical system? Or will the inconsistencies and paradoxes of human behavior mean that axiomatic formalization will always elude astrology?

More clearly defining and modeling the axioms of the different astrological branches using paraconsistent logic could open up opportunities for discovering unexpected relations between various branches of astrology. Debates around which house system or tropical versus sidereal zodiac could turn out to be more about different axiomatic assumption that reveals different dimensions of a valid astrological reality rather than any ultimate truth about which house system or zodiac is right or wrong. Different axioms create different branches of math, which end up being connected to each other in surprising ways.

Reflecting upon these philosophical questions and interfacing with other disciplines can not only help bring insights to astrology, but also help us better understand whether astrology could be thought of as a branch of mathematics, how astrology could provide insights into the philosophy of math, the nature of mathematical objects, and the relationship between Platonic realms of reality with the nature of consciousness and human experience.

Conclusion

The astrological community has a powerful skill-set that can be used to not only understand patterns of reality, but to actively participate in helping to imagine and implement an optimistic vision of the future. By 2025, I envision astrologers working side by side with the most exalted aspects of mainstream society using the magic, power and insights of astrology to help build a better future for everyone. We need more storytellers and world-builders to create interactive stories and immersive experiences that allow people can have an embodied, direct experience of themselves and the world. Astrology is pivotal for realizing this vision.

Endnotes

1 Steve Almond, *Bad Stories* (Pasadena, CA: Red Hen Press, 2018), 6.

2 Jennifer Zahrt, "The Astrological Imaginary in Early Twentieth Century German Culture," (PhD thesis, UC Berkeley, 2012).

3 Mark Colyvan, "Indispensability Arguments in the Philosophy of Mathematics," *The Stanford Encyclopedia of Philosophy*, edited by Edward N. Zalta (Spring 2015), available online: https://plato.stanford.edu/archives/spr2015/entries/mathphil-indis/

Kent Bye hosts the industry-leading *Voices of VR* podcast featuring over 850 interviews with VR pioneers, developers, and academics. He is capturing an oral history of virtual reality, documenting the evolution of immersive storytelling, and developing an experiential design framework inspired by astrology. He also hosts the *Esoteric Voices* podcast about astrology, *Voices of AI* about artificial intelligence, and the *Voices of Math* about the philosophy of math. You support his research into the future of astrology and development of open source, immersive astrology software at https://patreon.com/voicesofvr

Celestial Interpretation[1]

by Count Hermann Alexander von KEYSERLING

Translated by Jennifer Zahrt

Newly Translated from the Past: The following text is a lecture delivered by Count Hermann Alexander von Keyserling (1880–1946) in 1910, and printed for the first time in 1911. We are proud to publish the first-ever English translation.

IT IS A PREJUDICE without any real background that modern natural science represents a closed and complete world view: it is closed only in so far as it excludes, and complete only within narrow limits. All systems that exact research has led to and that withstand scientific criticism suffer from the common affliction that they leave little else of the world. The world of the physicist is closed enough, but only masses and movements find place in it, and there are many other things in nature; the energetic worldview proves to be complete only as long as the many things that are not understood as energy are ignored. Today, a system that is to include the whole and emanates from a single, all-conditional principle can no longer be put forward in the sphere of phenomena: the more research advances, the more insistently it analyzes the facts, the more inconsistent the universe appears, the more questionable its real coherence.

¶ The more unsatisfactory, of course, our worldview. Critical philosophy has well taught that the question of unity only arises from the standpoint of thought, and that our comprehension is only commensurate with a narrow slice of reality: the naïve, primitive man, who also dwells in the depths of the most conceptual scholar, does not know how to cope with a world foreign to him. He does not come to terms in a reality in which his laws are not dominant, which does not accommodate his understanding, whose meaning does not lie in the human. With all the tenacity of a deep-seated instinct he struggles against it, he seeks to force, to outwit it: the world must, be it as it may, be a seamlessly linked nexus, must be comprehensible by people. In earlier times, researchers had no difficulty in asserting their sense of self against such inhumane facts: the Christian order of salvation gave all mechanism meaning, and the reality of this order of salvation was beyond doubt. Today belief in the dogma is shaken, we know too much about the origins. And because that which is not dogma, which is not presupposed as being beyond any possible criticism, cannot achieve footing, religion lost its miraculous power to counterbalance science. Even those world syntheses of an abstract nature, that could comprehend everything and satisfy the spirit in bygone days, are no longer capable of doing this today: they have been destroyed by criticism, their foundations have been undermined, they have lost their background. We are without redeeming religion, without reassuring metaphysics; we feel homeless in infinite space, disappointed by all stars. What remains there for the tortured spirits, who, too weak for modesty, cannot live in a dehumanized world? Only one thing: to believe in those connections, which are not situated in the sphere of pure belief, since their presupposed reality is to be revealed in the order of nature, which however are neither unambiguous to prove, nor to refute because they cannot be directly derived from the phenomena: connections of a mystical nature. It is logical and easy to understand that precisely today, at a height of scientific knowledge, those seemingly long-dead disciplines, which were forged by the germinating spirit of inquiry, are awakening again: astrology, magic, and spirit lore; it is no less logical that we encounter as their most ardent adepts, the men of exact sciences, famous physicists, doctors, philosophers: for they are most closely and painfully touched by the inhumanity of nature.

¶ No, the mind is not called to serve, it is born to rule. Where it serves, it does so out of politics: only he is the master of his material, who knows its laws. The mind wants objective truth, as long as it proves its power. As soon as it turns out that nature does not obey it, does not recognize its norms, the tyrant awakens, overturns the constitution, belts the world into the bonds of the imagination. From the outset, nature was incomprehensible to the first humans, therefore they put a more humane one in its place, at first. Our cognitive power fails only in the depths of the world, only there are we compelled to have visions, to create correspondences that the spirit demands. And this compulsion functions as a liberation, as salvation; subservient knowledge is an abomination to the spirit. Everyone, even the most modest researcher, who spends his days as a servant of hard facts, basically merely lives off the desire to be able to conjure one day. It is this hope that sustains him. The magician is indeed the master of nature, he shapes it as he pleases; the magician cannot err, for his will first creates truth; his spirit, foremost, is spirit in the full sense of the word for it is unbound. Let's explore what our soul secretly loves: the world of fairies and goblins is more familiar to it than the Copernican system of the world. Every magical world is more intelligible to us than objective nature, since it is spirit of our spirit.

⁋ The most wondrous world system ever conceived by the imagination is that of astrology; it is the most coherent, cohesive, and complete system that can be imagined. It organically comprises nature and the intellectual world, coincidence and necessity, arbitrariness and fate, and all cosmic events possess deep human meaning. For the astrologer, the universe is a clockwork, in which each individual points back to the whole, and the whole is reflected in every single one of them. The cycles of the stars emerge in the germinating souls; what will and should happen on Earth, can be read up in the sky. The stars in their positions and wanderings are the projection of life into space, they are the dial of the world clock. Visible and invisible, living and lifeless, cosmic and human necessarily correlate in such a way; the meaning of it all, however, lies in man.

⁋ Astrology allows free will to exist. The configuration that determines the form of the soul at birth and whose progression signifies fate, is but the visible expression of those last immutable features which form the layout of character and persist beyond any free decision. The future presaged in the stars even glimpses—though less clearly—from the eyes; the compulsion of the stars is of one mind with the blood. Far from asserting an arbitrary influence on man through strange forces, astrology in fact establishes a coherently linked, watertight, intimate and necessary connection of all cosmic elements—a cohesive Becoming, down to the last detail. The flywheel of this becoming is the starry sky, a tiny cog in the work of every individual freedom. On the premise that the stars possess meaning, the world process is not a blind activity, rather a regulated development, not a senseless event, rather a meaningful fate. In such a world, spirit manages without difficulty: for it meets itself again everywhere. Everything is connected, makes sense, has a human, plausible meaning. The whole is so artfully arranged that no one is able to overlook it, and its possibilities are so rich, so dazzlingly ambiguous, that the principle does not have to be considered as failing in any questionable individual case. No wonder, therefore, that the astrological world appears to be more firmly established to all those who tend toward it than a theory to any researcher: it corresponds to the basic requirements of the spirit, the most urgent needs of the mind. What does it matter that the elements of this worldview—the specific meanings of the stars and their combinations—seem nonsensical in and of themselves and arbitrarily determined? From a purely human standpoint, arbitrary are a fortiori the products of nature. These could surely be different, nevertheless they always exhibit the same properties according to experience; exactly in this way the specific meanings of the stars in their being [*Dasein*] cannot be explained further, but have been proven to be accurate through millennia of research. Since ancient Chaldean times, science has not stopped testing its premises on reality; as much as induction can prove, it must have proven it here. The astrologer, supported by the oldest wisdom of humanity, presupposes the virtues of the stars just as naturally as the stars themselves.

⁋ The astrological worldview has never been surpassed in beauty. At the same time, it is the most arrogant thing ever created by spirit: The paths of eternal suns as curves of fleeting fortune, the starry sky as the emblem of personal, human fate—Prometheus has never been more proud of himself than he is of this belief, never more defiantly has he stood up to nature. Nature, however, has bowed to spirit, who knew how to violate it so splendidly: what was written above in the heavens has, for the most part, happened on Earth.

⁋ Celestial interpretation has proven itself for millennia as a source of knowledge. This is a fact, cannot be denied. And yet: anyone who searched for the cause for this in the stars, he struggled fruitlessly: the elements of astrology have no conceivable relation to the world of experience; in the framework of natural order there is no room for them. The truth of astrology is arguably of another origin; it is not rooted in nature, it arises from the human soul. It is a real work of the mind. But it is no less true. The germ of every truth emerges from the imagination; the world was first created by spirit. Reality is initially foreign to us, we do not see, understand it; we only see what we invent. We imagine ourselves in an inhuman world, grasp from it only that which fancies our concepts, our world is a child of our imagination. Thus the astrologer strikes a chord with only those facts, which must confirm the veracity of his art; so everywhere he must rediscover the relationships that correspond to his set of beliefs. It is not possible to refute a worldview if it corresponds to subjective reality; the subject exposes the object; where no light falls remains invisible. Thus many worlds have replaced each other, all of them really in their time; they all dissolve into darkness as soon as the magic lamp of the imagination settles on new desires and expectations. In our epoch, the human world may be fundamentally the same as the inhuman order of nature. Our world has become immortal. But nature is strengthened at the expense of spirit, it threatens to suffocate the mind. Our imaginations are weakened, our courage is sapped, we hazard, we cannot do any more. Out of creators, we have become observers, out of conquerors, envoys. We move further and further away from the type of the first human, who was at once the greatest: from the demigod Prometheus.

Endnotes

1 Count Hermann A. von Keyserling, "Sterndeutung," first appeared in a publication called the *Hyperion Almanac* in 1911, and was reprinted in Keyserling, *Philosophie als Kunst* (Darmstadt: Otto Reichl, 1920), 9–15. The title, "Sterndeutung" may be translated literally as astrology, but that obscures the resonance with Freud's 1899 book, *Traumdeutung*, (lit., dream interpretation), that was still quite topical in 1911, when this article was published.

Count Hermann Alexander von Keyserling (July 20, 1880–1946) was a renowned Baltic German philosopher who delivered this lecture on astrology in 1910, nine years before the Communists confiscated his ancestral home and property in Russian territory (now Estonia). In 1920 he founded the School of Wisdom in Darmstadt, Germany, gathering luminaries such as C. G. Jung, Richard Wilhelm and Rabindranath Tagore, among many others. Astrology was integrated as one of the wisdom traditions taught by the school, and it was a foundational site for the crosspollination of astrology with the newly emerging field of psychology. After the Nazis rose to power, Keyserling's School was shuttered, his citizenship revoked, and he was forced into virtual house arrest. He died in Innsbruck, Austria in 1946.

Translator Jennifer Zahrt, phd stumbled upon this text in 2009, during her research at the University of California, Berkeley. Zahrt's mission is to bring facets of German astrological history to the English-speaking world through translations and publications. To this end, she currently serves as an Honorary Fellow at the Sophia Centre for the Study of Cosmology in Culture and the University of Wales Trinity Saint David. This translation was also made by possible by the financial support of over 90 patrons through her Patreon campaign. Help her keep material like this coming: www.patreon.com/jennzahrt.

Paula Belluomini, cap, began studying astrology as a teenager in Brazil and moved to Southern California in the 90s to continue her studies through independent coursework. She completed the steps required to become a Certified Astrological Professional by isar in 2015, participated in several astrological conferences and local astrology groups. Her main areas of expertise and interest include horary, mundane, electional, modern and traditional astrology. In addition to providing astrology consulting services, Paula has a degree in marketing and is an experienced graphic and web designer who often creates artwork with astrological themes. For more information visit ocastrology.com

www.ingramcontent.com/pod-product-compliance
Lightning Source LLC
Chambersburg PA
CBHW050759110526
44588CB00003B/59